VOLUME EDITORS

MICHAEL BRUCE currently works in the non-profit sector with
at-risk youth. Previously, he was a teaching assistant at California
State University, Chico, and received his Master's degree from
San Diego State University, specializing in continental philosophy.
He has published articles in the pop culture and philosophy genre and
is currently editing Just the Arguments: 100 of the Most Important
Arguments in Western Philosophy for Wiley-Blackwell.

ROBERT M. STEWART is Professor of Philosophy at
California State University, Chico. He is the author
of *Moral Philosophy: A Comprehensive Introduction* (1994),
and editor of *Philosophical Perspectives on Sex and Love* (1995).
He has published numerous journal articles.

SERIES EDITOR

FRITZ ALLHOFF is an Assistant Professor in the Philosophy
Department at Western Michigan University, as well as a Senior
Research Fellow at the Australian National University's Centre
for Applied Philosophy and Public Ethics. In addition to editing the
Philosophy for Everyone series, Allhoff is the volume editor or co-editor
for several titles, including *Wine & Philosophy* (Wiley-Blackwell, 2007),
Whiskey & Philosophy (with Marcus P. Adams, Wiley, 2009), and
Food & Philosophy (with Dave Monroe, Wiley-Blackwell, 2007).

PHILOSOPHY FOR EVERYONE

Series editor: Fritz Allhoff

Not so much a subject matter, philosophy is a way of thinking. Thinking not just about the Big Questions, but about little ones too. This series invites everyone to ponder things they care about, big or small, significant, serious … or just curious.

Edited by Michael Bruce and Robert M. Stewart

COLLEGE SEX

PHILOSOPHY FOR EVERYONE

Philosophers With Benefits

Foreword by Heather Corinna

WILEY-BLACKWELL

A John Wiley & Sons, Ltd., Publication

This edition first published 2010

Blackwell Publishing was acquired by John Wiley & Sons in February 2007. Blackwell's publishing program has been merged with Wiley's global Scientific, Technical, and Medical business to form Wiley-Blackwell.

Registered Office
John Wiley & Sons Ltd, The Atrium, Southern Gate, Chichester, West Sussex, PO19 8SQ, United Kingdom

Editorial Offices
350 Main Street, Malden, MA 02148-5020, USA
9600 Garsington Road, Oxford, OX4 2DQ, UK
The Atrium, Southern Gate, Chichester, West Sussex, PO19 8SQ, UK

For details of our global editorial offices, for customer services, and for information about how to apply for permission to reuse the copyright material in this book please see our website at www.wiley.com/wiley-blackwell.

Library of Congress Cataloging-in-Publication Data
College sex – Philosophy for Everyone: philosophers with benefits / Michael Bruce and Robert M. Stewart (eds.); with a foreword by Heather Corinna.
     p.   cm. — (Philosophy for everyone)
   Includes bibliographical references.
   ISBN 978-1-4443-3294-0 (pbk.: alk. paper) 1. College students—Sexual behavior. 2. Sexual ethics. I. Bruce, Michael. II. Stewart, Robert Michael, 1952– III. Title: College sex – philosophy for everyone.
   HQ35.2.C645 2010
   176—dc22

                                                    2010004889

A catalogue record for this book is available from the British Library.

Set in 10/12.5pt Plantin by SPi Publisher Services, Pondicherry, India
Printed in Singapore

1   2010

CONTENTS

FOREWORD

In the late 1980s I attended a college whose core curriculum was rooted in the classics of Western philosophy. I also had sex in college and studied sexuality in college, between the pages, not just the sheets. For me, college sex and philosophy were largely inseparable, and I had both in equal measure.

Here's the crux of what I learned about Western philosophy in college: it is highly critical, systematic and relies upon – or states it does – logic and reason. It involves asking and exploring very big questions, sometimes about very large things, sometimes about very small things. It tended to mostly come from old, white men and be about men, even when those men are discussing women or others whose experiences they had not lived or had not lived lately.

Some of this stuff was seriously ancient, even when presented as shiny and new. Any given philosopher seemed to think that his – and with a hat-tip to Hannah Arendt, her – philosophical approach and ideas would make all others obsolete. Any given philosopher often used language (like the words "god," "he," or "moral") or approaches that made it sound like their language and approaches were the only right or reasonable ones.

Very few people seemed interested in it, but people still liked to argue about it a lot. Just when I thought I had a handle on philosophy, some approach to or experience of it spun my head around and made me feel like a newbie.

Philosophy often seemed to be coming from a bunch of dead people who were coming from a world that largely was not mine. But even when those folks were talking about something that either wasn't about them, or didn't speak to my experience, even in question or profound disagreement, I could learn a whole lot about myself and my world from it.

It sometimes also really made my head hurt.

Here's the crux of what I learned about sex in college, especially sex we have during the time of life when we're in college: it is largely uncritical (when it is, is more so after the fact than during the act), only systematic when it sucks, and most often relies upon a partial suspension of reason. It often involves asking for and exploring very big things, sometimes via very large things, sometimes via very small things. It tended to come from pretty much everybody of every age, though some men did like to think that it was mostly about them, even when they had it with women or others whose experiences they had not lived or had not lived lately. The older and whiter those men got, the more they seemed inclined to think that, something I hardly need to tell a generation that has come of age under the Bush administration. If you've already started college courses, you also know exactly what I'm talking about. If not, you will.

Some of this stuff was seriously ancient, even when presented as shiny and new. Any given sexual partner didn't seem think that his – or her – approach to and ideas about sex would make all others obsolete, but plenty seemed to hope for as much. Any given person often used language (like the words "oh-god," "sex," or "moral") about or approaches to sexuality that made it sound like their language and approaches were the only right, or reasonable ones.

Pretty much everybody was interested in it, but people still liked to argue about it a lot. Just when I thought I had a handle on sex, some approach to or experience of it spun my head around and made me feel like a newbie.

While the sex I personally had in college never involved dead people, it did sometimes involve those coming from a world that was not mine. But for the most part, sex in college was centrally about me and my peers and about our world, not the worlds or experiences of those outside it, even if to our great annoyance those outsiders invaded or policed that world. Yet, even when other folks were having sex or had a sexuality in college that either wasn't about me, or didn't speak to my experience of sex, even in question or disagreement, I could learn a whole lot about myself and my world from it.

It sometimes also really made my head hurt.

In some ways, college sex and philosophy are excellent bedfellows. In others, they're like those couples you see together and cannot figure out what the hell it is they see in one another. While adding sex to philosophy makes the latter far more compelling, the opposite is rarely true. Under the microscopic lens of philosophy, sex can sometimes appear nearly incomprehensible, painfully pat, or downright unappealing. Of course, some schools of philosophy are a better fit than others. Rationalism, analytic philosophy, or logical positivism? Highly incompatible. Skepticism or pragmatism? Not if you want to have a good time. Aesthetics, metaphysics, and existentialism? Sure. Poststructuralism? Depends on the sex you're having. Idealism? And how. Absurdism? Perfect.

Most of the Western philosophers who have explored sexuality often seem either like the folks who have enjoyed or experienced sex the least or who wanted to hide their enjoyment of it the most. When reading philosophers addressing sexuality, you may hear a voice in your head saying, with great exasperation, "Just get laid already!" or "For the love of gawd, come out of that closet." Many have seemed most focused on questions of what is and is not moral in human sexuality – and with infrequent self-analysis, mind – than the whole of the sexual experience or the more holistic sphere of what human sexuality entails. Much philosophy addressing sexuality can seem a determined attempt to take all the fun right out of it. For example, it's a testament to the fortitude of queer and women's sexuality and the drive we all have for pleasure that we of the female and/or not-hetero variety can still enjoy sex at all after reading and having culture influenced by most philosophical approaches to queer and women's sexuality. We also owe philosophy no gratitude for its endless fixation on what is normal and what is abnormal in sexuality, an enterprise so vastly diverse that the only thing we know about sexual normality is that either all of us are normal or none of us are.

Neither philosophy nor sex in college is new. In fact, much of what any given generation posits as sexually new in the next one is not, it just may be occurring in new contexts and frameworks or look different once one is beyond a given age. In the 1980s and 1990s, the 1960s and 1970s, in the 1930s, 1940s, and 1950s, people were doing the horizontal mambo in college, "hooking up," having or considering trysts with professors, sneaking or slinking home after staying out all night, communicating with long-distance partners, doing or utilizing sex work, sleeping with folks who weren't a spouse, fiancée, or "steady," having sex with and without romantic love. In short, they were exploring their own sexuality and sexual identity to try and find the right fit for who they were then and for who they wanted to become. Since most of the people applying philosophy to college sex are not college students having said sex (nor often sexologists), in some ways, I think the greatest information gleaned from philosophical analysis of young adult sex is what adultist attitudes and ideas about college sex and sexuality are.

Which is useful knowledge, really. After all, those not in college having sex have long been the greatest buzzkill of those who are, especially those who didn't have the sex in college they wanted and knew – or imagined – everyone else to be having. Let's be kind: adults who philosophically consider the sexuality of younger people probably had sex in college, too, and plenty of it was likely sex they enjoyed. (Or, being not so kind, did not have sex in college and are still royally pissed off about it.) Some of what you read in this book will be about your experiences with sex in college. Some won't: it may be about experiences others have, instead, or may be about someone else's perceptions of, ideas about, or even sexual fantasies of what you and your fellow students are doing. But whether it expands your mind or solidifies your own dissenting ideas, it's all good.

Outside philosophical perspectives on your sex life will tend to include one's own sexual history added to what they observe about yours now within the kind of rigorous structure philosophical approaches demand and require, and that's useful, both when on-target and when off-base. You can use them to see them coming and cover your tracks a bit better. Alternately, you can use them to apply a different perspective than your own to your own sexual life: seeing our experiences through different eyes and ways of thinking can provide potentially important tools with which to evaluate our choices.

As a sexuality author and educator, I find it frustrating when sex and sexuality are presented solely as pursuits of the body, when in fact they are also – sometimes great, sometimes not-so-great – pursuits of heart and mind. Furthermore, sex is not just what we do when we're engaging in it, it is what we think of it all, before, during, and after, in scarcity and in excess, about our own sexuality and sex lives and those of others, how we and everyone else contextualize, conceptualize, evaluate, enact, and represent it; how and if we say yes, maybe, or no, to whom and what we say it, what both our ideals and realities of sex – which often are not one and the same, nor universal for everyone – are. And having solid frameworks for thinking about something that can make us so dizzy in the head is mighty helpful. That is the aim of the authors of *College Sex & Philosophy*, and it's most certainly a fine one. As they were for me in college, sex and philosophy remain a heady mix, one that poses unusual and unexpected challenges for writer and reader alike.

So, I invite you to go ahead, open the pages of this book, put sex and philosophy in bed together and see what happens. And don't just lie there: let yourself really get into it and see where it takes you. Just like any other kind of "sexual experimenting," you may find it expansive or a yawner, you might get off on it or you might not. But you'll never know unless you give it a try.

Heather Corinna
Founder and Director, Scarleteen.com

ACKNOWLEDGMENTS

First, we would like to thank all of the contributors. They have been very patient and enthusiastic. We are impressed with the quality and creativity of their essays. The editorial process can feel grueling and tedious, amplified by the challenges of communicating electronically. We thank them for their persistence. Many of the contributors were writing during their summer break, and we thank them for using that precious time. We have an international group of authors, also authors specializing in different areas of philosophy, and interdisciplinary scholars from fields outside of philosophy as well. We are pleased with the collection of perspectives represented in this text.

Second, we would like to thank our publisher. Wiley-Blackwell has supported this project from the moment it was conceived. In particular, we acknowledge Fritz Allhoff and Marcus P. Adams. Fritz has been especially helpful, and we thank him for his patience and for believing in the project. Marcus was our invaluable resource behind the scenes, helping with careful manuscript preparation. We could not have realized this volume without help from both of you.

Third, Michael would like to thank Robert. Taking Robert's "Philosophy of Sex and Love" class as an undergraduate made a lasting impression. Philosophy, as a discipline, increasingly has to defend its relevancy and practicality, and Robert's class showed how philosophy can directly inform decisions and behaviors. Robert would like to thank Brenda Lowen for her technical help.

Finally, we thank you, the reader: enjoy the volume! The sexual dimension of human existence is a wonderful thing. We applaud your interest in exploring a topic that is unfortunately still taboo for many people.

Michael Bruce, Belmont, California
Robert M. Stewart, Chico, California

MICHAEL BRUCE AND ROBERT M. STEWART

CAMPUS ORIENTATION

An Introduction to *College Sex – Philosophy for Everyone*

College is a special time in Western culture. It is a unique social space where young adults are encouraged to sew their "wild oats," cultivate a sense of self, and be exposed to a global economy of ideas and perspectives. As many students are away from their parents and communities – and their enmeshed values – for the first time, they often experiment and explore themselves, their new autonomy, and the academic world. Sexuality and sexual practices are some of the most important and interesting areas students navigate. This volume in the *Philosophy for Everyone* series investigates contemporary sexual practices, behaviors, and mores of college students from a philosophical perspective. This introduction will highlight the features and history of the philosophy of sex as an area of research and then briefly introduce the essays and the organization of the book.

The philosophy of sex is a relatively new subfield. Although the works of some major philosophers in the history of philosophy have included important discussions of sexuality, often in relation to love and the family or broader social issues, only in the last forty years have professional philosophers recognized this subject as a significant focus of research in its own right. Many essays, books, and college courses have appeared since the publication of a seminal journal article by the noted philosopher Thomas Nagel in the early 1970s on the topic of sexual perversion.[1] Though widely criticized, and for good reason, in a series of subsequent publications by other philosophers, Nagel's use of the techniques of modern analytic philosophy to elucidate a controversial concept seldom addressed by his fellow philosophers working within the Anglo-American tradition was pathbreaking. Continental European philosophers such as Søren Kierkegaard (1813–55), Arthur Schopenhauer (1788–1860), and Friedrich Nietzsche (1844–1900), and later Jean-Paul Sartre (1905–80) and Simone de Beauvoir (1908–86), had written about the nature of sexual desire and relations between the sexes, but English-speaking philosophers had done little during that period on the subject of human sexuality. Nagel's "Sexual Perversion" was influenced by the insights of existentialist philosophers, particularly Sartre, but it had analytical rigor and clarity, advancing an argument for objective standards of sexual deviance and normality more liberal than one might find in orthodox Freudian accounts, for example, of homosexuality. His essay was thus an exercise in both conceptual clarification and applied moral philosophy.

Ethics, social-political philosophy, and philosophical psychology or the philosophy of mind are the main areas within the discipline of philosophy that contribute to the subfield of the philosophy of sex. Many of the questions falling within this subfield concern sexual morality – the ethics of premarital and extramarital sex, contraception and abortion, same-sex relations, and so forth. Some of the issues addressed by philosophers of sex are ethical but also involve social policy and the regulation of human practices and institutions, e.g., the sex industry. And there is a broad range of questions that concern the nature and aim of human sexuality itself, our desires and emotions, pleasure and pain, sexual identity, the normal and the abnormal, among other things. These are broadly psychological issues, yet philosophers approach them somewhat differently from the ways in which academic psychologists, clinicians, counselors, and psychiatrists do, and the matters of central concern are often not exactly the same. While the latter disciplines tend to involve theorizing about the causal origins of sexual behavior in our species and others, as well as effective treatment of sexual disorders or disturbances, philosophers – while usually interested in such empirical questions – are more likely to focus on the construction of conceptual frameworks for understanding and also evaluating human sexual phenomena. These frameworks draw from other important developments in other areas of philosophy, such as the philosophy of mind and philosophy of science. Ideally, philosophers and social or behavioral scientists benefit from each other's research, the conceptual and normative concerns of philosophers influencing the empirical research of scientists and in turn being informed

⁇   MICHAEL BRUCE AND ROBERT M. STEWART

by that research. Historical and literary studies of human sexuality have also significantly guided philosophical thinking about sex in recent years, especially by philosophers working in the Continental tradition.

Sex in the setting of modern college and university campus life is an especially fertile subject for philosophical reflection. Why is this? In part it is because the institution brings together larger numbers of people at the start of their adult lives and places them in a situation of relatively little supervision, one which is to some extent insulated from the pressures of the working world. Often they live together in dorms or apartments or houses; new relationships of various kinds are formed of necessity. Moreover, they will need to have considerable contact with faculty and staff, some of whom will not be too much older than they. Mentoring relationships will typically have a personal aspect that can lead to different kinds of intimacy. The college environment, of course, is supposed to provide the conditions for reflection about life and the world, to help students learn about themselves and others, and to establish their place in society. Depending on what a student chooses to study, some of her courses might deal directly with issues of sexuality.

Freedom and the leisure to reflect in circumstances of intense intellectual stimulation and constant interaction with many other people – often attractive individuals within the same age group – present students with many important decisions about how to share their lives with others. The choices they make can be central to the formation of character and life plans with long-term effects on their futures comparable to the decisions they arrive at concerning majors or careers. Emotional needs and aspirations will be central in motivating all of these decisions as students seek to create desirable lives for themselves. Sexual opportunities will force them to decide what they value and what their limits are, in the process learning about themselves as individuals and defining themselves as persons.

Philosophy has shaped the university environment over the centuries, going back to its origins in the philosophical and theological climate of the Middle Ages in Europe. The ideas of Augustine (354–430), Thomas Aquinas (1225–74), and other important thinkers of the Roman Catholic tradition, strongly influenced by Greco-Roman philosophy, determined the structure and curriculum of the early institutions of higher education into the Renaissance and the early modern period. The rise of Protestantism and the educational philosophy of John Locke (1632–1704) had considerable influence on the course of education in Western Europe and the United States. Today, American universities are dominated by a liberal political ideology that is secular and rooted in the pragmatism and progressivism of the late nineteenth and early twentieth centuries, represented by William James (1842–1910), Charles Peirce (1839–1914), and especially John Dewey (1859–1952). The social and political radicalism of the 1960s, shaped in part by the theories of Jean-Jacques Rousseau (1712–78) and Karl Marx (1818–83), continues to dominate thinking in much of the American educational establishment.

The "political correctness" of the late twentieth-century campus Left, now pervasive in our law, media, and educational institutions, has a dimension of sexual correctness defined by the radical feminism that developed out of the mid-1960s. A conception of women as a historically oppressed class, exploited and objectified by men, often collaborating in a state of "false consciousness" with male oppressors, has taken root in elite political thought and cultural criticism. Often it is tied to a critique of market capitalism, seen as the economic system most conducive to the treatment of female sexuality as a commodity. Pornography and other products and services of the sex industry are the most obvious form this sexual exploitation takes in our society, but from this radical feminist standpoint even conventional dating and marriage – indeed, perhaps heterosexuality itself – are permeated with power imbalances between the sexes and consequent subordination of the female.

While there has been some noteworthy criticism of these assumptions about the relative power of men and women in our society, as well as the need for greater institutional regulation to rectify the alleged imbalances and protect vulnerable females, these ideas are still widely accepted in American education at all levels.[2] Post-boomer generation women are less sympathetic to radical feminist ideology than were many of their parents, especially those who were college educated. Still, college students of both sexes today are sometimes confused and uncertain about what is appropriate behavior in many social situations having a sexual aspect. Institutional rules and policies intended to provide them with guidance are often ideologically motivated and overly instructive, even to the point of being ludicrous. A notorious sexual conduct code that was established at now-defunct Antioch College, an institution with a long history of progressive thinking since its founding in 1852, defined a series of sexual advances and required explicit competent consent before a student would be permitted to go on to the next stage. Attempts by liberal college administrators and faculty to regulate, for ideological or legal reasons, what most of us consider private behavior can be seen as heavy-handed and reminiscent of the conservative mores that supported the earlier doctrine of *in loco parentis*.

⁀⁀   MICHAEL BRUCE AND ROBERT M. STEWART

Religious beliefs may have once given some guidance to most students in previous times, but the present generation, shaped by decades of secularism and liberalism, is no longer as influenced by strict Judeo-Christian teaching about sexuality, even at many religious educational institutions.[3] Faced with tempting opportunities among a range of sexual possibilities in the permissive, generally tolerant setting of a typical American college campus, with a male-female ratio favorable to men (especially those of high status, e.g., fraternity members and athletes), and the easy availability of alcohol and drugs, young students of both sexes and different sexual orientations have serious choices to make. How can philosophical reflection be of help in arriving at intelligent decisions that can be defended ethically and not regretted in retrospect?

Philosophy, for most of its history in the West, has been primarily concerned with the definition, clarification, and critical analysis of basic concepts and theoretical frameworks that are fundamental to our understanding of the natural and social world. To live rationally, we must come to know ourselves. We are not merely thinking beings but also sensing, feeling, emotional, appetitive creatures with needs, desires, and aspirations for our lives. Our capacity for pleasure and pain, as with many other animals, is central to our existence. And among the chief sources of human pleasure (and pain) is our sexual experience and the emotional, social, and moral consequences that follow from the choices we make with regard to our sexual activities and relationships.

Having a clear conception of what sexuality is and what it means to us as individuals is essential for most of us to live a good life. Confusions, ambiguities, and contradictions in our ideas and beliefs lead to painful dilemmas, conflicts, and generally bad decisions; this is particularly true in sexual matters. Human beings typically live with others in often complex networks of different sorts of relationships. Normal sexual gratification, if it is anything more than masturbation, involves relating to other people, if only temporarily. What counts as normal sexuality and what kinds of obligations define intimate relationships are, at least in part, philosophical questions, i.e., they are not merely psychological, but call for *normative* standards. Arriving at acceptable standards means going beyond an uncritical acceptance of existing norms, reflecting on them, and perhaps rejecting or modifying them in light of what one learns from experience, scientific research, and the rational consideration of other points of view.

How we are to think of sexual desire, its connections to the various forms of love, marriage, and friendship, and its relations to our identity and sense of ourselves are basic philosophical questions about life. What is the aim of sexual desire? Should it always be expressive of love or even be restricted further to those who are engaged or married? Are friendships to be kept free of sexual complications? Does our sexual orientation define us as individuals? What about unusual sexual inclinations or practices – can some objectively be classified as deviant, perverse, or unhealthy? What kinds of experimentation might be reasonable and acceptable as a way of finding out what we want and who we are? These are some of the questions young adults of a college age should be asking themselves. The tools and techniques of philosophical inquiry, along with the ethical wisdom of centuries of profound reflection by philosophers, can help us find thoughtful answers.

Many of the questions we have, or should consider, about sexuality are essentially moral ones, concerning not just our personal goals but our relations to others as well. When is consent to sexual activity given competently? What constitutes rape? How can we not use others in sexual relationships, but always treat them with respect and consideration? What does self-respect demand of us in sexual situations, and is it a moral issue? Is the preservation of virginity until marriage a moral matter, or just one of personal preference? What are the reasons to marry in today's society, and what responsibilities does it entail? Do non-marital sexual relationships involve the same obligations as a typical monogamous marriage, e.g., sexual exclusivity? Is promiscuity wrong even if one has no duty to be sexually faithful? What about possible bad consequences of intercourse such as disease and pregnancy – how is responsibility to be attributed? These are the kinds of questions that most college students need to face early in their lives, and they need considered answers to them – something for which philosophy can be very helpful.[4]

There are also questions about professionals' relations within the college community, e.g., between students and their instructors. Are faculty-student sexual relationships wrong either morally or from the standpoint of institutional ethics? Do differences of age or gender have a bearing on this, or is it mainly an issue of whether the student is currently enrolled in that professor's class, or might be in the future? Some feminist commentators insist that such relations are necessarily exploitive, given the power imbalances, especially if the faculty member is a male and the student female, but others disagree.[5] And what about students who work outside the academic community in the sex industry, e.g., on computer websites or in strip clubs? Is this morally objectionable, even if it is done to pay for tuition, fees, and other expenses incurred as part of getting one's education?

MICHAEL BRUCE AND ROBERT M. STEWART

Does using digital technology in more socially accepted ways also pose ethical issues for students' romantic and sexual lives, e.g., meeting and communicating mainly or even exclusively over the Internet or cell phones? Moral philosophy, social philosophy, and the philosophy of technology can be very useful in finding reasonable answers.

The essays in this book are divided into four units: Freshman Year: Hook Up Culture (experimentation, shame, and alienation), Sophomore Year: Friends with Benefits, Junior Year: Ethics of College Sex, and Senior Year: Sex and Self-Respect. This structure loosely parallels Abraham Maslow's (1908–70) "hierarchy of needs" – a psychological theory of motivation ranging from physical needs up to self-actualization. The themes of each unit progress as the social and intellectual skills of a college student would as he developed through his college years. The first unit looks at initial experimentation, technology, and clothing, while the second unit deals with "friends with benefits relationships." The third and fourth units revolve around more abstract ethical issues, characteristic of the changing and perhaps less egocentric perspective of upperclassmen. The fourth unit specifically accounts for self-respect and mutually respectful relationships, akin to Maslow's "self-actualization." At this stage, the freshman has journeyed through the wild space of college – experimenting with the different kinds of relationships and college culture at hand – and has matured intellectually into a college graduate who understands the complexities of sexual respect and communication.

The first unit deals with aspects of college culture, or *hook-up culture*, as some writers have called it. These essays explore the following: the motivations and risks of sexual experimentation, the way college dating and sexual practices are enmeshed in technologies like Facebook and text messaging, and how the clothing students wear can signal moral judgments. The first essay in this unit, "Sex and Socratic Experimentation" written by George T. Hole and Sisi Chen, describes an experiment given in one of Hole's classes. The experiment explores ways students can make meaningful changes in their lives by reflecting philosophically on their life choices. Hole and Chen make this concrete by providing several examples in which students described the despair to which naïve experimentation led them and, remarkably, how they used philosophical methodology to recover a sense of self based on reflective thinking and action. These examples are intriguing because they show how philosophy can positively impact one's life.

One of the sexual clichés that runs rampant is that college students, particularly females, will experiment in homosexuality. This cliché misses that the opposite is also true. "The Straight Sex Experiment," authored by Bassam Romaya, explores a widespread practice involving openly gay or lesbian college students who occasionally experiment with heterosexual sex acts. In tandem with their heterosexual peers, Romaya argues that the sexual experiments of gay and lesbian youth reveal a sense of mystery, intrigue, and social or sexual rebellion by stepping outside the limits imposed by group-specific expectations in matters of sexual conduct. Ultimately, these haphazard experiences serve similar beneficial objectives, such as confirming one's understood and accepted sexual persona, eliminating mundane adolescent curiosity, or simply strengthening and broadening individual understanding of human sexual diversity. Romaya's essay is a much-needed analysis of college sexual identity, and moreover it provides a window into an often unheard portion of the story of college sexual experimentation.

It used to be a big deal to get a girl's phone number, but with the popularity of social networking sites, has this step been bypassed altogether? Michael Bruce's essay, "The Virtual Bra Clasp: Navigating Technology in College Courtship," examines the ways in which technology influences sex and love for college-age people. He first argues that there are certain socially acceptable steps of courtship for different technologies such as text messaging, My Space/Facebook messaging, phone calls, talking through friends, and old fashioned face-to-face communication. The ways students initially meet, stay in contact, break up, and reunite are all commonly mediated by technology in a way that is unique to the age group (though it may continue afterwards). Bruce reasons that technology has a tendency to alienate people who employ traditional methods – "Just walk up and talk to her" – and these direct tactics are viewed by younger generations as creepy. Bruce's essay unpacks the layers of technologies in which modern courtship is enmeshed, and in doing so he argues that social networking tools often function in the *opposite* way of their intended function, namely, to further remove and disenfranchise people.

Some college students have "one night stands," and these can lead to incredibly awkward mornings. "Smeared Makeup and Stiletto Heels: Clothing, Sexuality, and the Walk of Shame" is both a light-hearted and compelling account by Brett Lunceford, a specialist in the field of communication. Lunceford uses semiotics, the study of signs and sign systems, to analyze the relatively new phenomenon referred to as "the walk of shame." This act is usually typified by a college coed walking home in the morning while still wearing her party outfit from the night before, suggesting a sexually promiscuous act had taken place the previous night. Having described the stigma surrounding the walk of shame, Lunceford argues that the clothing worn during the walk of shame functions as a specific type of sign of sexuality, which is marked, especially in young women, as shameful. Lunceford's analysis is unique because it provides a framework through which to understand the walk of shame, which, though it is a common occurrence in the life of many college students, is often neglected in academic discussions of college life and sexuality.

Many freshmen move to college and leave behind a significant other, daring to enter into the much discussed and much dreaded long-distance relationship. Bill Puka's essay, "Relations at a Distance," uses current cognitive therapy techniques to outline the range of personal difficulties and dilemmas, special anticipations, and delights of college couples trying to conduct relationships at a distance. The essay emphasizes the freshman experience of trying to maintain relationships that started in high school, but Puka also discusses more recent innovations that many couples use throughout their college years to keep the spark going during their long-distance relationships. These innovations include sexting, Skype sex, and phone sex. Puka's essay is grounded not only in philosophical argumentation but also in interviews he conducted. He provides an in-depth account of these college couples' long-distance relationships, and he argues that long-distance relationships are not only something that can last but moreover that can be enjoyable and highly fulfilling.

In the second unit, Sophomore Year, the essays investigate "friends with benefits" relationships. This is a phenomenon that has recently been getting a lot of attention in the media as well as in academic research. The introductory essay in this unit looks at this kind of relationship in light of ancient Greek philosophy, while the concluding two essays are philosophical commentaries on experiments conducted by scholars working in the discipline of communications. These essays look at how common these friends with benefits arrangements are and how and why they begin.

What would the ancient Greeks think about friends with benefits relationships? William O. Stephens' essay, "What's Love Got to Do with It? Epicureanism and Friends with Benefits," applies Epicurean philosophy to this aspect of college sexuality. The essay looks at the phenomenon of friends with benefits from the standpoint of the Epicureans, a school of thought based on the pursuit of tranquility through knowledge, friendship, and a modest life. Stephens writes that Epicureans regard good friends to be much more reliable than good sex, and therefore college students should refrain from sex in order to keep their friends.

In the first of the essays related to the field of communication, Timothy R. Levine and Paul A. Mongeau's essay "Friends with Benefits: A Precarious Negotiation" explores a variety of questions about friends with benefits relationships: What are they? Can people really have sex with friends and remain friends? Is friends with benefits a new type of relationship, or have people always had sex with friends? What are the advantages and disadvantages of friends with benefits? Why do some people have friends with benefits relationships while others avoid them? Levine and Mongeau survey the different modes of communication surrounding these kinds of relationships, e.g., how people talk (or don't talk) about friends with benefits relationships with their other friends. This essay does an excellent job of framing the friends with benefits phenomenon with data that show how common the relationships are and what the outcomes statistically will be.

The second unit closes with "The Philosophy of Friends with Benefits: What College Students Think They Know," penned by Kelli Jean K. Smith and Kelly Morrison. Smith and Morrison supply a philosophical commentary to a study they performed, the goal of which was to collect information about multiple dimensions of friends with benefits relationships. These dimensions include how such relationships begin, the motivations for them, obstacles and emotions related to them, the maintenance rules associated with them, the outcomes of these relationships, and how these relationships are discussed and supported by same-sex friend networks. Smith and Morrison conducted this research to further their understanding of friends with benefits by exploring personal accounts of these kinds of relationships. The data revealed the presence of relational, emotional, and sexual motivations and barriers, as well as a broad array of emotional responses. People who are in friends with benefits relationships, or contemplating doing so, will find the information in this essay invaluable.

The third unit, Junior Year, is centered on ethical and epistemological issues – what is ethical and how do we know it to be so? – relating to sexuality that arise in college life, both for the students and teachers. Andrew Kania's "A Horny Dilemma: Sex and Friendship between Students and Professors" argues that two plausible claims lead us to a dilemma about the ethics of relationships between students and their professors. First, there is no clear line between an intimate friendship and a loving sexual relationship. Second, sexual relationships often, perhaps ideally, develop out of close friendships. This suggests that either

❴❵ MICHAEL BRUCE AND ROBERT M. STEWART

professors and students should refrain from entering into friendships at all or we should condone sexual relationships between them. Kania's intriguing essay not only questions what qualifies a relationship as a sexual one, but also what constitutes the act of sex itself. This essay is a must-read for anyone interested in the sometimes blurry line between friendships and romantic relationships.

Danielle A. Layne's "Philosophers and the Not So Platonic Student-Teacher Relationship" presents historical examples (Socrates and Alcibiades, Abelard and Heloise, Heidegger and Arendt) within Western philosophy where students and teachers have become intimately involved. This essay is fascinating, as it covers topics ranging from Socrates' flirting with young men, the castration of Abelard, and a complicated affair between a Nazi sympathizer and his Jewish lover in an internment camp. Layne draws parallels to current academic policies regarding student-teacher relationships, arguing that policies against such relationships inhibit young adults from exercising their autonomous judgment.

How do you know what you think you know? Ashley McDowell's "Thinking About Thinking About Sex" is an enticing essay that draws from the area of philosophy called epistemology, which deals with the nature of knowledge and justified belief. McDowell's essay will provoke you into asking yourself questions like "Am I good in bed? Did she have an orgasm? How would I know for sure?" Insecurities beware – McDowell argues that if college students are to have healthy and good sex lives, they must improve themselves epistemologically. Epistemologists can help students recognize the difference between what one accepts on the surface and what one *really* believes. McDowell shows readers how to evaluate their own prejudices, inconsistencies, and blind spots. With a heightened sense of awareness of their epistemic standing, college students can start guiding themselves towards good thinking and in turn good sex.

For various reasons, both parental and institutional, children are often raised with the belief that sex is something reserved for people who are in love. In "Exploring the Association Between Love and Sex" Guy Pinku considers the classic relationship between sex and love and reveals hidden philosophical assumptions within this kind of relationship. Pinku argues that the connection between sex and love is based upon, and reflects, the complicated body-mind relationship, and he argues that even if sex may express love in some cases (which is controversial) there is neither a natural connection nor a normative one between love and sex; sex and love are different, not necessarily related phenomena. As a result, nothing is missing or wrong with sex without love. For Pinku, the connection between sex and romantic love is based upon a tendency to extend feelings towards the body and apply them to the mind; without this extension, sex – which is based only upon an affection towards the body – might be experienced as limited or even as vain.

Prostitution is said to be the world's oldest profession. College is expensive. It doesn't take a logician to conclude college students might venture into morally questionable employment to help fund their college education. "Sex for a College Education" by Matthew Brophy shines a light on a contemporary paradox confronting many college women: that to become autonomous through higher education, they must subjugate themselves, sexually, to afford it. Higher education increases one's autonomy, cultivates individual flourishing, and affords graduates greater opportunity. Paradoxically, the expense of a college education often coerces women to engage in sexual enterprises that betray a lack of autonomy, inhibit flourishing, and often results in personal degradation. Brophy argues that prostitution, even when undertaken to pay for college, violates the intrinsic value and dignity of the prostitute because the body is used as a means and not an end in itself. As evidence for this claim, Brophy highlights the practices of college prostitution and webcam pornography and considers philosophical theories of autonomy, eudaimonia, utilitarianism, and Kantian and feminist ethics. To make his argument more concrete, Brophy presents examples from several recent cases, such as Natalie Dylan, John Getcher, and Ashley Dupré.

The final unit, Senior Year, examines notions of self-respect, mutually respectful relationships, and personal freedom. Robert M. Stewart's "Meaningful Sex and Moral Respect" uses Tom Wolfe's title essay in *Hooking Up* and his recent novel *I Am Charlotte Simmons* to examine the view that much of the sexual activity that involves students with other students – as well as with faculty – on college campuses today is devoid of meaning in addition to being self-destructive or abusive in many instances. This leads to a broader exploration of meaning as it relates to sexuality and respect in general. Stewart argues that, in the strict sense, sexual activity need not have meaning in order to have value, i.e., to contribute to the participants' wellbeing in some significant way. Love, Stewart concludes, is not the only value that makes sex objectively meaningful, and these meanings are not dependent on the meaning, or lack thereof, of life as a whole.

"Can Girls Go Wild With Self-Respect?" This is the question John D. Draeger asks in his essay. From skinny dipping, strip poker, and spin the bottle, to posting raunchy pictures online and "Girls Gone Wild" videos, Draeger examines different ways young women experiment with their sexuality and discover the sexual selves they want to become. This essay develops an account of self-respect through a discussion of various modes of experimentation, with a focus on highlighting gender asymmetries ("boys gone wild" doesn't carry nearly the same connotation). Navigating through "raunch culture" and depicting circumstances that often pit self-expression against self-respect, Draeger argues that girls *can* go wild with self-respect if they are conscious of their decisions and those choices are in line with informed standards and values.

A common question after sexual encounters during college when partners aren't as experienced is: Was it good for you too? "Mutual Respect and Sexual Morality: How to Have College Sex Well" by Yolanda Estes offers philosophical reflections on mutually respectful sexual relations. Estes first provides a brief account of sexuality and morality framed by human freedom and dignity. She then defines and defends reciprocal consent, desire, and concern as standards of mutually respectful sexual relations. Mutually respectful sex requires that each person clearly communicates voluntary participation, a concern for the wellbeing of their partner, and a willingness to attend to their partner's sexual desires. Estes then presents and applies a criterion of mutual respect to various sexual activities, including some commonly viewed as morally problematic, such as non-exclusive relationships, fetishism, and the combination of sex and alcohol. Estes concludes by providing additional reflections that broach the possibility of a morally sound, intellectually tenable, and perhaps even joyful account of human sexuality.

Do you ever deny your own freedom? Have you ever pretended to be someone else, or have you hidden your true potential? "Bad Faith or True Desire? A Sartrean View on College Sex" by Antti Kuusela explores the nature of sexual desire in college through the philosophy of the French existentialist Jean-Paul Sartre. Sartre claimed that sexual desire is quite different from strictly physical desires. According to him, sexual desire is something more than a desire for physical release. Kuusela asks that if students constantly have "sex on the brain" are they expressing real desire or is this desire better understood as an expression of "bad faith," a denial of one's freedom and choosing to behave like an object? This essay is able to get past philosophical jargon and clearly present some of Sartre's most influential concepts in relation to sexual desire and college students. Kuusela concludes via Sartre by underscoring the unlimited freedom college students have to be authentic individuals.

We hope that you enjoy the essays and that the philosophical perspectives within will help inform safe and morally respectful decisions.

NOTES

1 Thomas Nagel, "Sexual Perversion," reprinted in Robert M. Stewart (ed.) *Philosophical Perspectives on Sex and Love* (New York: Oxford University Press, 1995).
2 See Katie Roiphe, *The Morning After* (New York: Norton, 1993); Camille Paglia, *Vamps and Tramps* (New York: Vintage Books, 1994); and Rene Denfeld, *The New Victorians* (New York: Warner Books, 1995); for an opposing view, see Adele M. Stan, *Debating Sexual Correctness* (New York: Delta Books, 1995).
3 On current campus sexual mores, see Kathleen A. Bogle, *Hooking Up* (New York: New York University Press, 2008). Regarding the influence of religion in our colleges and universities, see Donna Freitas, *Sex and the Soul* (New York: Oxford University Press, 2009).
4 For detailed treatments of the issues involved in sexual consent, see David Archard, *Sexual Consent* (Boulder: Westview Press, 1997), and Alan Wertheimer, *Consent to Sexual Relations* (Cambridge: Cambridge University Press, 2003).
5 For a dissenting view from a prominent feminist scholar, see Jane Gallop, *Feminist Accused of Sexual Harassment* (Durham, NC: Duke University Press, 1997).

MICHAEL BRUCE AND ROBERT M. STEWART

PART I

FRESHMAN YEAR
Hook-Up Culture

CHAPTER I

SEX AND SOCRATIC EXPERIMENTATION

Where It's At

Young people have been experimenting with sex for a long time. Since the 1960s, colleges have become a laboratory for sexual experimentation. In addition to a perennial curiosity about sex among the young, social conditions have changed to allow for a wider range of experimentation. In college, students are free of parental supervision, and colleges no longer act *in loco parentis*. With students of the same age, with the same urges, and now often living in coed dorms, the conditions are ripe for experimentation not only with sex but with varieties of sexual relationships. Alcohol and drugs are readily available that can lower inhibitions for experimenting. (It is important to note that experimenting with sex and sexual relationships occurs at younger ages from high school even into middle and elementary school.)

Changes in social mores and technology have also affected attitudes about sex. Divorce no longer carries the stigma it once had. In light of the high divorce rate and second marriages, parents of current college students have had more sexual experiences than their parents and are likely to espouse more liberal attitudes: witness the surge in acceptance of gay rights. Sexual explicitness is evident in films, advertising, and contemporary dress. Significantly, the discovery and easy access to the contraceptive pill freed women from fear of pregnancy, so they could more safely engage in sex. Only the deadly reality of AIDS slowed the free love movement. Pornography is now easily accessible on the Internet that shows varieties of sexual acts that in earlier times were available only in esoteric books and art works, and so are "how to" books more graphic than the *Karma Sutra*.

Not only have attitudes changed about sex itself, there is a subtle change between sex and romantic love. In the "old days," sex was legitimate only within marriage. It then became acceptable (with grudging parental acceptance) for couples to live together, to have a love-sexual relationship that mimicked marriage except for the absence of state or church sanction. Living together, like marriage, presumed commitment, especially sexual fidelity, for both parties. Now, it seems, there is a further development in the connections between sex, love, and marriage or committed relationships: not only is there widespread acceptance of sex outside marriage, sex has become detached from both love and committed relationships. "Hooking up" and "friends with benefits" are new phenomena in the history of sexual relationships. Sex is no longer doing something special with someone special – it is a matter of "getting off" or "busting a nut," even if you have to "put a pager bag over his head."

The Internet has affected changes in sexual practices. If a student wants to check out a potential love or sexual prospect, Facebook will give information about whether the person is hot or not. Facebook has also changed the meaning of "friend." When many people on Facebook have long lists of friends, sometimes in the hundreds, "friend" no longer means a person one knows intimately and can count on for support. Also, texting has changed the landscape of human expression, closeness, and privacy. If a student can find a hot Facebook person and immediately text a brief message about hooking up, the landscape of relationships has certainly changed. Hooking up differs from wife swapping of an earlier generation, insofar as swapping maintained the marriage commitment and presumed a love commitment even as it allowed for variety in sexual partners. Hooking up is sex, free of love expression and relationship commitment.

In this essay, we will use the practice of hooking up to consider in what sense college students experiment with sex. Since experiments can go wrong, our main focus will be on a different kind of experiment, a Socratic one, as a way to make a significant healing change in one's troubled sexual life. We will describe the experiment format and give examples of two students' experiments.

Let's Experiment

Generally understood, experimentation includes any action motivated by curiosity or the intention to change something old or experience something new: for example, to try being a friend with benefits. A more carefully constructed practice of experimentation occurs in the sciences. It includes such general components as a field of inquiry with a background of theory and history, a scientific community with standards for data, objectivity, and, more specifically, evidentially supported inferences about hypotheses, based on controlled and replicable experiments that result in new knowledge or modification of accepted knowledge. At first glance, a student's experimentation with sex seems quite different from scientific experimentation; however, like scientists, students are motivated by curiosity. They seek new knowledge. They have a community that shares background beliefs about sex and relationships, shares "data" about sexual experiences, and makes inferences based on the results of their sexual encounters. So, a practice like hooking up at the individual level looks like a kind of experimentation, although it differs from Masters and Johnson's experiments that involved hooking up: they hooked up monitors to a female subject's anatomy, like a Plexiglas dildo (named Ulysses), to document a vaginal sexual response.[1] They also hooked up people, in the contemporary sense, for further experimentation that included watching subjects having sex. Their objectified approach to sex in *The Human Sexual Response* is more like college students' practice of hooking up and both are different from another attitude-changing book, *The Joy of Sex*.[2]

College students may not be objective like scientists. If they were subjects for self-experimentation, their self-interest in sexual pleasure would bias results that have general scientific credibility, though they may make discoveries about what pleases them. In contrast, a social scientist might study hooking up as a group phenomenon with conformity pressures. Accordingly, hooking up might also be seen as an individual's initiation rite into an elite group, "bad" college student or "cool" individual or, more simply, being a real student, not a "goody-goody." As a different kind of initiation rite, hooking up allows females to enter into the males' world of power and privilege by acting like horny males eager to get it on with virtually anyone.

When females start to realize the power over men that they hold in their loins – they do not have to "give it up" unless they choose to – a power struggle often ensues. Nonetheless, a female may still feel pressured or obligated to hook up so that the male does not move on to the next easy lay or so she does not feel guilty for frustrating him for not "getting any."

It seems many college students do not realize that experimentation can go badly wrong. Among the many examples we know about, this one is not unusual. Denise, a freshman, from a strict home, quickly became a sex performer. After she got wasted every night, she would invite guys to her room to give lap dances and strip tease, only to be confronted, nearly naked, by her hometown boyfriend of five years. After a public fight and failed classes, she returned home under even stricter supervision.

One of the authors (Chen) conducted an experiment, based on a dare, to abstain from sex during her freshman year. A male friend predicted "the guys are going to jump all over you." So she decided "if a guy is willing to wait a whole semester to have sex then he will prove himself worthy of being laid; the circumstances will wean out the assholes who only want sex (and want it now)." She realized the risk: "I would be missing out on the complete sexual freedom of my first semester at college; someone else may get to the guy I want first since I cannot offer anything sexual." Although it was a hard bet, she won. Her account is as follows:

> It was hard to abstain when there was a lot of alcohol and drug use almost every day of college. I have to admit there were some close calls due to a blurred conscience at times. I feel that I probably upset or frustrated a few guys because they had their hopes up about getting laid. Many guys, who are out to get laid, actually do expect to get laid. Not having sex showed me which guys are true friends and which are only out to get laid. Since promiscuous sex is so easy, there is so much of it, sex is devalued.

As a result of her experiment, Chen learned the following about herself (and transferred colleges):

> I do not want sex to be cheap. Sex should have physical and emotional worth. In the past, when I have engaged in meaningless sex, I would be left feeling emotionally unsatisfied. This would leave me feeling cheap, which lowered my sense of self-worth. In relationships or hook-ups where there was consensual feelings or attachments and love, I would feel like I was worth the guy's time and wait (to have sex). When a person I want to have sexual relations with waits to do it with me (and not other people while he is waiting), I feel special to that person.

Hooking Up Closer Up

Hooking up is simple, consensual sex with no romantic involvement. It is not prostitution, not only because money is not involved. (Some females do hook up in exchange for "a good time out" or other gifts, especially if the male is wealthy.) Prostitution has unsavory connotations, unlike hooking up. Hooking up does involve the satisfaction of sexual desire, but since either party can initiate the "date" neither can be identified as the prostitute or the John. Neither looks down on the other as being in a lower moral class, at least in theory. Insofar as males hook up, yet want eventually to be in a relationship with a female who does not hook up, there is still a double standard that affects male attitudes about female hook ups, even as they enjoy their sexual freedom and satisfactions. The male who hooks up a lot is envied by other males and given "props." Females will often think he is a pig or player and secretly desire sex with him. When a female hooks up with several males, other males will think that she is an easy lay, slut, or they might like to "ride the neighborhood bicycle." Other females will think she is a slut or infested with STDs and secretly be jealous of her. Both males and females enjoy the spectacle of the "walk of shame," when, before classes start in the morning, females are seen sneaking back to their dorm rooms, disheveled and wearing male clothing.[3]

While hooking up has an appeal of being edgy – "There's a sort of thrill when it's someone you don't know"[4] – in practice it seems more subdued. In theory, hooking up is just for sexual pleasure; emotions, intimacy, spontaneity, and commitment are deliberately marginalized and not expressed. From a survey of 43 female students, one student wrote:

> When I was involved in my hook-up relationship, I would never call him up for a sober booty call. It was always when I was drunk and wanted sex. This is also how I knew there was no emotional attachment because I wasn't even interested in hanging out with the guy unless I had been drinking. He wasn't really my type. He just wasn't someone that I wanted to be in a relationship with. We didn't have a lot in common.[5]

Almost all of the women surveyed said that alcohol was their gasoline for hooking-up sex.[6] As one recounted, "I was drunk. It's almost like a free pass." And:

Alcohol has a huge impact on my sexual activities. If I drink enough I have no moral rules with myself anymore. The next day I can wake up and make it okay by just saying, "I was drunk. It's a sign of liberation."[7]

Being drunk or pretending to be drunk allows these females to disclaim responsibility or, more radically, to pretend afterwards that sex did not happen. Drugs are used by males to seduce and enhance their experience. Hooking up also has its disappointments, as the following account indicates:

The hook-up guy never, ever, asked me how it was for me. He always quit after he finished, and there was rarely foreplay. You could tell it was strictly sex. My boyfriend always asks how it was for me; he is always worried that he is not doing it good enough.[8]

In spite of disappointments, hooking up is assumed to be a valuable phase in which females and males can experiment and enjoy sexual experiences as a prelude or interruption in more typical romantic relationships. However, for some people, sex, like any human activity, has unforeseen harmful consequences.

Problems and Socratic Experimentation

One of the authors (Hole) teaches a course titled "The Philosophy of Love and Sex." As part of the course, students conduct an experiment to engage in a meaningful change, definitely one of their own choosing.[9] The first format item for the Socratic experiment is to "briefly describe a change you are willing to make and evaluate what you are currently doing about it." Below are two sample experiments and their results.

EXAMPLE I

I have realized an unhealthy and self-destructive pattern in my love life that is directly related to alcohol. I seem to attract or get myself into one unstable and unhealthy relationship after another. In each relationship I find myself trying desperately to do whatever it takes to make the other person happy. I avoid the fear of being alone by trying to escape it by drinking or becoming involved with people

❪❫ SISI CHEN AND GEORGE T. HOLE

that I know will only bring stress and sadness into my life. My last attempt at a relationship failed because of this reason, and I cannot keep making the same mistake.

I would like to stop this cycle and be happier with other things in my life like school, my friends, and my future plans. I would like to be a wiser lover to myself by slowing down and only allowing healthy things and people into my life and my body.

Results

I was honest with myself and I asked, "Am I really accomplishing everything I want in my life?" My answer was no. Drinking was one factor that was getting in the way of being healthy. When I started the experiment I had to find an alternative to drinking when going out and socializing. I could no longer escape myself in that way, instead I did the opposite. Not drinking forced me to really take a look at myself and really see the people who surround me. I saw good people who were just as lost and confused as me. I never noticed how thoughtless I was until I took a step inside. I did not feel alienated from my wider circle of friends like I thought I would. I actually had conversations with my close friends that connected us on a deeper level. I replaced desperate attempts to finding a romantic relationship with stronger friendships.

I was honest with myself and redefined some of my core values. It is important for me to have stability in my life and routine; drinking was getting in the way of that. It weakened my morals and gave me excuses in romantic relationships. I feel that eliminating alcohol will keep me on a more stable romantic relationship path by giving me time to think and do things that are healthy. Even after two weeks of not drinking I have felt more emotionally stable and confident in myself.

EXAMPLE 2

One change came to mind when I first received this assignment, and it deals with my inability to trust people. I have an extreme difficulty opening up and sharing myself with another person. For the last few years my life has been following Murphy's Law, and when I was given the assignment, it had not even hit the peak of things "that could go wrong." I decided to change the relationships I have with men, because I feel that it has the greatest impact on my emotional wellbeing, which is rocky at best. I do not allow myself to become close to men in the emotional aspect, but have no problems being physically close to them. This creates relationships purely based on sex with a highly "no strings attached" policy. For the past few years, since a devastating break up with an abusive ex, I have not been able to trust a man past the point of getting my pants off. I am willing and able to change that part of me, because I feel that I hurt men with revenge in mind, punishing them for actions of my ex-boyfriend. At the time the assignment was given, I was seeing two men at the same time, neither of which I am extremely attached to.

Results

I have seen Mr. M every day since Halloween and about three times before that. He is now my boyfriend, and the experiment worked pretty well. On our first "date" we went out for Chinese food, and he began to ask me questions about my previous lovers. Normally when people ask me these kinds of questions, I either do not answer or I lie, because I've cheated on pretty much every boyfriend I have ever had. I told him the truth, explained a few of the situations and he seemed to understand. He loves me already I think, and I am positive it is because I started caring. I also slept with him (like fell asleep with him) which I never do, ever. When I am asleep, I will answer any question and tell anyone anything they need to know because I am a talker to the extreme. There is no way not to avoid my sleep talking, and I get nervous that people are going to ask me things while I sleep that I do not want to answer. (Paranoid, I know.) I have spoken to both of my other lovers since I started the relationship, and actually slipped up once. In the very beginning I started to get discouraged because I am a very negative person. I had sex with one of my usual men and felt terrible afterward. For the first time, I felt guilty for sleeping with someone else who I was not even dating at the time. I barely knew this person before I decided to experiment on him and from just the beginning, to let him into my life, I started to gain a deeper love relation than I had ever had.

These examples are far more serious than the usual ones, though many touch on troublesome aspects of a love relation, though not necessarily romantic love, since we consider many kinds of love. Many focus on a frozen relation with a parent or on self-love.

How did these two students make such significant life transitions? In the experiment format, after identifying their desired change, students plan their experiment by responding to the following items:

- State specifically what you will do, with whom, when, where and for how long.
- State what obstacles or excuses you anticipate in carrying out your experiment.
- Estimate how committed you will be in completing your experiment.
- Identify what risks are involved, both in doing your experiment and not doing it.
- Predict the results of your experiment, both positive and negative. Indicate what difference it will make if you are successful in your experiment.

The purpose of these questions is to focus on specific actions that are possible to engage, with respect to which a student can identify specific barriers that stand in the way of a clear sense of success. Typically, students see big barriers and give a low estimate of achieving success. In spite of their pessimism, they are often surprised at the high degree of success they achieve. They are successful because they move from entertaining a change hypothetically with negatives that inhibit action. As they identify the risks of not making their experimental change, they are better able to overcome the risks of doing it.

There are two more items to complete in the planning stage. They are to "identify one 'big' or essential, universal or philosophical question present in your experiment." While they initially find this instruction vague, they are able to identify questions like "Am I really free?" "What is romantic love?" and "Can you love more than one person at a time?" The "big" questions from the two student examples are as follows: "What makes a relationship or lifestyle unhealthy?" and "What is trust?" The other item to address is:

- Describe how your experiment is related to love or being a better, wiser lover.

In answering this question, students establish a reference point for assessing their experiment. Consequently, they think about their ideals in relation to not only the details of their planned experiment, but more generally about the meaning of love from a, perhaps, new perspective of "better and wiser." Once they complete their experiment they can tackle the following:

- Based on your experiment, describe what you have learned or concluded about your "big" question and being a better, wiser lover.

In principle, the experiments are Socratic. Students engage in a dialogue with themselves to clarify a concept at issue for them. (In the course, they are given critical thinking skills that help them to clarify meanings, test how they know what they believe is true, and reflect on their values.) They are also engaged in actions that give them results about their commitments, their assessment of obstacles and risks, and any differences between predicted and actual results. Consequently, students clarify what is involved in making a life change and explore the meaning of a concept embedded in their thoughts about the change. They often discover mistaken assumptions, like "I have nothing to talk about with my parents."

A Daring Ideal

Early in the course, students are asked to make a commitment that is part Zen mindfulness and part Socratic. Throughout the course, they are encouraged to adopt the ideal of being a wise lover. The ideal is both alluring and confusing. After class discussions, many students embrace the ideal and attempt to clarify its meaning in various contexts. The ideal certainly gives them pause when making choices: when they consider being a wise lover they shift from impulsive or habitual action to a more reflective perspective. In effect, they become more philosophical as they engage their "real" life. They often recognize what is obvious to an outsider: alcohol, another substance, or peer pressure has affected their capacity to make wise choices for themselves. Students typically make a distinction between academic and "real" life. Their sexual practices are often disguised or withheld in their academic discussions and not touched on significantly in course lectures. Philosophy courses can provoke heated discussion, but it seems there is only a weak connection between academic ideas about sexual practices and students' actual sexual practices. In the standard Philosophy 101 lecture-discussion survey course of "perennial" philosophy ideas, it is easy for students to keep separate (and unexamined) their "real" life ideas and practices.

In summary, we are offering our experimental model to connect critical thinking and troublesome aspects of their lives about which they are willing to risk making a change. They identify obstacles and excuses, like fixed ideas about a situation and about themselves, and their fears, and low expectations for meaningful improvements. Good experiments involve the virtues of honesty, courage, and foresight, which strongly contrast with the alcohol, conformist motivation, and disregard of consequences so characteristic of the college student's experimentation with sex (and other temptations like drugs). In our experience, the experiment works for many students. The two examples we have used are evidence that students can make profound changes in their lives.

We have focused on using this experiment to make changes in actual problematic areas in a student's life. It is also possible to use the experiment as a thought experiment to reflect on potentially troublesome choices facing them. By modifying the experiment format, students could imagine hooking up in detail, to consider obstacles and excuses for doing it, as well as predicted results or consequences if they did. Thinking about their "big question" and being a "better, wiser lover" in this format can be instructive for self-knowledge. In regard to experimenting in general, a big question is the value of Socratic experimenting itself. We have not presented an argument to show that philosophical thinking and deliberate experimenting is better than impulsive or compulsive experimenting. Any reasons bearing on the issue would have to appeal to examples. That is, an ideal experiment would involve trying and comparing both kinds of experimenting. So, in order to appreciate its value, we recommend experimenting with the Socratic experiment.

NOTES

1 William Masters and Virginia Johnson, *The Human Sexual Response* (Boston: Little Brown, 1972).
2 Alex Comfort, *The Joy of Sex* (New York: Crown Press, 1972).
3 For a discussion of the walk of shame, see chapter 4, this volume.
4 Paul Joannides, *Guide to Getting It On* (Oregon: Goose Foot Press, 2009), p. 763.
5 Ibid., p. 763.
6 Ibid., pp. 763–76.
7 Ibid., p. 763.
8 Ibid.
9 For an earlier version of the experiment see George T. Hole, "An Experiment To Make Your Life More Meaningful," *Teaching Philosophy* 14, 3 (1991): 223–39.

CHAPTER 2

THE STRAIGHT SEX EXPERIMENT

New Frontiers for College Sex

Discussions of college sex experimentation commonly focus on same-sex conduct performed in the context of haphazard "bicurious" interludes brought on by intoxication. In a new educational setting where much exploration awaits, it is not surprising that many incoming students partake in behaviors formerly unknown to them. An uninhibited social climate, coupled with inquisitive mindsets, fosters exploration in other domains as well, be it recreational drug use, vegetarianism, or unchartered political associations. It is much like yielding to an insatiable urge to explore unfamiliar sites, flavors, or customs while traveling in foreign lands. A more tolerant and welcoming environment generates newfound interests, inclinations, and inquiries; it supplies much needed courage to act on volitions.

In this spirit, the present essay seeks to explore a lesser-known phenomenon across college or university settings, namely, opposite-sex experiments involving self-proclaimed gay or lesbian students who, for one reason or another, engage in sporadic heterosexual sex. Much like their straight counterparts, homosexual students take advantage of opportunities that new college settings bring. Traditional accounts that attempt to explain same-sex experimentation do not convincingly apply to opposite-sex encounters. It will simply not do to extend a hypothesis regarding such experimentation about one student population to another. While there are some points of intersection between the two groups, such as acting on mere adolescent curiosity, opposite-sex experiments are distinct and complex practices that powerfully undermine both heterosexual and homosexual notions of sexual identity. In this essay, I argue that straight sex experiments of gay and lesbian students are unique practices that reveal important insights into the depth and diversity of college sex. I attempt to show that opposite-sex experiments challenge the notion of sexual identity more effectively than same-sex encounters, by mimicking yet rejecting both heterosexual and homosexual norms. Additionally, I discuss some of the reasons why opposite-sex experiments have consistently been ignored in academic settings as well as mainstream society. Lastly, in an effort to avoid needless complication, the discussion will not address college sex experiments of transgendered students, self-proclaimed bisexuals, or other groups.

"I'm no queer!" The Paradox within Identity and Practice

The running social, cultural, and theoretical focus on sexual identity might lead one to think that there is some corresponding relationship between sexual identity and sexual practice. The quandary is that one's sexual practice often does not cohere with one's self-proclaimed sexual identity, thereby challenging our widespread belief in a static notion of sexual identity. It is no mystery that many self-identified heterosexual students, at some point or another throughout their college careers, engage in same-sex practices. Straight college girls sometimes make out with other girls just to arouse their own boyfriends. Some of these encounters are voluntarily pursued out of curiosity, while others might be unintentionally brought on by inebriated stupors. Yet still, other encounters arise in a volatile climate of peer pressure, attributed to accepting one's dare or fulfilling frat hazing rituals; this might include mild acts like a quick peck on the lips or licking another guy's nipples, to serious moral and legal violations such as being sodomized by a broomstick handle or other household objects while frat brothers cheer on.[1] At other times, straight students simply seize the opportunity to experiment while they can, especially since future moral obligations that come with marriage and parenthood may prohibit them from indulging in same-sex relations.

Similarly, self-proclaimed homosexual students are likely to experiment with an opposite-sex encounter, albeit for different reasons, such as striving to imitate or fulfill mainstream sexual norms or undermining group-specific expectations of homosexual norms. Of course, this does not mean that members of this camp exhibit signs of bisexuality or latent heterosexuality. In most cases, it is a young lesbian bewildered by her first straight kiss or the daunting task of her first fellatio, or a gay man curious about submerging himself in a woman's bosom. It doesn't "convert" the experimenter and soon enough he reverts back to whatever was familiar to him. These sporadic acts, on the part of gay or lesbian students, further call into doubt the notion of residing within the limits of a static, clearly defined sexual identity; this is an especially relevant assertion for this population group since it has already taken the additional step of renouncing "mainstream" sexual orientations, prior to embarking on a journey to acquaint themselves with any possibilities mainstream sexualities may have to offer.

Attempts to resolve the disparity between sexual identity and sexual practice have busied aficionados of sexology for decades, especially in the area of study known as "queer theory." Within this monumental body of work, there are generally two dominant views. On the one hand, many argue that there is something unique about being gay or straight, namely, that there is in fact a clearly defined sexual "identity" (this is sometimes called the "ethnic model"). The view seems to have been influential in the early days of gay, lesbian, bisexual, and transgendered (GLBT) liberation movements, but was abandoned at some point in more recent decades. On the other hand, opponents of this view argue that the concern with identity is too restrictive, for it does not include variations such as situational sexual experimentation, episodic bisexuality, transgendered individuals, and other incidental sexualities or obscure categories that cannot be easily subsumed under strictly defined sexual or gendered boundaries. At some point, it was further realized that the notion of sexual identity is far too exclusionary, in that it overlooks key differences within groups, especially ones that cut across race, ethnicity, culture, gender, class, age, and sexual tastes. Thus, the use of the word "queer" (literally, "strange" or "odd") entered the lexicon of GLBT studies so as to account for any and all possibilities that might emerge, irrespective of identity or practice.

The queer designation has received its share of criticism as well. While it certainly opens up the possibility for introducing a more inclusive concept, it is frequently argued that the classification "queer" errs in the opposite direction; that is, it lumps too many groups together that otherwise have little in common with one another. As an open-ended umbrella term, queerness welcomes all; it is equally applied to overlapping sexual minorities (e.g., lesbian sadist and urophiliac pederast) as well as groups having little or nothing to do with sexual practice (e.g., vegan communist, Muslim feminist, and cannibal poet). While sexual identity is rejected for being too narrow, queer is renounced for being too wide.[2] As far as situational or context-specific sexual behavior goes – chiefly, same-sex or opposite-sex escapades – neither the static model of sexual identity nor the boundless excess of queer theory has much to tell us about erratic college sex experimentation among gay and lesbian student populations.

"You just might like it": The Straight Sex Experiment

Ever since Alfred Kinsey introduced his sex scale during the mid-twentieth century, a vast majority of sex research has perpetuated the social, cultural, and intellectual fascination with sexual experimentation in American society. The infamous "Kinsey Scale," as it would later be known, outlined a seven-point numeric system which attempted to diagram a seemingly diametric opposition between exclusively heterosexual and exclusively homosexual identities. The scale functioned so as to establish a continuum between two distinct counterparts, where zero stood for exclusively heterosexual identity, and six indicated an exclusively homosexual one. Since the vexingly complex nature of human sexuality is not easily bifurcated into two distinct halves, the sexual space between one and five accounted for alternative combinations, with bisexuality, or something close to it, usually placed around level three. As it turned out, a large portion of Kinsey's subjects fell somewhere along the spectrum, rather than some clearly marked division between heterosexual and homosexual.[3] Results from the Kinsey studies were initially met with surprise and hostility; social norms at mid-century were not quite ready to accept same-sex behavior as part of an ordinary developmental process, much less as part of an ordinary sexual identity, and given that these studies were published in the heyday of McCarthyism, cautious or ambivalent public reception was rather understandable.

Kinsey's respondents confirmed what social and sexual conservatives of the time feared most, namely that homosexual inclination, more specifically experimentation, was much more prevalent than previously imagined. The scale was, and continues to be, of great historic significance because it spearheaded the notion that same-sex experimentation forged a commonplace rite of sexual passage for many adolescents and young adults, especially since a significant portion of Kinsey's sample consisted of college students, as well as college-aged respondents more generally. The key role played by sexual experimentation achieved previously unrecognized cultural or clinical status. Sexual experimentation was gradually being recognized as a crucial ingredient in healthy sexual development. Of course, this minute achievement did not result in greater social acceptance of homosexuality. Nonetheless, Kinsey's studies helped reinforce the notion that human sexual behavior is fluid and developmental rather than fixed or stagnant. The studies continued to challenge "identity ideologues" and their unhealthy preoccupation with compartmentalizing human sexuality.

Toward the latter half of the past century and well into the present, a great deal of social, cultural, and academic attention has focused on the prevalence of same-sex experimentation throughout various stages of sexual development. With endless questionnaires, statistics, surveys, and studies, there is somewhat of a social and cultural obsession with same-sex experimentation and homoeroticism more generally. In popular culture and the entertainment industry, frequent use of lesbian eroticism caters to widely shared heterosexual male fantasies (Madonna's infamous nationally televised lesbian kiss with Britney Spears comes to mind). Heterosexual pornography commonly features lesbian sex so as to validate sexual desires many heterosexual men have but may never actually experience; entire series depicting drunken college girls "gone wild" on spring break lesbian sexfests are not uncommon. Of course, the heterosexual male's interest in lesbian sex does not translate into same-sex desire, but exhibits a fetishistic preoccupation with same-sex behavior between women. Though some heterosexual women likewise take an erotic interest in gay sex between men, it is to a much lower extent. The plethora of pornographic material showcasing straight college athletes seduced by gay sex is largely aimed at a gay male audience. Sex plots featuring naïve and desperately cash-strapped college boys coerced into gay sex (i.e., "gay for pay") similarly function so as to pay homage to pervasive sexual fantasies shared by many gay men. It is no mystery that there is public erotic interest in same-sex experiments at all levels, especially ones encountered by presumably drunk or confused straight college kids.

Despite the march toward increased social acceptance of homosexuality throughout the past four decades, there continues to be a great deal of enchantment or mystery, and to some extent latent repulsion, with same-sex practices. It makes tabloid news when straight-as-a-ruler celebrities or politicians get caught in the act; it enlivens otherwise mundane social science research and mind-numbing daytime talk shows. One does not have to search far and wide for examples of this. Recall the media frenzy that unfolded when British pop singer George Michael was officially "outed" after being arrested for lewd conduct in a Los Angeles men's room, or the more recent political spectacle that unraveled when former Idaho Senator Larry Graig was charged with a similar crime in a Minneapolis restroom.

By contrast, when high-profile gays and lesbians have an opposite-sex encounter, it is perceived differently. Rarely does the act evoke any reaction. Whatever media time one might elicit usually dismisses the act as a brush with bisexuality or some harmless PR stunt. The scandalous uproar one might expect to find is entirely missing. Iconic gay and lesbian celebrities such as Ellen Degeneres or Elton John should not be expected to ignite similar firestorms because any such acts are publicly non-essential (especially in John's case, since he was once married to a woman many years before coming out). The trend in high-profile gay and lesbian opposite-sex experimentation, being largely a non-issue, applies equally to low-level or commonplace communities. Opposite-sex experiments of ordinary, self-proclaimed gays and lesbians bring forth no social controversy. In fact, virtually no attention has been paid, socially, medically, politically, culturally, or otherwise, to opposite-sex experimentation among gay and lesbian college students. What are the reasons behind such glaring omissions?

Across college towns and university communities, initial departures from the norm merit some scrutiny, though any additional departures from a seemingly unconventional "norm" generate no additional concern. It has been customary to describe a sexual norm and simply focus on behavioral modifications that deviate from that norm. Homosexuality, once considered a mental disorder, is now clinically described as a "normal variant." However, behaviors that depart from the variant, or psychologically speaking, "variant of a variant," do not warrant an equal or serious degree of social or medical attention. That is, opposite-sex experiments (i.e., "variant of a variant") undertaken by self-identified gay and lesbian students are not significant enough to merit sustained analysis; after all, they're usually dismissed as mere adolescent confusion or evidence of latent bisexuality. The idea here is that once you have crossed the normative line (of heterosexuality) it matters little what other lines might be crossed along the way, since you have already been tainted by the greater stigma of homosexuality. Moreover, it is assumed that mainstream cookie-cutter gay and lesbian personas commonly venture into unconventional fetishistic territory anyway, be it cross-dressing, pederasty, incest, sadomasochism, bestiality, or "polymorphic perversions" widely believed to cross the moral line. According to this line of reasoning, once one is perceived as having willfully renounced mainstream sexual practices, attempting to understand one's motivations or intentions for experimenting with mainstream sexuality is a bit uninteresting, for it adds little value to the study of human sexuality.

For opposite-sex experiments of gay and lesbian college students to go unnoticed as they commonly do, might initially signal the dawn of an uninhibited sexual utopia. This is not the case at all. Today's gay and lesbian students have not arrived at some great political achievement by overcoming a climate of social opposition to their opposite-sex experimentation. Rather, its absence is cause for concern, likelihood for further neglect, and evidence of severe bigotry. Opposite-sex experiments merit no vilification or public outcry because gays and lesbians are doing what social and cultural norms have prescribed for them. They are habitually encouraged to experiment with the opposite sex in hopes that they "just might like it" or "turn straight." Better still, they may only stand to benefit from the process; after all, they might save their souls from sin and pathological perversion, or free themselves from an otherwise self-destructive lifestyle. Consider the rise in American "ex-gay" movements and their gay gulags scattered around the country, which further attest to a sustained social, cultural, and political effort to turn homosexuals into straights. Unfortunately, these largely unregulated sexual orientation conversion camps harm and screw up the helpless youngsters sent off to them.

It helps to recall that the American university setting has only recently been welcoming to gay and lesbian students, staff, and faculty. Despite strides toward greater social acceptance, many private and religious institutions continue to discriminate overtly against homosexual students, staff, and faculty in admission, promotion, or hiring practices, and many now require signed statements of "faith" or "ethics" which demand compliance with the institution's prohibition on homosexual conduct, and adherence to broader religious or ideological foundations. Many who apply for admission or employment may not even be aware of their university policies on these issues. This is especially the case for undergraduates and younger college-aged populations. College students enter university life in the face of innumerable challenges, many of which are unknown and unfamiliar to them. They are required to take on a great deal of financial, academic, and personal responsibilities all at once. Anyone who is accustomed to working in an academic setting must realize that college life, and by extension college students, drastically changed with the times. Factoring in additional complications brought on by being gay or lesbian magnifies challenges a student might face, such as the awkwardness of dorm life, forcible "outing," homophobic settings in intercollegiate athletics, or unwelcoming fraternities and sororities. Fortunately, there are now GLBT student unions on most campuses and even nationwide gay fraternities such as Delta Lambda Phi and lesbian sororities like Alpha Chi Upsilon.

It is clear that contemporary gay and lesbian students have a greater social space in which to affirm or express their sexuality. Notwithstanding this newfound freedom, the potential does exist that many will and in fact do experiment with opposite-sex encounters for a variety of reasons, some of which markedly differ from reasons applicable to straight counterparts – no lesbian is expected to make out with a man in order to please her girlfriend. A gay man is not worried about straight sex experimentation defiling his image in the way a straight man might worry about the stigma of gay sex, tarnishing an otherwise pristine reputation; so long as he doesn't "suck cock" and only plays the active role in anal sex, he continues to "preserve" his heterosexuality – or so the story goes. The reasons for gay and lesbian experimentation with straight sex might not be due to hazing rituals, pledging, or initiation requirements commonly found in heterosexual frat contexts. In fact, Delta Lambda Phi has a strict "no hazing" policy.[4] In such contexts, there is no peer pressure and no need to submit to asinine, often illegal and life-threatening initiation rituals to impress one's colleagues.

Unlike same-sex experiments, opposite-sex experiments, directly or subconsciously, seek to accommodate social expectations of being straight. The act fulfills a socially idealized role through simulation. While there is no social pressure to be homosexual or engage in same-sex encounters, there is tremendous social, cultural, and psychological pressure to conform to the status quo of heterosexuality. As one strives, be it unsuccessfully, to appease the hegemonic standard of heterosexuality, one's effort is usually welcomed by onlookers. The act is not met with repugnance, resistance, or intrigue, and no invasive or deeply personal questions are asked. Indeed, there is a double standard at play; just as lesbian eroticism is more socially or culturally acceptable than gay eroticism, a controversial reaction is more readily available to same-sex experiments of straights than opposite-sex experiments of gay and lesbian students.

The often disingenuous effort to accommodate social and sexual norms functions so as to mock said expectations by imitating same-sex experimenters. Just as same-sex experiments challenge rigid designations of heterosexual norms, opposite-sex experiments undermine sexual identities prescribed by homosexual norms. More to the point, opposite-sex interludes subvert notions of sexual identity by departing from dominant social expectations governing the status quo, as well as group-specific norms governing sexual conduct within gay and lesbian communities. Whether pursued in the spirit of shock value or sexual rebellion as same-sex experiments often are, opposite-sex experiments end up fulfilling some of the very same goals or curiosities, and ultimately, contribute to a healthy developmental gay or lesbian sexuality. While a social commotion may not be forthcoming, straight sex experiments of gay and lesbian college youth fulfill and reject mainstream heterosexual norms and further destabilize social, cultural, and political constructs imposed upon them from within, by their own "homosexist" communities that routinely frown upon deviations from self-imposed, group-specific expectations governing sexual conduct. Having the least to lose and "most to gain," self-proclaimed gay and lesbian college students take greater risks in their opposite-sex experiments by undermining both exoteric and esoteric conventions, as well as institutionalized religious fundamentalism that repeatedly bombards them with messages to "turn or burn!" They violate homosexual expectations by destabilizing their tightly knit gay and lesbian community's sense of pride, and ultimately succeed in neutralizing our ubiquitous, antiquated, and excessive faith in sexual identity.

Challenges to College Sex Experimentation

One might conjecture that opposite-sex experiments lack the strength or theoretical force to impact the types of outcomes illustrated in this account. While it is much easier to gauge increased social acceptance of same-sex experimentation in mass culture by considering analogous transformations in public perception of homosexuality, the same cannot be similarly assessed with respect to increased acceptance of running tendencies governing opposite-sex practices. There is no parallel social interest or clinical evidence to demonstrate this to be the case. On the one hand, we find a climate of fear and institutionalized intolerance, increasingly preoccupied with maintaining the status quo sexuality so as to discourage homosexual conduct. On the other, the proclivity to experiment with the opposite sex is frequently met with suspicion and hostility within gay and lesbian settings; in *either* camp, one must work hard at maintaining an identity convincing enough to those who value and avidly cling to it.

It helps to note that there is more focus on and interest in same-sex experimentation for two main reasons: first, it violates a greater taboo; and second, it is much more common. It stands to reason that since the heterosexual population is much larger than the gay and lesbian populations combined, more instances of same-sex practice are likely to take place; accordingly, more public attention is paid to it. However, the more crucial point is that it violates a more serious social taboo, whereas gay and lesbian experimentation with straight sex is barely a taboo at all, especially outside of its esoteric setting within gay and lesbian communities.

The strong emphasis on identity formation once played a dominant role in coming to think of oneself as straight, gay, or lesbian. At some point, same-sex sexual behavior became *not merely what one does but what one is*. However, globally and historically speaking, this is not how same-sex sexual relations have been thought of or understood. The predominantly Western (but now global) preoccupation with sexual identity among college-aged (or any other age) groups is still rather new. Whether or not this is the best method to understand human sexuality or seek social equality for sexual minorities remains a hotly debated topic. The emphasis on personal sexual identity, and by extension hyper-individualism, is much overemphasized, especially in mainstream American society.

Same-sex and opposite-sex experimentation is possible in the absence of identity talk or boundary blurring queer sensibilities. There are ways to preserve sexual selfhood without clinging to exclusionary selves. Such questions have ramifications for personal identity theory in general and not just personal sexual identity. There are schools of thought that have traditionally rejected the notion of identity altogether. Most denominations of Buddhism maintain that there is no fixed, unchanging, persistent self that exists through time (the view is sometimes referred to as *anatman*); thus, any association with a persistent, fixed self that exists through time is entirely contrary to Buddhist teachings. The influence of this view has also surfaced in mainstream Western philosophy, particularly in the Scottish philosopher David Hume's theory of personal identity (sometimes called the "bundle theory"). If these ideas have any merit, they ought to at least invite us to rethink our obsession with identity, sexual or otherwise. At least this much is vindicated by both same-sex and opposite-sex experiments.

Toward Alternative Notions of Sexual Experimentation

Despite countless social advances and increased openness toward sexual experimentation, there is much in our midst that continues to baffle us. Opposite-sex encounters invite us to consider a new social world and its accompanying generation, perpetually mesmerized by the allure of sexual experimentation. Kinsey's oeuvre entertained the possibility that human sexuality was partly fixed and partly fluid, contingent upon and determined by a variety of circumstantial factors – ideas still influential in our own times. Kinsey himself did not impose restrictions against sliding from one numeric slot into another, because behavioral frequency largely determined sexual identity. A Kinsey "one" may jump to a "two," provided that a few additional same-sex experiments were to take place. However, he and others before him did not envision alternative types of college sex experimentation that may tip the scale. We have moved beyond the sex scale age, and must further open ourselves to possibilities that college sex experiments take on, ones which may not even involve gender-based forms of experimentation at all.

Pervasive obsession with static identities and queer theory's historic preoccupation with their annihilation are both equally problematic dispositions; part of the solution to the quandary must lie somewhere within the two possibilities and perhaps outside of them. A new generation of experimentation portrays a disaffected population. Applying sweeping generalizations about human sexuality is risky business, because sexuality seems to be that type of thing, partly fluid and partly fixed, an inconspicuous, ambiguous matter, as diverse as human nature itself.

NOTES

1   See Cyd Zeigler, Jr., "The Gay Side of Hazing," *Outsports*, available online at www.outsports.com/campus/2006/0524hazing (accessed June 20, 2009).
2   I'm indebted to two drafts of Carol Quinn's unpublished manuscript, entitled "On My Reluctance to Defend a Queer Point of View," for some of these

points. Quinn's paper, along with my subsequent commentary on it, were both delivered at the group meeting of the Society for Lesbian and Gay Philosophy, in conjunction with the American Philosophical Association's (APA) eastern division conference in Philadelphia, December 2008.

3 Details of Kinsey's study are available at the Kinsey Institute website, at www.kinseyinstitute.org (accessed June 8, 2009).

4 Detailed information on Delta Lambda Phi may be obtained directly from their website, at www.sites.dlp.org/sites/national (accessed June 15, 2009).

CHAPTER 3

THE VIRTUAL BRA CLASP

Navigating Technology in College Courtship

College Sex is Tagged: Become a Fan

One clear way to reveal someone's age is by the technology they use. It does not take a genius to tell that the guy with the beeper or with the giant *Miami Vice* car phone is not fresh on the scene. Today, college kids are swerving in and out of traffic on their new iPhones, updating their Facebook status, Twittering "I just changed my Facebook status," and texting the guy or girl they met the night before. And don't tell me that in ten years people will think our Bluetooths are not hideous, but for now we're cool. Soon enough a new advance in technology, or a change in fashion, will have us signing up to the next social media website, uploading the "good" pictures, adding all the same friends again as they slowly follow our lead from the last place, updating our status – *this place is so much cooler!* – and it is business as usual.

If you are in college and are trying to meet a boyfriend or a girlfriend, find a husband or wife, a friend with benefits, a rebound, or the infamous one-night-stand, you have to be able to navigate an incredible amount of technology. It may help you or it may crush your chances; either way, you have to deal with it. The following essay is a phenomenological account of the technological hoops college students jump through every day in their quest for love and lust. A phenomenological account is concerned with attaining an understanding and proper description of the structure of our mental and embodied experience. Phenomenology employs a distinctive method to study the structural features of experience and of things as experienced; it does not attempt to develop a naturalistic explanation, i.e., an explanation that is justified insofar as it rests on empirical evidence, or causal theory.[1]

"That will get you slapped!"

Think back, way back, when people were less mediated by technology. I do not know if it is true, but I have heard stories that people used to meet other people, even ask them out on dates, by just walking up and talking to one another. Can you believe that? What a rush that must have been – the Wild West! But wait, how could that work? Did they quickly look at each other's online profile from their smart phone with the Facebook application? Would they see those awesome pictures from Cancun when I was tan and all my hundreds of hot friends? Would one person walk over to the other and say "Want to text?" followed by flirty finger-work?

Of course, that could never happen today; when was the last time you saw someone walking alone who did not have their phone glued to their ear? Walk across most college campuses and you will be shocked by how many people are on their phones. I feel sorry for the poor guy who tries to approach directly a college girl on campus, or vice versa. A girl walking through the quad on her Blackberry might as well be in a bubble.

If I saw a girl sitting on a campus bench, drinking coffee and reading my favorite book, and I walked up and started talking to her, I think there is a good chance that she would find it very awkward. There is a sense in our current customs that meeting "random" people this way is highly suspect. People who do this must be creepy and desperate, and probably rapists. This kind of encounter is immediate and direct, so much so that our culture finds it uncomfortable. Sure, Johnny Depp could stroll through campus and none of this would apply to him, but that is Johnny Depp. There are a number of different reasons why this does not apply to all people. The model, the quarterback, the rich kid, and so on, may all be stereotypical exceptions, but I am concerned with the everyday, normal background practices of college kids trying to mate the hard way.

One theme I want to develop in this essay is how technology gives the illusion of bringing people together, when often it is doing the exact opposite. While someone is engrossed on their phone as they walk the fifty feet to the cafeteria – apparently engaged in an urgent conversation – they actually seal out the world around them by directing their attention elsewhere, privileging the virtual, non-present relationship over the environment at hand, the possibilities of chance encounters, of old fashioned social courtesy, and the quiet refuge or hell of the psyche.

If you are in college and want to find someone special, the old school, John Wayne mentality is not your best bet. But do not despair. This may be the best time in the history of history to be single. There are so many ways to meet people, but you have to know the technology! In any society there are a host of background practices or "forms of life" that its people learn in order to function; these are the rules and mores, ethics, and social customs that its people learn and develop from birth. Mating rituals and codes like who can court whom, what the proper steps are in courtship and marriage, initiations and permissions, and monogamy and fidelity are all issues in the fabric of social courtship, and college kids are no exception. With the advent of the Internet, and especially social media and networking sites like Facebook and MySpace – not to mention craigslist and Match.com – college students have chances to meet new people like never before. One hundred years ago college-aged kids had a mating pool the size of a tear drop. Technology has changed everything.

"Can I have your number?" A Short Genealogy of Stressful Situations

One interesting aspect I want to point out from the start is that if we again compare the old fashioned, direct mode of courtship with one enmeshed in technology, the trajectory is inverted. Let me explain. Let's say you strike up a conversation with someone after class (right before she gets on her phone) and it goes pretty well. If both of you appear to be interested in each other, then the classic tense situation arises: how to contact her again? Do you ask for her phone number? But which one? Cell, home, dorm? And if you get a number how do you know which one it is? You do not want to booty call the home phone at two in the morning. If you ask for her phone number or are asked for yours, chances are you will give or receive the cell phone number (because you love your cell phone so much).

Once you have the cell phone number, you are now mediated by a base technology. At one time, the phone level of courtship consisted only of a phone and waiting for the phone to ring. It was simple, but

❦ MICHAEL BRUCE

torturous. Then came the answering machine; you could now leave the house and not be afraid that you would miss the call. You could also leave a voice greeting, which I think paved the way for sharing small tidbits of information. At first, people would just have something generic like "You've reached 555-5555, please leave a message." Then, later on, people might leave a family greeting ("You've reached the Johnsons!") or tell you where they went ("We're on vacation/Out of the office" – just like a Tweet).

The cell phone was a massive leap forward. One of the fancy new perks of a cell phone was that everyone with one also had caller ID. The advent of caller ID was a double-edged sword. It let you know who was calling you, which was great since it hopefully meant no surprises or fishing for a person's name or number. On the other hand, if they knew you had caller ID, there was no way of missing a call. Even if you did not pick up the phone, like you could have done before the answering machine/voice-mail to avoid calls, the caller stills showed up on your call log. In some ways caller ID replaced voice messages. Why leave a message? They can see I called. This was also the downfall of many over anxious suitors who called too much, thus scaring away their potential mates.

Even more importantly than caller ID, cell phones changed the land-scape of modern courtship by adding another dimension. By leaving his cell phone number on the answering machine at home, he thereby redi-rected you to another level of technology. In homage to Mario Bros., I will call this level jumping. Now you are mediated by two levels of tech-nology, the land line and the cell phone. To the nervous freshman, there are so many questions: if she doesn't answer at her dorm, do I leave a message? Should I call her cell? Do I leave a message there or both places? Or should I not leave a message at all; she will see that I called?

But let's go back for a second to our couple talking after class. Let's say now that the couple doesn't exchange phone numbers. Oh no, they are not nervous freshmen. They are way too hip, they have MySpace and Facebook. I think the sentiment among college kids is that if you have the resources, use them. Now, instead of dealing with the potential pitfalls of phone calls, voice mails, or even the possibility of him not giving his phone number at all, you take it to another level: online. You search for him on MySpace or Facebook, probably both, and enter a higher level of mediation. The risk is much lower and the amount of control you have over the contact is surgical. You may send him a message, "poke them," or add them as a friend. Now that you have access to his online profile, you can sculpt your witty message, maybe even through a quote from his favorite movie. You've got access to detailed information about him, the likes of which your grandparents don't know about each other.

But again, you have to know the customs of the technology. For example, it would be a bad move to write a message that was too long. It is not an email, and also having the right amount of online casual grammar, unfortunately, is the norm. Another advantage to pursuing someone through the online level is the ability to network. If you have a mutual online friend this gives you the appearance of credibility. It also is a conversation piece and a reference (for better or worse!). You also have possibly your greatest tool: your profile. Having an online template to tell the world how special you are, how cool, how eccentric, how buff, how smart, and so on, can be a great asset.

If you are online using a social media website, you have a profile and this can make or break you. In a sense, you are enslaved to your ability to present yourself through the online technology. You can have a profile that has music and video blaring, stunning background images, inspiring quotes, and a blog detailing all of your awesomeness. Or at the other extreme, you can have the default layout with an old cropped picture, a couple of sentence fragments about yourself, and be friends with four of your cousins and Tom from MySpace. Once again, suitors must advertise enough of their personality to attract interest, but not too much as too annoy or over share.

Treating Objects like Women, MySpace Pics, and Level Jumping

The interesting part of the online profile is the acknowledged unreality of it all. Everyone agrees to play this game where we realize people's profiles are often misleading and the product of the person projecting their ideal self for others to see. A profile is a text. No, not a *text message*, but a literary object. This kind of text conceals as well as reveals, has no fixed meaning, and is subject to the interpretation of its author and readers. Personal statements from an online profile, for example, are often crafted for effect, trying to highlight and emphasize a person's perceived attractive strengths.

With the biographical statements, the profile pictures, and a seemingly infinite amount of information available, a suitor must be a philosopher and detective. This online text is critically analyzed and deciphered.

The consequence of this is that the love interest becomes an object. Through the investigation of the profile, combined with whatever everyday information and contact a suitor may have with a person, that person is objectified. But isn't this a cardinal sin in our culture – to treat someone as an object? Or worse, a sex object? What makes things even more interesting is that both are implicated. As a suitor objectifies his potential mates, he has objectified himself in the process of engaging in the online community; the suitor has a profile as well. Instead of a couple learning about each other through intimate personal dialogue, suitors are challenged to interpret vast collections of data and have a refined "bullshit detector." At its worst, this kind of evaluation is reminiscent of a physician reviewing a patient's medical history.

Nowhere is this more clear than with profile pictures. "MySpace pictures" is a phrase that depicts certain poses, angles, and lighting that are used to frame a picture in such a way as to focus only on part of the subject. These kinds of pictures have served as ammunition to numerous online parodies and have trained the suitor's eye. Of course, not everyone online has less than truthful pictures or information. Nevertheless, this kind of behavior is rampant and is more or less unavoidable for people looking for love or lust online. The funny thing is that everyone in the online community seems to know profile pictures are often misleading, but it seems that as long as "I" get to post my own misleading picture for my benefit, everything is just fine.

This process, where one has the intention of getting to know and court someone, ultimately leads to an alienation of both parties. The online technology has mediated them to the extent that courtship is entrenched in two virtual personalities, interacting as objects, and further distancing each other through what was supposed to *connect* them. And remember that "connecting" online is a metaphor, and obviously quite removed from the embodied face-to-face encounter that suitors desire to have.

It might seem after all of this complicated nonsense that it would be impossible for people to hook up using online tools. But people are getting together left and right, and using social sites is essentially mandatory for college students and is gaining popularity across all ages. Moreover, dating sites like Match.com and eHarmony.com are quickly losing any taboo that used to be associated with them. More and more college students are joining these communities and people are hooking up like rabbits. On the dating sites there is a culture of extreme objectification, and even *expert objectification*. It is common on these sites to have professional photography done specifically for your profile. How do you take a

"MySpace picture" without it looking like one? Hire a professional. And with "29 dimensions of compatibility" as eHarmony advertises, suitors are further distanced by not having a text, but instead, a multiple choice questionnaire.

Let's recap the potential trajectories of courtship so far:

Face-to-Face → Get phone number → Calls or texts → Face-to-Face → Calls/texts or online

Face-to-Face → Online → Private messages or profile posts → Calls or texts → Face-to-Face → Calls/texts or online

Online → Private messages or profile posts → Calls or texts → Face-to-Face → Calls/texts or online

The type of communication following hanging out or hooking up is often an indicator of how things went. If things went well, or at least was perceived that way by one of the people, direct contact like a phone call or text message is likely. This immediate gesture signals that he is very interested and wants to continue in courtship. The response to this act is equally important. If the call is taken, which is a large clue already, the status of courtship or attraction, and so on, is normally obvious by the conversation. If the call is not answered and a message is left, the technology the person replies with – if he does at all – points to his level of interest. If a phone call is responded to with a text message, if a text message is responded to with an online message or email, if an online message is responded to with a public profile post, this would be a huge sign showing a lack of interest or a sense of uneasiness. This move, which may not be consciously chosen, creates distance and brings the relationship into a "safe" place of objects where a battery of technological gestures can help him manage the situation. In sum, it is easier to give and take bad news online. The alienation of people by the distancing and objectifying technology makes it easier for people to break up or brush people off.

Shy college students use level jumping to their advantage. There are a number of reasons why college suitors prefer to use online media for courtship, especially when it comes to meeting and introductions to new people. A person who may be socially awkward or have challenging interpersonal skills may be much more successful using the text-work of the Internet. The incredible amount of control over how she can frame her information and online persona gives rise to an alternate online-ego or confidence, behind or through which the suitor may exploit opportunities not available ten years ago. Shy and soft spoken sensibilities can become, often comically, robust and aggressive when enough distance and subterfuge is in play.

When Internet dating was still relatively new and heavily stigmatized, popular culture had a running gag: a new and exciting online romance would be depicted, followed by the first face-to-face meeting ... and ... neither person would be anything like they described themselves to be. The butt of the joke was often a geeky college kid. The mode of communication used by these shy suitors is also used in relationships where someone cannot express themselves in person. Many important conversations, fights, and love letters are enacted this way, because they might be too upset, intimidated, or flustered to articulate it in person.

It can be hard to judge if "level jumping" is disrespectful or not. Prior to the social media craze, the moral standard was that breaking up was done face-to-face. Doing it over the phone was not acceptable, and there was a level of respect perceived when breaking up in person. From this perspective, brushing someone off via online message would amount to a slap in the face. But I am not sure online junkies would agree. If most of the relationship, however brief it may have been, takes placed via indirect technologies, then perhaps online is an appropriate space to give bad news. This is also much more acceptable if the couple met online; courtship here still has a level of unreality associated with it. It would be completely normal to hear a rationalization like, "It was an online thing. I met them on that website; it didn't work out, no big deal." Now it may have been the case that these people just did not have a connection, and meeting online was not a factor. However, I suspect that framing relationship reports with technology like this can be used to lessen the social stigma of a failed relationship – "It was just an online thing."

Black Holes

There are some places where technology is seemingly abandoned and college kids revert to the glory days of face-to-face courtship. The Mecca of this wild space is the bar and club scene. Here caution is thrown to the wind and kids will sweet talk and "hit" on each other, grind on each other, and suck face until the lights come on. This is one of the few social spaces where someone has a chance to talk to a stranger without the creepy or rapist vibe associated with the random campus walker.

That being said, of course the bars often do house weirdos, creepsters, and maybe even actual rapists – but that is not who I am talking about.

Going to a bar is like signing a social contract: within these walls it is okay to dress slutty (without being slutty), talk to strangers, and say things that would otherwise get you fired at work for sexual harassment. And college bars are king. Bar culture is a fascinating world to visit. There is a separate code of appropriate behavior, a sexual ethic much different and more direct than non-bar communication and courtship. Try this experiment: in the middle of the day, strike up a conversation with a stranger you find very attractive. After the initial brief introduction or small talk that gets their attention, tell them that you find them extremely attractive, that they are "hot," and that you want to go back to your place and hang out with them. It is not likely that this will be successful. However, this style of communication is commonplace at the club.

Outside of the bar, verbal expressions of attraction are usually much less interesting. It seems that complimenting a person on their physical appearance must have a clinical matter-of-factness, "Sally, you look very pretty today; I like your sweater." A lot of this has to do with the "political correctness" in our society at large and isn't isolated to younger folks. My point is just to highlight the radical incongruence of morally appropriate discourse at different places within a single community. One of the significant differences that contributes to this is use of technology, specifically the lack of use in the bar scene.

Alcohol, the best and worst friend a college student may have, plays a crucial role here without a doubt. The wildness, debauchery, and glorious inhibition are all accelerated by derivations of this magical elixir. It could be argued that alcohol is the technology of choice here, and that the change in behavior is purely chemical. While acknowledging the clear biological impacts of the drug – inhibition, beer goggles, better dancing – I think it is only part of the equation. My counter example is that the same actions are deemed appropriate in the club no matter if you are drinking alcohol or not.

After college and even more so in graduate school, coffee shops replace many of the functions of the college bar. Cafés are still a place where society approves of outright flirtation for singles of all ages. Instead of buying someone a beer or cosmopolitan, people are buying black coffee or a triple *venti* non-fat macchiato. With a caffeine buzz and their favorite books in hand, single people love their coffee shops. However, the plot thickens. It is becoming popular to bring a laptop to the café! Customers maneuver for the seats with the electrical outlets, where they will remain for hours on end. The bright screen emits an aura of light around the customer that acts as a don't-bother-me force field. This is the sibling of the student walking across campus glued to their cell phone.

Someone quietly sitting, reading a book in a café is exponentially more approachable than the person at the next table squinting at her laptop. First, a suitor has many clues to engage the reader. The person's choice in literature often sparks interests in a suitor and gives an easy "ice breaker." There are no such clues when dealing with the laptop zombie. The black box gives the impression that he is doing something important. The loud noises of the keyboard mimics a real conversation people do not want to interrupt. With enough laptops in the room, the friendly café is turned into a computer lab that happens to have good coffee. Once again, technology pushes people away.

Wrap It Up

College students master an enormous amount of technology. The limitless sex drive of college students has never had a better chance for satisfaction. There are so many things to know, but technology creates opportunities that abound for the young lovers. The nature of online profiles and the "objectification" of people online raise many interesting questions, warranting more research. The entrenchment in technology of college lovers will be a fascinating spectacle to follow. It is clear that video chatting like Skype will be the next massive leap forward, which will most likely minimize the role played by written text online.

I leave with an analogy that attempts to tie the broader technological issues of college courtship with sexual foreplay and intercourse. Understanding each layer of technology in courtship can metaphorically be seen as lovers undressing each other. There is a microcosm of courtship within this most intimate of rituals:

The couple meets and kisses passionately, the initial face-to-face encounter. They take off their shoes next and start to get more comfortable – the exchange of information and early flirting. Topical layers of clothes are removed, shirts, pants, and so on; their guards are down, mutual interest and attraction signaled. The incredibly tough snaps, buckles, and hooks of undergarments and lingerie are next – carefully navigating technology (form) and saying the right things (content).

At last, the two lovers are fully revealed to each other and sex ensues; the couple meets and continues courtship, in person and unmediated.

NOTE

1 See Dermot Moran and Timothy Mooney (eds.) *The Phenomenology Reader* (New York: Routledge, 2002) and Dermot Moran, *Introduction to Phenomenology* (New York: Routledge, 2000).

‼ MICHAEL BRUCE

CHAPTER 4

SMEARED MAKEUP
AND STILETTO HEELS

Clothing, Sexuality, and the Walk of Shame

7 a.m.: These Boots Aren't Made for Walking

When I mentioned to my students that I was writing an essay on the walk of shame, some responded with knowing looks and smirks while others responded with a bit of confusion. Others in the class responded to their confused classmates by explaining that the walk of shame is when men and women make the trek back to their apartments or dorm rooms after a night spent elsewhere. "All you have to do is wait outside a frat house or a sorority house on Sunday morning to see the walk of shame," one student explained. Once the explanation had been made, they immediately recognized the phenomenon.

There is a good reason why the walk of shame is not quite so prevalent at my current campus. Ours is mainly a commuter campus with a small percentage of students living near or on campus. However, at Penn State, where I received my doctorate, a large percentage of students lived either on campus or within a few blocks of the university. As such, the walk of shame was an institution. For example, when I taught a course in small group communication, I had an assignment where students had to create an infomercial selling some product of their choosing, either real or imagined. One group developed a "walk of shame kit." In doing so, they polled 100 women who lived in the dorms with them and asked questions such as "Have you performed the walk of shame?" "If so, how many times?" and "What do you wish you had brought when you performed the walk of shame?" They found that many had performed the walk of shame at least a few times, and one woman confessed to doing so 50 times. I expressed doubt that such a number was accurate, but was corrected when one of the students explained that that response had come from her roommate. "It's definitely accurate; she's had an interesting semester," she explained.

A former colleague at Penn State reported that he would go out to breakfast with his roommates on Sunday morning and watch as people performed the walk of shame; for them, it was like breakfast and a show. People performing the walk of shame are easy to identify – they are wearing clothing that is calculated to attract sexual attention that seems out of place in an early morning walk. As such, women are much easier to identify. As Laura Baron notes, "Everyone knows black-patent leather stilettos, jeans, and sequins isn't a morning jogging outfit."[1] This essay will focus mainly on women who perform the walk of shame because they are particularly held up for ridicule because of their transparency. My students reported that people in the dorms would mock the women who performed the walk of shame, calling them "whores" and "sluts." Elsewhere, I have discussed the rhetorical and semantic aspects of defining this behavior as the walk of shame.[2] In this essay, I take a semiotic approach. Semiotics is the study of signs and sign systems, which makes it particularly well-suited to examining aspects of the walk of shame, such as the clothing, that mark such behavior as shameful. Specifically, I will consider how the clothing worn during the walk of shame functions as an index (i.e., a specific type of sign) of sexuality, which is marked, especially in young women, as shameful.

Dressing for (Sexual) Success

Dress is the first indicator that a woman is performing the walk of shame. When I was an undergraduate, I had a housemate who would often go to the Peacock tavern to the "Top of the Cock" where there was dancing on frat night. She would come to my room if she wanted an honest opinion on her outfit for the night. On one such occasion, she asked my opinion and the exchange went something like this:

"How do I look?"

"You look like a slut."

"OK, but how about the specifics?"

"The shirt is good – it shows off the cleavage well."

"OK, good. How about the pants?"

"Turn around. They make your ass look big."

"So lose the pants?"

"Lose the pants, but the top is good."

In this exchange, she was not terribly concerned about the appearance of looking like a slut, so much as she was concerned about looking like an *attractive* slut.

The clothes that a woman wears during the walk of shame fall into a particular category; they are generally more revealing, accentuating her body in such a way as to invite desire. The shoes are not the sensible shoes of the workplace, but rather the "hooker shoes" or "fuck-me pumps" of the club scene. Even the fabric itself is more sensual, clinging to her body in some places, and flowing and gauzy in others. The colors are likewise selected to denote sexiness; this is not the place for bright flowery prints or whimsical patterns. Instead, she chooses dark, serious colors that evoke the mystery of the *femme fatale* or bold colors that draw the viewer's eye to what lies beneath the clothing, rather than the clothing itself. As a society, we are in general agreement concerning what certain articles of clothing are trying to communicate. Let us now examine the typical outfit for a night at the club or the bar to see what is being communicated and, more importantly, *how* it is being communicated.

Philosopher Charles Peirce described two types of signs that are relevant for our discussion of the walk of shame: indexes and symbols. Peirce explains that an index is "a sign which refers to the Object that it denotes by virtue of really being affected by that Object."[3] The typical analogue of an indexical sign is a thermometer; as the temperature rises, the mercury rises. A symbol, on the other hand, refers to an object because we have agreed that the symbol refers to the object.[4] For example, a flag may represent a nation, but it has no resemblance to the nation; the association is essentially arbitrary and held only by mutual agreement.

Generally, the woman's clothing reveals much more flesh than everyday clothing. I suggest that such clothing functions as an index of sexuality because the more flesh that is revealed, especially flesh that is considered taboo to reveal, such as the breasts and buttocks, the more sexual the outfit is considered to be. It is not uncommon to see women wearing low-cut or backless shirts, short skirts, or tight-fitting pants that hug the hips. When the woman performs the walk of shame in such an outfit, she demonstrates a potential for sexual behavior by displaying herself in a manner deemed to be sexual.

Yet it is not simply the display of skin that codes an article of clothing as sexual, but rather what particular area of skin is displayed. In jeans, the woman may wear a pair of low-rise pants that bare the midriff and ride just below the pelvic bone, drawing attention to the pubic area that lies just beneath the waistline. The skirt, however, functions to draw the eye upward from the lower hem to the pubic area or buttocks that are hidden (in the walk of shame, often barely hidden) just above.

The underwear (or potential lack thereof) likewise functions as an index of sexuality. The halter top or backless shirt may call attention to the lack of bra, which allows the breasts to move freely, also calling attention to her body and potentially highlighting her nipples. The woman's underwear may ride up displaying the "whale tail" of the thong or g-string that she wears beneath the pants or skirt, likewise calling attention to what lies beneath. Such clothing may also help to reinforce the idea that the woman is sexy not only in the minds of the observers, but herself as well. Such underwear is meant to transcend practical needs of support and coverage; it is meant to display sexiness. In this way, the undergarments function as another part of the costume that reinforces the image that the woman seeks to display, but, unlike the rest of her costume, a part that will be seen fully only by the person with whom she will go home. Other more visible undergarments such as stockings, pantyhose, or leggings compress the leg to make it appear leaner and alter the color of the skin, or, in the case of colored tights or fishnet, draw attention to the leg. Stockings or hose also conceal blemishes, body hair, or other imperfections of the leg, providing the illusion of perfect smoothness.

Some articles of clothing may seem to function more as symbols than as indexes, such as high heels. High heels are worn not only at the club, but also in the workplace, and as such could be coded as professional wear, but despite their presence in the workplace, high heels are coded as quintessentially feminine and as sexy. Moreover, the heels that the women may wear during the walk of shame (or simply carry, thus reinforcing their discomfort) are not the heels of the workplace, but rather the stiletto heels of the club that are associated with sexiness. Yet, I suggest that these heels serve not only as a symbol, but also as an *index* in that they actually reshape the body to more fully conform to societal norms of attractiveness by elongating the leg and creating the illusion of leaner, sexier legs. Moreover, such shoes cause the wearer to walk in such a way that hip motion is accentuated, thus drawing attention to the pelvic area. Once again, this sign may be directed not only outwardly, but also toward herself.

Some ornaments do seem to function as symbols, such as jewelry, makeup, or sequined tops. These objects signify that the outfit is constructed for a different time and place than the everyday. Perhaps this is why the outfit seems so jarring to witness in the morning. For example, where modest earrings are common in the workplace, the woman may choose to wear large, dangling earrings that move with her body and accentuate her face. She is less likely to choose the demure strand of pearls and more likely to choose the necklace with the pendant that hangs between her breasts, drawing the eye to her cleavage. Likewise, she coifs her hair for work, but when seeking sexual conquest, her hairstyle is crafted to portray a sense of glamour or beauty in ways that may not be present in her morning grooming ritual.

In order to understand how these elements function with the complete outfit, we must consider the outfit as a syntagm. In semiotics, systems constitute a class of like kinds of individual elements, such as different types of skirts. Elements of a system cannot be used together – in other words, one generally wears a long skirt or a short skirt, but not both.[5] Combining different elements of systems forms the syntagm, and each element of the syntagm contributes to the meaning of the whole. For example, Barthes notes:

> The language, in the garment system, is made (i) by the opposition of pieces, parts of garment and "details," the variation of which entails a change of meaning (to wear a beret or a bowler hat does not have the same meaning); (ii) by the rules which govern the association of the pieces among themselves, either on the length of the body or on the depth.[6]

For example, a woman can choose to wear a flowing skirt or a micro-mini skirt and this decision affects the system that includes pants, shorts, skirts, and dresses. But one cannot look at individual choices of a system, such as skirts, in isolation, even though these elements alter the meanings we ascribe to the outfit. One must look at what the entire ensemble – the syntagm – signifies, because a long, flowing skirt paired with a skin-tight, sheer top and no bra would still signify sexuality. In the case of the woman who performs the walk of shame, the syntagm almost always signifies sex.

Shamefulness and the Walk of Shame

In the morning, the observer notes that a woman who dressed in a way to attract sexual attention spent the night at someone else's home and the chain of reasoning begins. It is important to note that the accuracy of the judgment is not the issue. Witnesses are only able to draw from what they observe, as well as their personal experiences. The unspoken idea here that becomes obvious to the observer (despite what actually occurred) is that the woman is coming from a sexual encounter with someone she is now leaving. Many fragments of experience go into this judgment. First is the assumption that sexual people do not spend the night at someone's house without having sex with someone; certainly, such an outfit is not something that one wears when spending the night with a friend. Second is the assumption that the sex that was had was a random hook up rather than sex in a committed relationship. After all, why would the woman slink out of the house shortly after dawn if she and her partner had a relationship? This line of reasoning is likewise accepted by the woman performing the walk of shame. Sarah Morrison, writing in *Cosmopolitan*, states, "What makes those slinks back to safety so totally unbearable is that most of the time, all we're dressed in is our skimpiest manhunt ensembles and last night's makeup. Hell, we might as well be wearing a sign that says 'I just came from a sexy sleepover.'"[7]

Thus, the walk of shame is not only a function of the clothing that the woman wears, but also the time and space she occupies. Peter Berger and Thomas Luckmann suggest that "the canons of proper dress for different social occasions … are taken for granted in everyday life."[8] There is a time and place to look sexy. For example, *Chicago Tribune* columnist Gina B. described the disheveled state of her college suitemate, "Miss Bedhead," who "crept in at 6:30 a.m. looking like she'd been run over by a truck," wearing revealing clothing, smeared lipstick, and tousled hair.[9] Yet for the author of this narrative, Miss Bedhead's transgression was not the sex itself but rather the sin of impropriety. In response to Miss Bedhead's statement, "I can't believe I hooked up with him!!" the author recounted that "I had no problem with the hook up – I couldn't believe she actually walked around on campus looking like that."[10] However, I would suggest that the author is much more forgiving than others who may have viewed this spectacle, because such behavior transgresses social norms of femininity. Shannon Gilmartin notes that "'Hook ups,' or casual sexual interactions that are familiar to many undergraduates today, leave some women feeling awkward and disappointed, feelings no doubt engendered by the 'proper' code of feminine conduct (women are not supposed to act on their desire, especially outside of a romantic relationship)."[11]

Because the clothing functions as an index of sexuality in a time and place where the woman is forbidden to display such desire, the act is coded as shameful. Yet this is not merely a function of the woman herself; the viewer may also be complicit in the act. Kenneth Burke suggests that those who hold up scapegoats as objects of ridicule often conceal their own tendencies toward the act in question: "When the attacker chooses for himself the object of attack, it is usually his blood brother; the debunker is much closer to the debunked than others are."[12] These women become scapegoats for the viewer's own potential desires and failings. After all, we must disabuse ourselves of the notion that college is where young adults begin experimenting with sex; public health researchers estimate that almost half of the adolescent population has engaged in sexual intercourse.[13] By the time they reach college, about half of the observers who mock the woman engaging in the walk of shame are no longer virgins themselves, and even those who are technically virgins may have engaged in some form of sexual behavior. This, more than anything, explains why the walk of shame is considered shameful – in order to maintain one's own supposed innocence, those who observe *must* cast derision on those who display their sexuality openly. That women are allowed to wear clothing that openly signifies sexuality in the evening, yet not in the morning light, reinforces the idea that they can seek sex, and can portray themselves as sexual beings, but they are not actually allowed to act on those desires or to *succeed* in their efforts. A woman can be desirable but cannot consummate that desire.

With such sanctions leveled on women who perform the walk of shame, one is left to ask, "Why do they do it?" The simplest answer is because women are sexual creatures who, like the men with whom they have sex, sometimes act on their desires. But it is also illustrative to consider what Susan Bordo describes as the "receptive pleasures traditionally reserved for women," such as "the pleasures, not of staring someone down but of feeling one's body caressed by another's eyes.... Some people describe these receptive pleasures as 'passive'.... 'Passive' hardly describes what's going on when one person offers himself or herself to another. Inviting, receiving, responding – these are active behaviors too, and rather thrilling ones."[14] Women have been socialized to be attractive and desirable, and it is acceptable and enjoyable to be observed as an object of sexual beauty, to be seen as desirable. Yet women must negotiate a paradoxical imperative to be sexy but not sexual, desirable but not desiring. Once a woman appears to have acted on her sexual desire, she is persecuted and shamed by her peers.

There is, of course, nothing intrinsically shameful about the walk of shame. Alan Soble argues that "the sexual permeates our Being. But this does not make sexual ethics *sui generis*, even if this ethics is important. Nor need it be restrictive; if our being is sexual, that could be just as much reason for a relaxed, as for a restrictive, sexual ethics."[15] Sexuality is a natural part of life, but the walk of shame is not merely about sex. One does not perform the walk of shame when one returns from the home of a lover; rather, the walk of shame takes place when there is a tinge of regret. This shamefulness is inscribed on the body itself.

In the evening before the walk of shame, the woman moves in such a way as to draw attention to herself. She moves in close to the target of her affection, whispering in his (or her – there is always the assumption that it is him, however) ear, a subtle touch on the arm, a brush against the thigh, a quick toss of the hair, a laugh. All of these behaviors stand in stark contrast against the next morning, where she hurriedly gathers her belongings, attempting not to wake the object of the previous evening's affections. She attempts to return home as inconspicuously as possible, yet she is thwarted in this effort because her clothing still loudly proclaims her sexuality by drawing attention to her flesh. Much as when someone lowers his voice and others strain to hear what is so interesting, she draws attention to herself by attempting to avoid attention.

Her movements in the evening reinforce her sexuality, even as her movements in the morning attempt to deny it. The walk of shame itself would not be shameful without the observation of others. Gilles Deleuze observes, "A body affects other bodies, or is affected by other bodies."[16] This works both ways in the case of the walk of shame. The woman's body is a body out of place, which causes a jarring effect on those who recognize her for what she performs (not necessarily what she is). They see her as a breach of feminine codes of conduct, and as such, other women are implicated in her transgression. Other bodies gaze at her, disciplining her through knowing looks and slurs muttered in her direction. Her clothing and her own adoption of a shameful affect testify against her. At this point, her clothing acts as an index of *actualized* sexuality, while her recoiling away from the weight of observation functions as a signal of her shame.

You Can Walk, But You Can't Hide (The Shame)

What seems, more than anything, to make the walk of shame shameful is its transparency. The walk of shame is a manifestation of feminine sexuality which is simultaneously required and forbidden. Such paradoxical norms are shaped early in our development and women are as likely as men to sanction other women. Yet the reason we know that such an act is worthy of shame is the semiotic codes displayed by the woman as she performs the walk of shame. Such codes take considerable effort to alter. Naomi Wolf observes that attitudes toward clothing are indicative of women's position in society:

> Clothing that highlights women's sexuality will be casual wear when women's sexuality is under our own control. When female sexuality is fully affirmed as a legitimate passion that arises from within, to be directed without stigma to the chosen object of our desire, the sexually expressive clothes or manner we may assume can no longer be used to shame us, blame us, or target us for beauty myth harassment.[17]

Still, so long as a double standard concerning sexuality remains, college women all over the country will attempt to look sexy on Saturday nights, they will engage in sexual behavior, they will attempt to slink home unobserved, and the walk of shame will continue to be shameful.

NOTES

1 Laura Baron, "Sex on the First Date? Be Respectful: Talk About It," *Chicago Tribune*, September 9, 2004.
2 See Brett Lunceford, "The Walk of Shame: A Normative Description," *ETC: A Review of General Semantics* 65, 4 (2008): 319–29. Despite its ubiquity, little scholarly attention has been paid to the walk of shame. The only other article I could find that discusses the walk of shame at all was Elizabeth L. Paul, "Beer Goggles, Catching Feelings, and the Walk of Shame: The Myths and Realities of the Hookup Experience," in D. Charles Kirkpatrick, Steve Duck, and Megan K. Foley (eds.) *Relating Difficulty: The Processes of Constructing and Managing Difficult Interaction* (Mahwah: Lawrence Erlbaum, 2006), pp. 141–60. Even so, the main focus of Paul's essay was not on the walk of shame, but rather on how college students described "hook-ups" or sex with random people; the walk of shame was a peripheral aspect.

3   Charles S. Peirce, *Collected Papers*, 6 vols. (Cambridge, MA: Belknap Press of Harvard University Press, 1960), vol. 2, p. 248.

4   Ibid., p. 249.

5   For a concise explanation of the differences between system and syntagm, see Roland Barthes, *Elements of Semiology*, trans. Annette Lavers and Colin Smith (New York: Hill and Wang, 1968), p. 63.

6   Ibid., p. 27.

7   Sarah Morrison, "When I Did the Walk of Shame," *Cosmopolitan* (February 2002), p. 128.

8   Peter L. Berger and Thomas Luckmann, *The Social Construction of Reality: A Treatise in the Sociology of Knowledge* (New York: Anchor Books, 1966), p. 148.

9   Gina B., "Turn Walk of Shame into Walk of Pride," *Chicago Tribune*, December 2, 2005.

10 Ibid.

11 Shannon K. Gilmartin, "Changes in College Women's Attitudes toward Sexual Intimacy," *Journal of Research on Adolescence* 16, 3 (2006): 429–30. Here, Gilmartin quotes the following: E. L. Paul and K. A. Hayes, "The Casualties of Casual Sex: A Qualitative Exploration of the Phenomenology of College Students' Hookups," *Journal of Social and Personal Relationships* 19 (2002): 639–61; Norval Glenn and Elizabeth Marquardt, *Hooking Up, Hanging Out, and Hoping for Mr. Right: College Women on Mating and Dating Today* (New York: Institute for American Values, 2001).

12 Kenneth Burke, *A Grammar of Motives* (New York: Prentice-Hall, 1945), pp. 406–7.

13 John Santelli et al., "Trends in Sexual Risk Behaviors, by Nonsexual Risk Behavior Involvement, US High School Students, 1991–2007," *Journal of Adolescent Health* 44, 4 (2009): 372–9.

14 Susan Bordo, *The Male Body: A New Look at Men in Public and in Private* (New York: Farrar, Straus and Giroux, 1999), p. 190.

15 Alan Soble, "Sexuality and Sexual Ethics," in Lawrence C. Becker and Charlotte B. Becker (eds.) *Encyclopedia of Ethics* (New York: Garland, 1992), p. 1146.

16 Gilles Deleuze, "Ethology: Spinoza and Us," in Mariam Fraser and Monica Greco (eds.) *The Body: A Reader* (New York: Routledge, 2005), p. 58.

17 Naomi Wolf, *The Beauty Myth: How Images of Beauty Are Used against Women* (New York: W. Morrow, 1991), p. 273.

CHAPTER 5

RELATIONS AT A DISTANCE

Moving Apart

Two high school students, dating since tenth grade, get accepted to different colleges. They hear that college is a time to be free from entanglements, meeting all sorts of new and interesting people, but they want none of it. And so they lay complex plans on how to keep their relationship alive with frequent contact, train trips, and even flights, whether or not these break the bank.

A college student (you?) meets someone at a mixer. He's the friend of a classmate there, just in for the weekend. It's attraction at first sight, growing with second and third sightings. But just when she starts to feel involved, he's gone – his far-away campus called, classes are back in session. She can think of little else until they next meet. He feels the same. But does she really want her attentions focused elsewhere, absenting herself from the life she chose and built on campus, compromising her studies?

One member of a college couple gets an amazing one-semester internship in a foreign country. On campus, they are joined at the hip, doing everything together, but the internship is a once in a lifetime opportunity, a dream come true. "I want you to go," says the partner being left behind. "Don't worry, our love is too strong to let a semester separation part us." (Anyone who has seen the film *Family Man* may doubt that.)

These are typical entry points to the infamous realm of distance relationships. Why infamous? I interviewed a host of college students to find out.

Their most common depictions were "very hard to pull off" and a "real challenge to couples" that "takes a constant toll on both members." They added, "Only the strongest relationships can survive." But while this overwhelming response marked normal interviews, "think-loud protocols" revealed some surprising information. (These stream-of-consciousness interviews elicit psychological associations that don't come up in normal conversation.) More couples were *told* by others about the hell of distance love than actually experienced it that way. In fact, a major challenge for distance couples was overcoming the dark expectations they'd been saddled with, and crediting their direct experience instead. Positive associations to distance were revealed as well, though rarely shared with distance partners. Emphasizing the benefits of not being with one's lover doesn't tend to enhance togetherness.

Philosophical exploration rarely begins with psychological interviews, but much in philosophy rises from common observation, and philosophy's golden age of exploration included all the sciences. Why give these up when analyzing daily life? Our analysis of college sex and love focuses on philosophical process, the thought strategies of comparative interpretation, critical questioning, assessing a view's pros and cons, and tracing out its implications in illustration and argument. (I don't mean personally contentious argument, but the kind that draws inferences and good reasons to believe.) Philosophy is especially keen on seeing matters in new ways to reveal hidden realities. These suggest alternative paths for penetrating matters, opening up on new grounds for mutual understanding. In distance relationships, this can be a saving grace for better communication and meetings of minds. "Let's look at what we're doing as...."

I offer a supporting case for distance relations, built by first running them down in comparison with up-close relations, then reshaping our picture of them to include recent media of communication. We consider the capacity of these media to become integral parts of relationships, shaping their actual conduct, and their promise for overcoming distance deficits.

On First Reinterpretation

Sacrifice, longing, and the frustrations of separation and miscommunication compose the reality of distance relationships, but reality can be interpreted in many different ways. To start, we may ask whether viewing distance relations as stretched and mangled versions of "normal," up-close romances makes sense. Is it more useful and accurate for understanding than seeing such relations in their own terms, as wholly different kinds of relationships? Isn't it likely that we view and experience distance relationships as difficult because we judge them by the standards of close-up ones? Imagine if we afforded them their own standards of quality and success the way we do marriages as opposed to dating relationships, for example.

Isn't it true also that up-close relationships in college are typically distanced by class schedules and study routines even for partners at the same college? Aren't couples driven apart by too much togetherness, needing space? And doesn't scheduling time together within class and study routines get as complicated and burdensome as commuting to a distant campus? The whole relationship can begin to seem like an exercise in logistics: "Every time we talk, the topic is basically planning when and where we next meet." It is the up-close relationship that is traumatized by a traveling semester or foreign summer internship. The distance relationship can handle it in its stride, merely shifting geographical direction. The same trauma marks the normal up-close college routine of winter breaks apart and long summer breaks away. Such relationships are a figment of semesters, not a fixture of a couple's real lives. Lovers at the same college likely have homes far apart, spelling long separations each year, and on key holidays. Long commutes are required to get together. By contrast, high school couples, separated by college, usually spend summers and other breaks in the same town – an advantage of the distance relation.

Couples joining the "real [work] world," after college, spend more time at the office, and working weekends, than with each other. Commutes are a daily exhaustion causing a different, more permanent sort of distance to dominate. "We never see each other, and when we do, we're half dead, needing space to recover for the next workweek." Sex? What's sex?

The Real: From the Mouths of Babes ... and Dudes

Three college students bemoan (and praise) their distance relationships:

> My girlfriend and I started dating at the very end of our high school careers.... After a mere two months together we were catapulted to college, her at a school two hours from mine. The relationship was strained at first

but with social utilities like AIM and Facebook … we soon realized that we could still communicate as though we lived close to each other. The journey to visit each other was a taxing one. Besides the expense, three separate modes of transportation had to be employed in order to see one another. A taxi, train, and bus ride later we could be in each other's arms. The intimacy level was through the roof, being that we were young freshmen, and we hadn't seen each other usually for a month at a time. After our freshman year, she decided to transfer to a nearby school. With the distance cut from hours to a few minutes, this was great. We could see each other much more often and even during the week. At the same time our experiences with the previous year allowed to not be upset when we couldn't spend time together.… After that year, my girlfriend transferred again, this time to a school almost two hours away. With the distance increased our relationship has become strained again. It seems now that we can no longer settle for the times we are apart. When we don't see each other for a few weeks our phone conversations become shorter and our other interactions almost become non-existent. But when we get together the distance is erased, and we are instantly in love again.

The distance is hard. We miss each other. We want to be together, in every sense of want. But there are a few upsides to being apart, too. Since we see each other about 4–5 days total a month, things don't go stale as easily. Since we don't see each other as often, it makes those times that we do see each other much more special and significant. Also, since we are in love and enjoy each other's company, the entire time is not spent having sex, and we actually get to do other things. Of course, since we're deeply in love, the separations and rough spots are manageable. If we weren't so in love with each other, maybe not.

Thank God for Skype, that's all I can say. The visual communication is key. My fiancée tells me that my voice is hard to read when we talk on the phone. She needs to see my body language and facial expression to really see what I'm saying.… I survive sometimes by putting it out of my mind. But it's a real test of strength and will. Being apart makes you appreciate the other person more when you get together. That's the up side. But mostly it's hard because the two of you change over time, which is easy when you change together, side by side. It's not easy when you get together after a separation and things are different. If we didn't understand that, and plan for it, we'd be in trouble.

Sound familiar? Notice the surprising pros alongside the cons here, but also the common theme of strain, requiring strength. Notice the appreciable role of technology as well – "all you need is love" … and the ability to videochat on your laptop.

Reconnecting and Misconnecting

These typical tales of struggle recall my own college-day love-commutes back in the day: traveling between Hofstra in Long Island and Syracuse upstate to see my girlfriend; next from Rutgers in New Jersey to Cedar Crest College in Pennsylvania; then between Brown in Rhode Island and New School in Manhattan – one weekend at her apartment, one weekend at mine – then finally from Harvard to "the city" for almost two decades. Even as a professor, there were the long train rides between Hartford, Washington, and Boston, then upstate New York and South Bend, Indiana – great strains of relationships played out in Chicago train stations.

Too much growing, while separate, led to growing apart. New love partners brought similar commutes, each visit anticipated long beforehand with a mixture of hope and worry, and often a vague sense of foreboding. The return trip held a raft of small satisfactions and disappointments, a sense that the visit swept by so quickly, requiring anticipation of the next reunion to fill the coming void. "Next time" dominated the conversation on leaving, at the bus stop, or when pulling away in my car – if New York City's finest hadn't towed it away.

You might expect the loss of a normal sex life to be the most discussed sacrifice in such relationships. That's how distance relationships are billed, but loss of an emotional connection was of primary concern to me and also to my college interviewees. Late night phone calls could not quench a longing to be close and to feel direct connection with partners. Stretching these calls generated too many words, words that lost meaning; we'd say anything to maintain connection. A careless wordiness sometimes spawned misunderstandings and conflicts that our bleeding hearts never intended. In person, the problem could easily have been resolved: we could have shut up and sat happily in silence together, touching, kissing, or just holding hands. But geography wasn't this kind.

Occasionally, the call from afar arrived at the wrong time; the caller had to be rushed off the phone. "What does that mean?" the caller wondered. "Is she with someone else?" "Am I not important enough to stop everything for?" "Am I becoming an intrusion – calling too much, seeming clingy and pathetic?" Or "Is she simply drifting away, into newer and more interesting things and circles?"

The rare in-person visits were occasionally jolted by conflict. Perhaps conflict arose at the beginning of a visit, requiring what was left of our time to get beyond the issue. Final resolution was followed by an immediate goodbye. When such a rough patch marred the end of the visit, there was no time to smooth it out. The parting was not "such sweet sorrow," but a sour note that lingered.

When we laid eyes on each other, after a separation, we expected an instant restoration of connection – the in-person version of close bonds tied over the phone while apart. We soon realized, instead, that we'd gotten closer while apart – closer at a distance. Our in-person contact was clumsy and awkward by comparison, making the actual relationship seem the more artificial one. A feeling of alienation permeated – a horrible feeling of "separation together." Again, we wondered, "What does this mean?" but feared to express it, compounding our anxiety. Or we did express it, and the process of "talking things out" was rewarded by prompt and wrenching separation at a travel terminal. A looming sense of disconnection haunted the ride home. "We fell apart." "It's over." What could be more encouraging than waiting weeks for a visit, then fighting? What could revitalize us more, facing weeks of study ahead, than a grieving trip home? Such were the tales of woe recounted in interviews.

Keeping at Arm's Length

Many commuting visits go well, of course. There is a smooth reentry, complete immersion in the moment, with no underlining worry over loss to come. The eventual parting is filled with a "see ya soon" type of optimism, and the interim is marked by stepping back a bit and realizing just how valuable the relationship is. Distance relationships suit the rigors of college life in key ways. We find ourselves concentrating more on studies when apart, and concentrating more on our relationship when together – "quality time" both ways. We can afford to slack-off on our work during weekends together due to concentrated work done apart.

Contrast the up-close relationship in which there is constant pressure to study while we're "just hanging" together. This causes anxiety and impatience. We distract each while studying together, so work never seems to get done. Then there are too-much-togetherness problems. What's left to say when we've just seen each other a half-hour ago? Conversations become ridiculous, superficial. "It's as if we have nothing worthwhile to say to each other anymore." Too few "spaces in our togetherness" can also cause sex to get old as well. In such contexts, distance imposed by geography can be a saving grace. Commuting to renew love and intimacy can become the special delight of the month.

But there is a catch. The problems of togetherness, while delicate to raise, can be addressed by up-close couples. They are akin to other problems these couples work out – balancing time with friends, family, and one's lover on campus. The couple will likely grow during such resolution processes, making both partners feel stronger and more mature. The same cannot be said for problems of distance. Some are simply unbridgeable, or too cost prohibitive. Associated personal issues are too delicate to address at a distance, requiring unaffordable time in person.

Then there are special problems of sex at a distance, severe enough to outweigh distance assets all put together. While sexual intensity is often boosted by separation and delayed gratification, having to perform on a schedule can be a nightmare. It increases performance anxiety, which diminishes the quality of sex and sexual experience. Weekends together may not catch distance couples in the mood. Or one partner might be over-sexed while the other is anti-sexed. This means hurtful arguments, a sense of being intruded upon sexually, or being rebuffed in one's advances and made to feel foolish. Not being around each other enough diminishes our ability to pick up cues of being out of sync.

Failing to click sexually can devastate a long-awaited reunion. What was to be the prime testament to our love falls flat. Where does that leave our love? Sex is the most concrete fruition of the distance relation, making our relation concrete only on rare weekends. When it fails, our relation itself fails in the most tangible way. How else can it feel to couples? How can abstract sentiments like "these things happen, let's forget it" grip us as powerfully as "look at what happened?"

But can we really assume that this one sexual con likely outweighs the positives of distance relationships? Reams of supporting testimony supply the answer from "people of all ages." "The heartbreak of sexual timing" is the reported bane of young couples trying to get pregnant or having difficulty doing so. Needing to make love constantly during ovulation periods yields well-known complaints. Consider, also, men taking Viagra and the need for aging couples to make love before its effects wear off. Most couples of all ages routinely wait too long while "in the mood," and then lose it when finally going to bed. For at least one partner, the sleepiness of the other bodes a cold shower. Time constraints place out-of-sync college lovers in the ranks of couples for whom the thrill is gone, or of women raised in prudish traditions, feeling obliged to go through the motions of sex. "I don't enjoy it at all (anymore)," a wife confides to a friend, "but we can't simply never make love and stay together, can we?"

So which perspective on distance sex seems more plausible – "separation fitting the rigors of college life," as posed above, or "distance relation as a recipe for emotional and sexual doom?" If we were creating a design for such stressful roller-coaster rides of emotions, or a prescription for breaking up, wouldn't distance relation serve us well?

Aristotelian Trauma

One-third of the way through my annual ethics course, we complete Aristotle's account of *philia* – love and friendship.[2] For him, love is a potential virtue – not a feeling or a passive state one falls into, but a team of abilities. As an interpersonal virtue, love does an artful dance-a-deux in which both partners are called to perform at the top of their game.

I pose an unusual implication of *philia* to students – that when we're not *doing* love together, as an ongoing practice, we're not actually in a loving relationship. To be in love is to make love, to do and dance love together, not just to feel love or feel ready to resume the dance. Love can be felt alone, but not *done* alone. Making love is the only form of love for Aristotle, from infatuation and passionate lovemaking through tender companionship in old age. Thus, being far apart for long periods is not just a strain on love, it is a destroyer (a murderer) of it. And this is so whether or not the love resurrects on the next visit.

As a result, distance relationships don't really exist because distance love doesn't actually exist, any more than distance coitus does. (One does not play soccer at a distance, nor musicians an orchestral piece.) As jolting as this news may seem, as much as we'd like to dismiss it as mere semantics, we're dimly aware of its insight in the darkest moments apart. "Where is he?" Where are we?" Alone in our rooms we look for our "us" in tangible terms, but in vain.

Those of us who saw *Dan in Real Life* heard Aristotle's view recalled, *Amor no es un sentimento … es un abilidad* (love isn't a feeling, it's an ability). The boyfriend of Dan's daughter may have "thought this up," as he claimed, but it originated quite a few centuries before. A commuting encounter in the film marked the relevant scene. Dan's daughter's boyfriend crashed a family reunion-weekend at the shore, arriving unexpectedly by bus, and was sent packing by a disapproving dad. Dan's apt reward for this intervention? The title his daughter screamed: "Murderer of love." ("Murderer of sex" was implied.) And "murderer" doesn't mean merely "delayer" or "suspender" of love, does it?

Students jump on my Aristotelian inference from *philia* with rare gusto, claiming to find it preposterous. "While apart love surely persists," they protest, "merely in latent form." How else could it magically resurface the second we see each other again?" I counter: "Powerful feelings are latent in love indeed, and can be rekindled into flame, but the flame is emotional self-expression in each partner. Whether the love *relationship* resurrects depends on how couples interact from then on. Either way, loving interaction was not going on in the interim. Continuing to feel in love inside does not make love so in reality." Doesn't college commuting experience bear this out when a particular visit shocks us with the sense that we're over? And doesn't that sense in fact pan out? We go on to visit, and return no longer in love.

Talking Sexy

In the vacuum of relational space, caused by distance, can we find a more central and relational role for phone conversations to play, or for texting and email? Perhaps they are not simply a way to feel less apart. Perhaps they are not merely a lifeline for the relationship. Instead, consider them the relationship itself. They are its integrated components, its means of interactive expression from a distance. Even close up, our love must voyage across a psychological bridge extended in psychological space, from one partner to the other. Our minds and feelings do not touch directly, but are conveyed in words or body language. When we hold each other in full embrace, we are trying to convey our full selves to each other in a way linking particular body parts cannot. That is what makes such embrace so emotionally consuming.

When full physical embrace cannot reach across the miles, these new electronic media cross the psychological bridge for us, allowing us to make love in ways that past lower-tech "embraces" could not. Previously, media were like parts touching – a handwritten letter symbolized thoughts, a phone call provided sound and voice. But now, in addition to "non-stop" talk (via phone, text, and email), we have real-time visual images via videocam. A lover can almost reach out and touch, as some do, moving their hands over our moving images, a step up from kissing spindled photographs. (Could Aristotle ever have imagined?) All hail the future of hologram (and holodeck?) technology, the "doctors of love" for a truly new millennium.

If communication media are the primary forms of distance relationships and embrace, Aristotle's previous prescriptions would have us put great effort and practice into perfecting their fine arts – the arts of texting, email, and videochat. Think of how carelessly we use these media, even when sexting. We may "say" arousing things, but only as if we were saying them in person, simulating in-person talk. Do we consider how e-talking and video talking (with body language) speak their own romance languages? (What font do you use for e-love letters? What colors or combination of colors?) One can simulate the classic love letters of old online – elegant cursive on sepia-tinted parchment. But is "going old school" the best this technology can achieve? Classroom "power-point" simulates blackboards, with jazzy motion added? Is that a fine educational art of computer graphics?

Graphic Sex

Making sex at a distance seemingly awaited tech-assisted communication. Phone sex, sexting, and especially Skype sex may surpass the floweriest of love-letter rhetoric if done right, and it is far more timely than snail mail. One can't "get naked" in letters, after all, even when baring one's soul. Video-chats currently advance forbidden sexual purposes – partners stripping for each other, mutual masturbation, mutually observed. Couples can enhance these communications by transporting in-person sexual rituals to their media embrace – playing the same music, producing the same aromas (incense) and bedding patterns in each locale. A key here is how difficult it is to go in the other direction – emailing each other while wrapped in bodily embrace. Thus, distance relation has the advantage. Enhancing up-close relation via such technology feels inherently inappropriate, as those few who Skype or film each other sexually at close quarters can testify. (I asked.) Doing so has its thrills, but couples are unable to hurdle the intrusive qualities of such media for in-person relating. Not so for distance coupling.

Does it seem perverse to nurture excellences in the arts of electronic lovemaking which merely simulate the real thing? Isn't authenticity what marks true love? The idea posed, however, is that such lovemaking should not be mere simulation. It is art's perfect new lovemaking form. Regardless, there's a lot more to sex and love than true love, and artifice is a part of all art, the art of love included.

Many couples get a sense of using each other for sex as the depersonalizing features of passion increases, and the most creative media lovemaking can be accused of enhanced depersonalization to some degree. As we get addicted to email and sexting, so we may get addicted to videosex. We may crave its graphic appearance at the expense of less visual romance and tenderness on screen. "As soon as the Skype call is connected, all you want to do is get naked."

As one interviewed student regarded in-person reunions, "We get together, the sex is great, wild, intense, but it seems to take over the visit, even before we can really reacquaint. It becomes all we seem to do during our visits. It's like we barely "saw" each other when leaving. Raw sex isn't really heart to heart communication, much less head to head." And another student: "As much as I ached for sex while we were apart ... it felt like we almost got that out of the way at first each visit. Then we could really talk and just hug each other.... Sometimes later in the visit, I don't even want to have sex again. But I feel like we have to since we can't soon.... It feels like a great gain at the time, but it's really a loss." Still another student: "Sex is the glamour part of reunion. And you feel, 'how can I trade that for something as mundane as taking a walk together, holding hands or whatever.' But then you're sorry later you didn't make that trade more."

Making this trade has consequences however, given our "glamour" expectations for reunions and videochats both. What if sex is unexpectedly delayed at the start of a long-awaited visit or call? (Arriving during a must-see college event can cause this, as can some big news to convey on a Skype call.) What if the first opportunities to be alone bring estranged feelings rather than sex, or sex without the anticipated passion? In person, this is predictable psychologically. Our subconscious is not as reasonable as we are. It may want to punish our partner for abandonment just for being so geographically distant from us for so long. Videocalls leave us geographically distant the whole while, a subconsciously punishable offense. And while a certain kinkyness to video lovemaking may spur passion, some partners may have difficulty responding to it. What if the evening goes on, during a visit, but without sexual accompaniment? If sleeping together then only brings sleep, there is more estrangement. *Far Away, So Close*, says the movie title. Having a videochat end with just chat, when more was expected, can leave an empty, disappointed, even resentful feeling.

The Ideal

How can we turn a distance relationship into a masterpiece of a relationship? Student interviews said little on this topic. And, of course, they never took up this Aristotelian challenge regarding media-assisted love. In part, excellence rises from the pursuit of goals – ultimate goals of ultimate value. Integrating true love with hot sex seems the college *summum bonum* (highest good). But may I pose two alternatives? First, consider sex, not love, as the distance-ideal. The burdens and sacrifices we considered for the distance relationship all stem from deep feelings and strong bonds – love delayed and denied by separation. It's simpler from afar. It allows easier compartmentalizing of work and play, along with greater fantasy delight from afar. There's far less anguished tugging on heartstrings when things are amiss, and less complicated reunions as well. Space between couplings often enhances sexual thrill, keeping sex fresh – not so love. Loving sex may be more elevated, but at a distance, it is a more difficult stretch.

Second, consider infatuation as a distance ideal, too often short-sold. Infatuation holds the greatest intensity of joy and excitement love offers. It sustains "flow" and "peak experience" for unimaginable durations, even in fantasy. And it provides nothing short of hormone-raging ecstasy on contact. Adults seem to relish calling this state superficial, childish, and fated to fade. So what? What happens afterwards makes infatuation no less spectacular and all-consuming while ongoing. (We're not asking it to rival the pyramids after all – short but sweet is nice too.) And how credible is the "infatuation fade theory" on analysis? When questioning adult know-it-alls on this matter, I noticed that they couldn't recall prior reflection on how infatuation could be extended. Much less had they ever tried to extend it in practice. The possibility had never occurred to them. They never considered the Aristotelian prospect that infatuation fielded a team of abilities that we can learn to wield and perfect.

The fading of infatuation may seem natural and inherent to the condition, but it noticeably marks a general failure of diligence and proper care, like the pervasive adult tendency to lose curiosity and wonder, or let one's figure go. Laziness in passion may be the best explanation for why love "matures" into "tender companionship" at older ages, trumping "a time for all seasons" rationale. As adults, we slowly retire our love and lives, neglecting the arts of keeping life fresh and romance alive.

No wonder kids typically respond that "parents just don't understand" when they criticize infatuation. Young, immature, "irresponsible" love is also wildly intense love, as is young sex, once kids get the hang of it. Hormones, freshness of anticipated experience, forbidden pleasure, and the breaking of taboos make young love the perfect storm of emotional obsession and whole-self involvement.

The Arts of Distance Loving

Aside from goal-direction, the art of the distance relationship requires polished performance-abilities, "excellences" or "virtues," and the motivations for nurturing them ably. On the matter of peak performance – on expressing our nurtured excellences in masterful action – the Aristotelian keywords are style and timeliness. To wit: doing the right thing, in the right way, at the right time, with the right people. A student interview addresses the matter:

> Long, drawn-out phone calls every night from far away can become monotonous and, consequently, draining. We're blessed with a variation of technologies that can mix up the styles of communication, providing the feeling of multiple activities together. And in fact, we communicate differently via each one – short emails, videochats, text messages. An intimate relationship should be full of those minor, trivial comments that can be shared freely, not for practical reasons or adherence to social norms but just for off the cuff thinking out loud. If two partners can casually text message throughout the day ... both members stay a part of each other's lives in real-time. It's like the real thing of being together where the little things count most. Mixing in a short phone call at night, a videochat now and then, that's wonderful. It's just the right combination.
>
> We found that visiting each other every three weeks worked best. If we saw each other more often it would have interfered with opportunities to have meaningful friendship with other students on our campuses. Then we'd feel like outsiders in our own homes.... There'd be too much pressure on the relationship and the partner to deliver during those brief visits. Better balance this way. And it also means that when we talk at night, we have something worthwhile to say.

I leave you to discover the artful particulars here for yourself, which Aristotle perceptively left to each person's exploratory experience and self-development. No general principles or formulas are likely here to allow general evaluation – at least none that avoid sounding like cheesy self-help programs. Completing the comparative case for distance and up-close relations awaits a comparative justification for these possible ideals, and the previous love ideal. It also requires evaluating the challenges of pursuing them – how hard they are to master.

The Last Word

Perhaps distance relationships should be avoided by most of us where feasible. Perhaps the case for them must always play catch-up to up-close alternatives. Still, some couples, I suspect, should consider marrying into them. I've met couples who have done so permanently, and to good effect. All of us may be meant to love, but some of us only as hermits. We are the hermit type and too picky to accommodate others' little quirks. We live too much "in our heads" to summon the constant attention needed for constant interacting. And so, living together is a really bad idea! Such couples have worked out creative arrangements to live largely apart, dating each other (exclusively) from the privacy of separate abodes, 'til death do they part. Seeing much less of each other, missing each other occasionally, not only keeps their love alive and untrammeled, but romantic and vibrant. And over time, with increasing age, they stop caring "how it looks."

NOTES

1 I'd like to thank my Rensselaer students for information on distance relationships, especially Kyle Monahan, James Letteney, Cale Hays, Josh Seldin, and John Mazza, as well as my sweet Mt Holyoke daughter, Emma Puka-Beals, and her NYU boyfriend Dave Seaward.
2 Aristotle, *Nicomachean Ethics*, in *The Basic Works of Aristotle*, ed. Richard McKeon (New York: Random House, 1968).

PART II

SOPHOMORE YEAR

Friends With Benefits

WILLIAM O. STEPHENS[1]

CHAPTER 6

WHAT'S LOVE GOT TO DO WITH IT?

Epicureanism and Friends with Benefits

Epicureans and Pleasure

The ancient Greek philosopher Epicurus and his followers believed that the good, the ultimate goal of all our actions, is pleasure. By nature all animals pursue pleasure and avoid pain and behave appropriately in doing so. Since human beings are animals too, and particularly intelligent ones at that, the good life for human beings is, the Epicureans argued, the pleasant life. This conception of the good life has an obvious appeal, and not only for college students. But the best strategy for achieving this pleasant life may not be quite so obvious. It may seem safe to suppose that Epicureans would consider all kinds of gratification, including sex, to be worth pursuing, but in fact they rejected the idea that all pleasures should be sought equally. Epicurus writes: "No pleasure is a bad thing in itself. But the things which produce certain pleasures bring troubles many times greater than the pleasures."[2]

Epicurus and his followers also rejected the common opinion that the more pleasant something is, the more vigorously one should go for it. The Epicureans believed that the best kind of pleasure is the purest kind, and the purest kind of pleasure results in no pain at all. They argued that happiness consists in freedom from pain and in particular from pain caused by unfulfilled desires. Consequently, we need to understand the nature of different kinds of desires and use reason to distinguish among them in order to lead a happy life. Epicurean ethical philosophy thereby provides a conceptual framework that enables us to fulfill those desires that need to be fulfilled, to avoid pursuing those desires that are difficult to satisfy, to avoid pursuing those desires which tend to result in greater pains than pleasures, and to eliminate altogether those desires that are impossible to fulfill or that always result in more pain than pleasure.

What did the Epicureans think about sex? In this essay I will explore how Epicurean philosophy applies to sex and the idea of friends with benefits among college students. I will argue that Epicureans regard good friends to be much more reliable than good sex, and so college students ought to keep their friends by avoiding having sex with them.

Freedom from Anxiety and Types of Desires

The Epicureans distinguished between two kinds of pain that our natural powers of reason can remove: physical pain and mental distress. Physical pains afflict us only in the present. Mental distress includes present unpleasant memories, present regrets about the past, present fears, and present worries about the future. Whereas present pangs are ever transient, the scope of past and anticipated future pains is much broader. Consequently, the Epicureans believed that mental suffering threatens a pleasant life much more than physical pains do. Physical pains, they argued, tend to be either mild (and so easy to bear) if they are chronic, or relatively short if they are intense. Mental distress includes all kinds of emotional upset and perturbation, including fear, frustration, anxiety, and grief. So the Epicureans offered a set of principles from which they derived arguments designed as therapy for the mental afflictions that ruin peace of mind and painless living. To rid oneself of all those desires which disrupt mental tranquility is to attain what the Greeks called *ataraxia*, that is, the ideal state of freedom from anxiety. The fear of death, fear of a future harm, the Epicureans considered to be the greatest obstacle to this life free of anxiety. So the Epicureans developed strategies for eliminating false beliefs that occasion worries about the future and for dispelling false beliefs that generate painful thoughts about the past.

If pleasure results from getting what you want and displeasure results from failing to get what you want, then two strategies suggest themselves

WILLIAM O. STEPHENS

for dealing with any desire that arises. You can try to satisfy the desire or you can work to get rid of it.[3] If a certain kind of desire cannot be eliminated because it arises from the natural constitution of human beings, then that desire counts as natural for the Epicureans. Natural desires may be either natural and necessary or natural but non-necessary. Of natural and necessary desires some are necessary for life itself, some for freeing the body from troubles, and some for happiness. When one is hungry or thirsty, it is because one's body lacks food or drink necessary for its healthy operation. All animals require food and water. Consequently, desires to eat and to drink are natural and necessary for life itself. Eating eliminates the lack of food, thereby removing the pain of hunger and satisfying the desire to eat. Eating thus has a natural limit. Drinking water eliminates the lack that is dehydration, thereby removing the pain of thirst and satisfying the desire to drink. Drinking, too, has a natural limit. Similarly, wearing clothing and inhabiting shelter to protect oneself from the elements satisfy desires natural and necessary for freeing the body from troubles. But so long as one's clothing and shelter remove the troubles of being too hot, too cold, or too wet, these desires are satisfied, since they too have a natural limit.[4]

Sex, Shoes, and the Needs of College Students

Now the ordinary college undergraduate won't worry much (or at all) about suffering from lacking the clothing, shelter, food, and drink needed to survive. Yet she may still have a host of concerns about certain *kinds* of food, certain *kinds* of drink, certain *kinds* of clothing, and various kinds of fun possessions and entertainments. Moreover, the ordinary college student is likely to have urgent concerns about whether, when, and with whom to engage in sexual activity of one kind or another. Is having sex with a friend a good idea? Other concerns may include grades, papers, lab reports, deciding on a major, roommates, friends, drinking alcohol, and how to behave at parties. All these concerns and associated desires can easily generate many serious worries and thereby threaten her tranquility.

Are all these desires on the same footing? The Epicureans hold that vain and empty desires are not natural desires because they do not arise from any depletion of the body and so have no natural limit. Consequently, desires for political power, fame, wealth, luxuries, jewelry, toys, art works, and the like count as "vain and empty" for the Epicureans. All too often the more of these things one gets, the more one wants. Consider an example. A person can wear only one pair of shoes at a time, so wanting to own many pairs of fashionable shoes is vain and empty, from the Epicurean perspective. A pair of feet does not hunger for more than one pair of shoes at a time for shelter, yet one can be fooled by advertisers and fashionistas in our materialistic society into falsely believing that getting more shoes will make one happier. But in fact wanting more shoes than one's feet need endangers one's *ataraxia*. Fancy, trendy, expensive clothing keeps one's body no more comfortable than basic, cheap, readily available clothing. Jewelry, iPods, gaming stations, stereo systems, and plasma TV sets provide neither calories nor nutrients for, and remove no pains from, the body. Therefore, desires for such things are neither natural nor, Epicureans would argue, necessary for happiness. Since inability to satisfy desires for these kinds of things frustrates and perturbs us, the Epicureans urge us to eliminate all such vain and empty desires and limit ourselves entirely to natural desires and mostly to necessary desires.

To maximize our chances of achieving *ataraxia*, wouldn't the Epicureans advise us to limit our desires *entirely* to the natural and necessary ones? Here they make modest room for natural but non-necessary desires. These include expensive, gourmet foods and beverages: truffles, caviar, filet mignon, lobster, fine wines, elegant desserts, pricey chocolates, and the like. After all, champagne, espresso, and milkshakes fail to quench thirst better than water. One can enjoy these delicacies if they happen to be available, since as food and drink they do remove the physical pains of hunger and thirst by replenishing the body.[5] But to foster a habitual desire for extravagant goodies so as to make one's happiness depend on getting them inevitably causes mental distress whenever such treats are unavailable. Consequently, harboring such a psychological dependency is wildly imprudent because it considerably and unnecessarily risks one's *ataraxia*. So the Epicureans recommend that we be wise and cautious about our natural and non-necessary desires. The pleasures they afford are real, but they are necessary neither for our survival nor for our peace of mind. Being ever mindful of this reality enables us to be happy in both plentiful times and lean times. We must not allow occasional indulgence in a special treat to undermine our habituated satisfaction with simple food and drink. To believe that we ever *need* rich foods or costly beverages is to be deluded.

The Dangers of Sex

The Epicureans considered sexual appetite to belong in the class of natural but non-necessary desires. Sexual appetite arises from the body and its hormonal activity, and so it is natural. But one can live serenely without satisfying sexual desires, the Epicureans believed, so they are not necessary. Orgasms are undeniably pleasant, but in order to preserve one's *ataraxia* one must be careful and selective about satisfying one's sexual desires. Epicurus writes:

> I understand from you that your natural disposition is too much inclined toward sexual passion. Follow your inclination as you will provided only that you neither violate the laws, disturb well-established customs, harm any one of your neighbors, injure your own body, nor waste your possessions. That you be not checked by some one of these provisos is impossible; for a man never gets any good from sexual passion, and he is fortunate if he does not receive harm.[6]

First, notice that Epicurus' friend's natural inclination toward sexual passion is *excessive*. Passions are dangerous because of their extreme intensity, and this extremity usually creates trouble. One kind of trouble would be violating the law, since excessive sexual passion could lead one to commit adultery, incest, or other illegal acts like date rape. Another kind of trouble is disturbing those well-established customs that facilitate harmonious, cooperative, and pleasant social living. The pursuit of sexual passion could also result in harm to one's neighbor, either physical harm through a minor sexually transmitted disease, or emotional damage, or both, say through a serious STD or an unwanted pregnancy. Indulging one's sexual passion could also result in injury to oneself. This could take the form of an STD, an unwanted pregnancy, or emotional anguish when one is spurned or betrayed by one's lover, or physical injury at the hands of one's lover's jealous ex-lover, or even an assault by a lover one has jilted. Finally, Epicurus warns that excessive inclination to sexual passion could result in squandering your possessions and money in wooing the person(s) you lust after. Epicurus thinks it impossible to avoid every single one of these possible harmful consequences. Sooner or later, at least one of these harms will afflict the person who gives in to his excessive erotic inclination. Though the *appetite* for sex in itself is natural, according to the Epicureans, sexual *passion* is fraught with many dangerous consequences. So not only is it not necessary to satisfy sexual passion to live a happy, untroubled, peaceful life, it is wiser still to *eliminate* this hazardous disposition. Epicurus concludes that a person never gets any good from sexual passion, and is lucky not to receive harm from it. In short, sexual passion is of no benefit.

The Roman poet Lucretius, inspired by the wisdom of Epicurus, elaborates on this topic in his magnificent poem *De Rerum Natura (On the Nature of Things)*. The third book of this monumental work includes an account of the annihilation of the mind in death and an extended attack on the superstitious fear of death and the afterlife as anathema to rational living. At the end of Book Four, Lucretius' exploration of the inexhaustible human capacity for delusion leads him to target what he takes to be the most debilitating of desires, sexual passion.[7]

Lucretius begins the finale of Book Four with an account of how images received in dreams cause sleepers to groan, struggle, speak, and wet their bed clothes. Adolescent boys whose bodies are beginning to produce semen receive images of fair faces with beautiful complexions that trigger ejaculations in wet dreams. Lucretius describes how "the desire arises to emit the seed toward the object of our dire craving" (line 1048),[8] and "the body seeks the object that has wounded the mind with love" (line 1049). So while sexual arousal and climax are harmless, pleasant biological events, Lucretius considers love to be a wound injurious to the mind. He compares a body pierced by a weapon gushing blood in the direction from which the wound was inflicted to the man "wounded by the darts of Venus" moving toward the beautiful (male or female) body that fired those darts into him. Love is not a benign pleasure unmixed with pain; rather, love lacerates the mind. Though love might seem sweet at first, it is in reality pernicious because even when your loved one is absent, images of her continue to invade your thoughts, and her name rings incessantly in your ears. These relentless stimuli plague the mind with emotional turbulence, robbing it of peace. They are so aggravating, so disruptive of mental calm that Lucretius urges the afflicted lover to shun these images and to abstain from all that feeds the affliction. The treatment he prescribes is drastic:

> ... turn your attention elsewhere: you should ejaculate the accumulated fluid into any woman's body rather than reserve it for a single lover who monopolizes you and thus involve yourself in inevitable anxiety and anguish. The fact is that feeding the ulcer increases its strength and renders it inveterate: day by day the frenzy grows and the misery is intensified,

unless you obliterate the old wounds with new blows and heal them while still fresh by taking at random some random-roaming Venus, or unless you divert the motions of your mind into some other channel. (Lines 1064–73)

Lucretius sees love as a psychological obsession that must not be fueled. Feeding the obsession makes it grow into a frenzied madness. Lucretius prescribes two possible cures for the lovesick lover: either have intercourse with any woman *except* the object of his monomania, or think about something other than passionate love and sex.

Sexual activity with any partner satisfies the desire for orgasm, but sexual activity with the individual who inflames one's erotic passion only serves to intensify that agitating, passionate love without extinguishing or even diminishing it. By hooking up with any random partner, Lucretius thinks the lovesick lover can divert his mind from its obsession and heal the old erotic wounds of that obsession with "new blows." Alternatively, the fixated lover can divert his mind from its obsession by simply thinking about any subject other than sex. He can watch sports, play sports, walk in the park, do manual labor, play video games, listen to tame music, do laundry, or, what should be a daily priority for college students, work on one of his classes. This second strategy seems quite sensible.

Regarding the first strategy, however, we may wonder how getting new wounds could help old ones heal. How can casual sex with random-roaming partners quell an erotic obsession with one lover? Epicureans sharply distinguish the desire for physical gratification through orgasm from the passionate desire to fuse with one special mate. Since this fusion is both physically and psychologically impossible, such a desire is futile. The biological desire for orgasm is simple to satisfy and fully satisfiable since it has a natural limit. Any comely body can satisfy it equally well. It can even be satisfied solo. But I think it would be a mistake to derive from Lucretius' comments an Epicurean policy recommending to college students a series of meaningless sexual encounters with random strangers. Lucretius suggests this *only* for the lovesick and only as a means of diverting the mind *away* from its obsessive, lustful fixation. One-night stands with passersby would be particularly reckless today because of the much greater likelihood that they would run afoul of most of the troubles Epicurus detailed. Ignorance about most facts about one's unloved sex-partner greatly increases the chances of laws being violated (e.g., unwittingly committing statutory rape), or beneficial customs being disturbed, or the parties involved (or their future sex-partners) getting harmed, especially by STDs. I argue that Epicureans today would reject sex with strangers as far too risky to be compatible with *ataraxia*.

Sex and Sensibility

Perhaps erotic obsession with a special individual stems from the opinion that *only* one person is a fully satisfactory sex-partner. The problem is that this fixated passion cannot be satisfied by any sex act because it is a stubborn, disordered condition of the *mind*, a delusion, not an innocuous, transient impulse of the *body*. Psychological obsession cannot be healed by sex with that body that is the very object of fixation. Sex satisfies the body and is a natural pleasure. Love crazes the mind and leads to heartache. So Lucretius thinks the lover's impassioned mind can be distracted by means of physically gratifying sex with persons that do not make it lovesick. This prescription aims to disabuse the mind of a fantasy, namely, the false belief that sex with she who monopolizes he who is love-crazed is a good thing because it heals the lovesickness and returns his mind to a calm, unfrustrated, happy state.

Indeed, Lucretius believes that sexual activity untainted by passionate love is better than passionate lovemaking. He says "it is undeniable that the pleasure of intercourse is purer for the healthy-minded than for the lovesick" (line 1075). So when college students embroiled in passionate affairs suffer heartache, would an Epicurean advise them to hook up with one (or more) of their friends for casual, loveless sex? Isn't this precisely a pitch for the convenience of no-strings-attached friends with benefits? Don't Epicureans believe that Tina Turner's 1984 single "What's Love Got to Do with It?" is right insofar as it claims that loveless sex is far better than erotic love, which is inevitably bittersweet and often agony? As tempting as it is to interpret Lucretius to condone loveless sex with pals, I will argue that, from the Epicurean perspective, this is not, in fact, wise for most college students in most situations. Before making that argument, however, further study of the Lucretian pathology of erotic love is needed.

In contrast to the unpenalized sex of non-lovers, Lucretius describes how impassioned lovers rush and fumble in frenzied, clumsy lovemaking, uncertain of what to squeeze and roughly kiss first, often hurting each other, spurred by their erotic madness. Lovers vainly hope that the same body that enflamed their passion can also extinguish it, but the reverse happens. The more ardent sexplay they have, the more fiercely their hearts crave more. Food and drink replenish physiological voids in the body, but the visual image of a beautiful face is an impalpable image, Lucretius explains; it fills no emptiness in the body and quenches no longing in the heart. Rather, "lovers are deluded by Venus with images: no matter how intently they gaze at the beloved body, they cannot sate their eyes; nor can they remove anything from the velvety limbs that they explore with roving, uncertain hands" (lines 1101–5). But their gazing and groping "is all in vain, since they cannot take away anything from their lover's body or wholly penetrate it and merge into it" (lines 1110–11). Even after their orgasms, the escape of the deranged lovers from their raging passion is all too brief:

> Then the same madness returns, and they have another fit of frenzy: they seek to attain what they desire, but fail to find an effective antidote to their suffering: in such deep doubt do they pine away with an invisible wound. (Lines 1118–21)

Sexual activity only satisfies sexual desire of the body, but passionate love is an invisible wound, a gash in the mind, for which there is no bodily remedy.

Many other ills multiply from love, according to Lucretius. Love consumes and exhausts the lover's strength. His life is ruled by his beloved. Love makes him neglect his duties and ruins his reputation. Love gobbles away his wealth as he buys for her lovely slippers, jewels, gowns, tiaras, imported cloaks, draperies, dainties, banquets, entertainments, drinks, perfumes, and flowers. Notice that with the exception of the fancy foods and drinks that count as objects of natural but non-necessary desires, all these other gifts are objects of vain and empty desires. Consequently, there is no natural limit for purchasing, owning, or wearing such superfluous items. They are entirely for show. Neither does gifting them promote the lover's *ataraxia* in any way, nor does receiving them enhance his beloved's *ataraxia* at all. They are not real benefits. In fact, showering the mistress who has mastered his heart with lavish gifts likely reveals rather than eases his feelings of doubt, regret, and insecurity. As Lucretius writes:

> Perhaps his conscience experiences a twinge of remorse at the thought of a life spent in sloth and squandered in debauchery; perhaps his mistress has thrown out an ambiguous word and left it embedded in his passionate heart, where it burns like living fire; or perhaps he fancies that her eyes are

wandering too freely, or that she is ogling some other man, while he detects in her face the trace of a smile. (Lines 1135–41)

Jealousies and anxieties like these undoubtedly flare up among college student couples, too.

Romance, Beautiful Illusions, and Sound Minds

So if a college Joey O'Montague finds himself falling passionately in love with a Julie Capulet in his entomology class, what advice would Joey's Epicurean advisor give him? I suggest that Joey would be sternly cautioned against being seduced by the bewitching fairy tales of romance peddled relentlessly by Hollywood and the popular media. Joey ought to rein in his wild-running imagination from insidious fantasies about how he and Julie will crash together in ecstatic union, serenaded by a swooning soundtrack, to become the Brangelina of their campus, self-heroized in their omnipotent, triumphant love. Such is the stuff that dreams are made of,[9] by the movie, television, and music industries that so richly profit by perpetuating these delusions on celluloid and compact discs for mass consumption. Commercialized, fairy tale romance is big business and a monstrous myth. Lucretius warns that images of idyllic, beatified, electrified, passionate love are ephemeral *images*, mirages, incapable of feeding our real, earthly, embodied human relationships but fully capable of poisoning them. Hollywood stars make horrible models for personal relationships among college students (or any other couples, for that matter). To fall prey to the delusion, the vaunted fantasy, that Julie will be for Joey O. what Angelina Jolie is (portrayed by Hollywood to be) for Brad Pitt and vice versa is to bury what could be a healthy, pleasant relationship under an avalanche of utterly unrealistic and ultimately impossible expectations. She is no Aphrodite, even if she is a Homecoming Queen. He is no godlike superhunk, even if he is a Homecoming King.

Hollywood filmmakers and Madison Avenue magazine moguls enlist armies of make-up artists and post-production wizards to erase all blemishes and tiny wrinkles from the complexions and sculpted bodies digitally perfected to bedazzle us. The media-bloated imagination of a college student can do as much for him when he finds a mortal to idolize and enshrine on his pedestal of love. The benighted, lovesick dreamer will be bitterly disappointed when his zealously constructed fantasy of a perfect

❦ WILLIAM O. STEPHENS

goddess is dissolved by the flaws and frailties of what was all along a mere mortal. This is why Lucretius thinks it is easier to avoid being ensnared by erotic love than to free oneself from its nets once entangled. But he believes the dangers of love's mania can still be escaped unless you prevent yourself by deliberately overlooking

> all the mental and physical imperfections of the woman for whom you yearn and long. For men who are blinded by passion generally do this and attribute to their mistresses virtues that in reality they do not possess. Thus we find women with numerous defects of body and behavior being fondly loved and held in high esteem. (Lines 1151–6)

To the poor fool deranged by passion, her swarthy skin is "honey-brown," if she is sloppy and smelly, to him she is "beauty unadorned," if she is gray-eyed (considered a defect by the ancients), to him she is "a little Athena," if she is wiry and woody, "a gazelle," if she's a dumpy dwarf, "one of the Graces, a charmer," if a giantess, "a marvel of majesty." If she stammers, she "has a lisp," if dumb, she's "modest," if a chattering, spiteful spitfire, she's "a sparkler," if she's wasting away, she's "slender and willowy," if she's half-dead coughing, she's "delicate." The bulging and big-breasted is "Ceres suckling Iacchus," the snub-nosed is "a she-satyr," the thick-lipped is "kissy-faced" (lines 1159–69). Lovesickness so distorts the manic lover's perception that his beloved's obvious flaws are hallucinated into traits so lovely that they approach godlike ideals. Love steals the lover away from reality, according to Lucretius.

Contemporary American culture sells different therapies for dissatisfaction with our looks. Today, college students pay for tanning treatments and painful hair removal and bleaching procedures. If Julie C. had more to spend, would she buy Botox injections, skin bleaching, liposuction, or plastic surgeries to alter her breasts, tummy, nose, chin, and eyes, and invest in whatever bodily "corrections" modern medicine sells? Ubiquitous stereotypes of "perfect" physical beauty, especially concerning body shape, brainwash many students into dangerous eating disorders and self-destructive behaviors, including smoking to control weight. Lucretius' message for us, I suggest, is that for our mental health, we *accept* our bodies and safeguard our physical health rather than worry about our looks.

What about Brangelina and other hyper-beautiful people? Lucretius insists that even if your beloved is totally gorgeous from head to toe, she isn't so special for the following reasons: first, there are others like her; second, you have lived without her until now; and third, she behaves no better than an ugly woman. New beauties, supermodels too, crop up like weeds, and you didn't and don't need any of them to live happily. Moreover, since supercouples divorce with the seasons (or faster), their outward beauty fails to reflect their inner characters. The Epicurean lesson is plain. Obsession with physical beauty is a pathological fixation with mere appearance, and such a psychological fixation is a debilitating disease. Planet Hollywood proclaims: image is everything. Lucretius wants to dispel this delusion with the sober wake-up call: image is illusion.

Skip the Sex and Keep the Friend

Lucretius claims that the many ills catalogued are experienced even in steadfast, successful love. But "when love is frustrated and unrequited, the miseries you can spot with your eyes shut are countless" (lines 1142–4). For college students, who generally are less emotionally experienced and under considerable academic, social, and sometimes athletic pressures, these miseries can include depression, drinking problems, drug abuse, eating disorders, crippling driving accidents, attempted suicide, and suicide.[10] These troubles ruin one's academic progress and worse. Therefore, the wise Epicurean advice is for Joey O. and Julie C. to cool it, to stay focused on their studies, to prepare for and attend every class, to take notes attentively and participate in class, and to complete and turn in their assignments on time. Better for them to remain study buddies, at least until the semester ends.

What if they really like each other a lot? I propose that the Epicureans would consider wanting friends to be in the class of natural desires necessary for happiness. Friendship is hugely important for achieving *ataraxia*. Epicurus beams about it: "Friendship dances through the world bidding us all to awaken to the recognition of happiness."[11] But friends are not just for happy times. When college students are distraught, to whom do they turn? When they need a sympathetic ear or a shoulder to lean on, on whom do they rely? When they are in conflict with their parents or siblings or bosses or co-workers, who provides emotional support? Amid romantic disasters so devastating that they may even consider suicide, who is there to help them regain perspective? Their friends, naturally. As Epicurus advises, "Of the things which wisdom provides for the blessedness of one's whole life, by far the greatest is the possession of friendship."[12]

WILLIAM O. STEPHENS

Desires to engage in sex with others are natural but not necessary for life, for freeing the body from troubles, or for happiness. Desires to have friends are natural and necessary for happiness. So I argue that the Epicureans would advise college students to avoid having sex with their friends in order to protect their friendships. Epicurus writes: "Do not spoil what you have by desiring what you have not; but remember that what you now have was once among the things only hoped for."[13] As tempting as it may be to upgrade a friend to a friend with benefits, friendships can be counted on to last much longer than either bouts of sexual passion or the flings which they punctuate. The conclusion of Book Four of *De Rerum Natura* seems to lend support to my argument. Lucretius explains that "a woman with little pretension to beauty" can, by what she does, by her obliging, gentle, and pleasing conduct, and by "the neatness of her person," accustom a man to spend his life with her (lines 1277–82). He adds that "mere habit generates love" (line 1283). I understand this kind of love not to be the tumultuous, crazed love of sexual passion, but rather the painless, soothing, abiding love of a person. This suggests that personable, amiable conduct, consistently *friendly* behavior, can sometimes create the kind of love upon which a strong, lasting marriage is founded. The best lifelong companions more often emerge from a group of good friends than from the stage of a beauty pageant. Perhaps a key insight of Epicurean philosophy is that good friends are far more reliable, and so ultimately more desirable, than good sex. If so, the wise Epicurean chooses to populate his tranquil, happy life not with friends with benefits, but with friends. Friends *are* the real benefits.

NOTES

1 I thank Tim O'Keefe, Jeffrey Hause, Al Spangler, and Berel Dov Lerner for their helpful comments on an earlier draft of this essay.
2 Epicurus, *Principal Doctrine* VIII, in Brad Inwood and L. P. Gerson (eds.) *The Epicurus Reader: Selected Writings and Testimonia* (Indianapolis: Hackett, 1994), p. 32.
3 See Tim O'Keefe, "Epicurus," *The Internet Encyclopedia of Philosophy*, available online at www.iep.utm.edu/e/epicur.htm (accessed July 9, 2009).
4 *Vatican Saying* 33 reads: "The cry of the flesh: not to be hungry, not to be thirsty, not to be cold. For if someone has these things and is confident of having them in the future, he might contend even with [Zeus] for happiness." In Inwood and Gerson, *The Epicurus Reader*, p. 38.

5   Epicurus says "we believe that … if we do not have a lot we can make do with few, being genuinely convinced that those who least need extravagance enjoy it most." *Letter to Menoeceus* 130, in Inwood and Gerson, *The Epicurus Reader*, p. 30.

6   Epicurus, *Vatican Saying* LI in R. M. Geer (ed.) *Letters, Principal Doctrines, and Vatican Sayings* (New York: Macmillan, 1985), pp. 69–70.

7   My explication of Lucretius owes much to Robert D. Brown, *Lucretius on Love and Sex: A Commentary on De Rerum Natura IV, 1030–1287* (Leiden: Brill, 1987).

8   Lucretius, *On the Nature of Things*, ed. M. F. Smith (Indianapolis: Hackett, 2001), p. 128. All subsequent quotations of Lucretius are from this edition and are cited parenthetically.

9   Respect for director John Huston (rather than spotty memory of Shakespeare) compels me to follow Humphrey Bogart's famous last line in *The Maltese Falcon* (1941) instead of Prospero's original line: "We are such stuff / As dreams are made on" in *The Tempest*, Act 4, Scene 1, lines 156–7.

10 For a physically healthy young adult to kill himself out of depression or despair would be unwise and unwarranted, according to Epicurus: "But the many … sometimes choose [death] as a relief from the bad things in life. But the wise man neither rejects life nor fears death. For living does not offend him." *Letter to Menoeceus* 125–6, in Inwood and Gerson, *The Epicurus Reader*, p. 29. "He is utterly small-minded for whom there are many plausible reasons for committing suicide." *Vatican Saying* XXXVIII, in Inwood and Gerson, *The Epicurus Reader*, p. 38.

11 Epicurus, *Vatican Saying* LII, in Geer, *Letters, Principal Doctrines, and Vatican Sayings*, p. 70.

12 Epicurus, *Principal Doctrine* XXVII, in Inwood and Gerson, *The Epicurus Reader*, p. 34.

13 Epicurus, *Vatican Saying* XXXV, in Geer, *Letters, Principal Doctrines, and Vatican Sayings*, p. 68.

CHAPTER 7

FRIENDS WITH BENEFITS

A Precarious Negotiation

Sex Talk

This essay is about "friends with benefits" relationships. We presume that the typical reader (an undergraduate college student) is already familiar with the term. Many typical readers probably have experience with a friends with benefits relationship (either in the past or the present) or know someone who has. We also expect that reactions to friends with benefits relationships vary dramatically, as some readers likely find the very idea difficult to imagine, offensive, or both, while others find them to have strong advantages. Still others, especially those who have been out of college for at least ten years, probably have no idea what the term means.

Sexual life on today's college campuses is seemingly dominated by the hook up.[1] In this context, our research suggests that friends with benefits relationships are common on college campuses.[2] It is important to note, however, that large random surveys on the topic have not been performed. Even if such a survey were done, rates would likely vary over time and across college campuses. However, prevalence rates in the 50–60 percent range are typical in our and others' research. Friends with benefits relationships are a relational fact of life for many unmarried American college students (and probably many non-college students in their late teens, 20s and early 30s).

In this essay, we explore a variety of questions about friends with benefits relationships. What are they? Can people really have sex with friends and remain friends? Is friends with benefits a new type of relationship, or have people always had sex with friends? What are the advantages and disadvantages of friends with benefits? Why do some people have friends with benefits relationships while others eschew such relationships? Finally, because both of us teach and research the topic of communication in relationships, we explore how people talk (or don't talk) about friends with benefits relationships with their friends. Answering these questions is more difficult than asking them, for a couple of reasons. First, friends with benefits relationships are a developing trend that morphs over time. Second, given the recent emergence of this phenomenon, there has not been much research on these topics.

Just Friends and Sex Too?

An obvious place to start our exploration is with the task of defining friends with benefits relationships. A definition identifies the meaning that a person or scholar associates with a word, term, or phrase. Defining a term can be difficult because the meaning or meanings associated with words is ultimately arbitrary and a matter of convention (i.e., agreement among a language community), not fact. The term "friends with benefits" came to mean what it does because someone (our guess is a group of fraternity brothers) made up the label and it stuck. This does not mean, however, that terms and their definitions should be thrown around carelessly. Some definitions will be more useful than others and more useful definitions are clear, help us understand what we are defining, help us differentiate between instances of a thing and instances that do not count as the thing, and help us communicate our understanding.

Therefore, here we present a definition that we hope facilitates understanding and our ability to communicate thoughts on friends with benefits relationships. We, however, make no claims that our way is the only or the right way to think about friends with benefits relationships because, as we will note throughout this essay, the use of the phrase "friends with benefits" varies substantially. We are trying to come up with a useful way of understanding friends with benefits relationships.

Too simply put, friends with benefits relationships consist of friends who have sex. This was the consistent answer Paul received when he asked

⁙   TIMOTHY R. LEVINE AND PAUL A. MONGEAU

undergraduates to define the phrase in both Arizona and Ohio in 1999. This simple definition, however, masks considerable variety and complexity in the nature of this relationship type. In particular, the simplicity of the label hides several difficult questions, such as what does it mean to be "friends," how are friendship relationships different than romantic relationships (other than having sex), what counts as sex, and how frequently does sex have to occur within an ongoing friendship for it to count as a friends with benefits relationship? These are not simple questions, and our answers are less than definitive. Understanding friends with benefits relationships, however, requires grappling with these questions.

As we discuss the meaning of friends with benefits relationships, it should be noted that our definition is not limited to heterosexual partnerships. Cross-sex friends with benefits relationships are likely more common than same-sex friends with benefits relationships simply because heterosexuals represent a greater proportion of the population. Our discussion here will likely reflect the heterosexual bias in the research literature. Despite this bias, most of the issues discussed here apply regardless of sexual orientation.

Defining friendship and differentiating between friends and romantic partners is something that is difficult to put into words, but nevertheless it is something that people usually (but not always) do with ease. Friends are people we know (i.e., we have some unique knowledge of them as a person), and like (i.e., we have positive feelings toward them), and this knowing and liking is, to some extent, mutual. Our friends know and like us, too. We have interacted with friends (perhaps in great breadth and depth) in the past and anticipate doing so in the future. So, friends are different from strangers and acquaintances because there is mutual liking and shared personal knowledge. Friendships are also consensual (i.e., relationships of choice). Friends differ from family because we choose our friends.

Given our definition, how do friends differ from romantic partners? Traditionally, one (but not the only) key difference between friends and lovers is sexual desire and interaction. Lovers, romantic partners, and romantic interests are people with whom we either have sex or desire to have sex. This is not typical for friends. People who are sexually involved, by some definitions, are not even considered friends. In fact, if you tell a boyfriend or girlfriend "let's just be friends" the implied meaning is, in part, no more sex together.

The distinction between friendship and romantic relationships, based only on sexual behavior, is challenged by friends with benefits relationships. If friendships are really non-sexual, friends with benefits relationships make no sense. Alternatively, if friends with benefits relationships are relationships involving friends who have sex but who are not romantically involved, then the act of sex alone cannot fully differentiate between friendships and romantic relationships.

Given this discussion, it should be clear that defining the term "friend" and differentiating it from "romantic partner" are surprisingly difficult tasks. What is more, one of us (Paul) has found that part of the ambiguity surrounding the friends with benefits label stems from the dramatic differences in the types of relationships between friends with benefits partners. Some cases are consistent with the commonsense notion of the friends with benefits label; good friends (perhaps best friends) who care for – and have sex with – each other, but for whatever reason are not in a romantic relationship. At the other end of the spectrum, what some people call a friends with benefits relationship is really little more than serial hook ups where partners engage in very little communication other than to arrange and carry out sexual rendezvous. In still other cases, friends with benefits partners used to be in a romantic relationship but broke up, but maintained the friendship and sexual parts of their relationship. In this case, friends with benefits relationships represent the smoldering embers of a past romantic relationship.

Casual Sex

A key to clarifying distinctions between friends, romantic partners, and friends with benefits likely resides in considering what the sex means to partners, specifically as it relates to the motivations that underlie the behavior. We believe that a distinction between romantic sex and casual sex can help to differentiate these relationships. In our view, romantic sex is motivated by passion, love, or at least the potential for love, and romantic interest, while casual sex is motivated by mere hedonistic sexual gratification. In other words, the goal of casual sex is to have sex as a purely recreational (i.e., fun) activity, while there are more relational implications inherent to relational sex. This distinction highlights some of the ambiguity in some friends with benefits relationships. In the early stages of a friends with benefits relationship, it may not be clear whether the partner (or even oneself) considers the sex to be romantic or casual. Moreover, as we will discuss below, partners may assign different meanings to the same behavior.

TIMOTHY R. LEVINE AND PAUL A. MONGEAU

One of the phrases we hear a lot from our students is that friends with benefits relationships come with "no strings attached." This suggests that the whole point of friends with benefits is to have sex without the romantic label and the commitments, emotions, and hassles that come along with it. For the most part, friends with benefits involves people who have sex with someone they know and like while attempting to avoid the romantic feelings and label that comes with romantic relationships. In the "no strings attached" ideal, the relationship is understood as a friendship, not a romance, and the sex is thought of as casual, not relational. Consistent with this notion, Tim's research indicates that friends with benefits partners have low levels of passion when describing their friends with benefits relationship.[3] Friends with benefits is not about "having the hots" for each other; it's about convenient, no strings attached sex.

All this raises the question of whether friends can really have casual, recreational sex without at least one of them wanting a romantic relationship. In one of Tim's studies, we asked college students this question.[4] While a little more than 60 percent of the survey respondents answered in the affirmative, answers differed strongly based on a person's actual experience with a friends with benefits relationship. Over 80 percent of people who had a friends with benefits relationship thought it was possible to have casual sex with a friend, while almost 70 percent of people who had not had a friends with benefits relationship believed that friendship and sex were incompatible. One of the interesting questions about this finding is the direction of causality: Does experience lead people with friends with benefits relationships to believe that friendship and sex can go together, or is it that beliefs about sex and friendship help determine who has a friends with benefits relationship and who does not? In any case, our data suggest that at least some people think it is possible to have casual sex with a friend, and people with a friends with benefits relationship are more likely to hold this belief than people who do not. But, clearly, there are those who firmly believe that friends with benefits relationships are impossible because they understand friendships as excluding sex.

A final set of definitional issues involve the nature and frequency of sex. If friends with benefits relationships are friends who have sex, then we need to know what counts as sex. Obviously, vaginal intercourse is sex. But what about other sexual acts? Many of our students tell us that in their view, kissing or even oral sex do not count as sex. Given this view, it is hard to know where to draw the line. Kissing on the lips probably does not count as sex, but how about a hand job or cybersex? A related issue is if someone has sex with a friend just once, does that count as a friends with benefits relationship? In defining friends with benefits relationships, both of us agree that sexual interaction must be repeated before the relationship can be considered a friends with benefits relationship. Our take is that if people engage in "one time sex" or consider it a "mistake" and do not intend to repeat it, then the relationship is not a friends with benefits relationship.

History and Prevalence

The label "friends with benefits" is relatively new (from our perspective at least – it might seem like ancient history to some readers). We do not know its origin or how long it has been in use. Paul first came across it when talking with his undergraduate students about campus dating norms at Miami University of Ohio around 1997. His students attributed the friends with benefits label to a song entitled "Head Over Feet" by Alanis Morrisette. Tim learned of the phrase more recently when Melissa Bisson, a recent graduate student at Michigan State University, wanted to do her MA thesis research on the topic.

An interesting historical question is how long have friends with benefits been around. Have friends always provided each other with convenient, recreational sex, or is this an invention of the current younger generation? While the friends with benefits label is relatively new, we suspect, there have always been people in these relationships, they just did not have a sexy label to describe it. Moreover, friends who had sex were probably less likely to talk openly about their relationship with family and other friends. Therefore, we suspect that given the current climate of casual sex on college campuses (the so-called hook-up culture), friends with benefits relationships are likely both more widely practiced and more openly discussed than was the case a decade or two ago.

A second related question is the extent to which friends with benefits relationships are limited to college campuses. Although no one has investigated this, we believe that the answer is most likely no. We suspect that people do not stop all friends with benefits relationships after they graduate from college, though opportunities for these liaisons are likely less frequent. It seems likely that recent college graduates are willing to defer long-term relational plans to begin their career trajectory, but still want a stable romantic relationship (and many want to get married). Therefore, there likely comes a point where friends with benefits relationships

TIMOTHY R. LEVINE AND PAUL A. MONGEAU

become less attractive and consistent with the desired lifestyle. So long as people are willing to eschew long-term romantic relationships to build their career and have a sufficient sample of attractive singles around them, friends with benefits relationships will likely occur off, as well as on, campus. We wouldn't be at all surprised, however, if friends with benefits relationships are *primarily* a campus-based (i.e., high school and college) phenomenon. Anecdotally, we have heard from high school counselors that friends with benefits relationships exist among high school students.

So, Why have Sex with a Friend?

We have already said that friends with benefits relationships seem to be about casual, recreational sex with "no stings attached." This appears to be their primary advantage. People wanting to have sex need a partner. But why choose a friend? One likely answer is simply convenience. Friends are frequently in the same social network and go out drinking together, which provides an opportunity for repeated sexual interactions. A friends with benefits partner may represent a sexual "plan B." Lots of college students go out to a bar (or party, or other event involving the consumption of alcohol) in the hopes of meeting someone to have sex with (casual, relational, or both). But in this typical college life scenario, failing to meet someone means going home alone without sex (or "striking out" in the slang of our youth). With a sexual plan B, even if friends are not together, one can simply drunk dial or text the partner at the end of the night to see if he is interested in sex. If neither friend meets someone, they have a workable backup plan. Failing to pick someone up at the bar or party does not mean going without recreational sex.

A second advantage is that having a friends with benefits relationship is more likely to lead to sexual success when compared with going out to find a stranger. Particularly if the partners have hooked up before, the odds of a "yes, let's do it" are better and a refusal is less ego threatening with a friend than with a stranger. That is, a "no" from a friends with benefits partner is likely interpreted as "I'm sleeping" rather than "Yuck, I have no interest in what you got" or "I can do better."

A final potential advantage of a friends with benefits relationship is perceived safety. Sex can be risky. Unprotected sex can lead to pregnancy, STDs, date rape, and stalkers (or worse). In many cases, partners already know and are comfortable with their friends. Therefore, within a friends with benefits relationship, issues of birth control and safe sex can be addressed with more certainty and less awkwardness than with a stranger (assuming, of course, that partners know ahead of time that they are going to have sex and aren't already drunk). Also, hooking up with a friend rather than a stranger may provide some protection against people with bad intents. Most people probably have confidence that their friend is not going to hurt them, but picking up a stranger while drunk is a considerably riskier proposition.

It is important to note that we labeled this potential advantage as *perceived* safety. It is hard to know how much of the perceived safety advantage of a friends with benefits relationship is real and how much is illusory. For example, if people think, "My friend would not have an STD, so there is no reason not to have safe sex with them," the perceived relative safety of a friends with benefits relationship is misguided. Moreover, some of Paul's data suggests that in many cases the first sexual interaction between friends was facilitated by the consumption of alcohol and was not planned ahead of time. Decision making in this sort of context (drunken and impulsive) is relatively unlikely to include safe sex.

So, the primary goal of a friends with benefits relationship is supposed to be casual, recreational sex with no strings attached. A major disadvantage of friends with benefits relationships, however, is that they can become considerably more complex than the simple no strings attached ideal would suggest. Sexual interaction without romantic feelings may create an irony and a catch. One of the primary downsides of friends with benefits relationships is the worry and, in many cases, reality that one (and only one) partner develops romantic feelings for his or her friend. In Tim's research, nearly two-thirds of people in friends with benefits relationships shared this concern. This isn't a great surprise that because the friends know each other well and enjoy each other's company, the addition of sexual interaction likely brings up desires for something "real." So, the major irony of friends with benefits relationships is that people have them precisely because they do not want romantic commitment with the person, but having sex creates the worry, and justifiably so, that romantic feeling will develop.

Another disadvantage of friends with benefits relationships is that they are not an effective way of establishing romantic relationships. In Tim's research, only about 10 percent of friends with benefits relationships transition into a boyfriend-girlfriend or some other type of romantic relationship.[5] This percentage may sound low to some readers, but remember, avoiding

❬❭ TIMOTHY R. LEVINE AND PAUL A. MONGEAU

TABLE 7.1   What became of the friends with benefits relationship

Stayed friends but stopped having sex	35.8%
Stayed in a friends with benefits relationship	28.3%
Friendship and benefits came to an end	25.9%
Became romantically involved	9.8%

being romantically involved with the person is the point of friends with benefits relationships. Friends with benefits relationships will likely transition to a romantic relationship only if both partners desire such a shift.

Another disadvantage of friends with benefits relationships is that they can create drama and damage the friendship. This worry is real. If neither partner desires a romantic relationship, the friends with benefits relationship might continue, or it might become "weird." When only one partner desires a romantic relationship, but the other person desires sex but not a romantic entanglement, the situation becomes difficult to negotiate. In Tim's research, about 25 percent of the people with friends with benefits relationships ended up losing both their friend and the benefits (both sexual and non-sexual) of that friendship.[6] Potential harm to the friendship is likely one reason why the most common outcome of friends with benefits relationships in Tim's research was that the friendship went back to just friends without the benefits. Friends consider their friendship to be more valuable to them than the sexual gratification that they receive. Apparently, finding an alternative sexual partner is easier than finding another friend. The outcomes of friends with benefits relationships in our research are summarized in table 7.1.

Communication in Friends with Benefits Relationships

Given that the point of friends with benefits relationships is sex without romantic attachment and that the most commonly listed disadvantage of friends with benefits relationships is the worry that the other person will become romantically attached, one might think that the friends would just talk about their desires and expectations for the sex and the relationship. Our research, however, suggests that those involved in a friends with benefits relationship usually don't do this. In relationships that might become romantic, the most frequently avoided (i.e., taboo) topic is about the relationship itself.[7] This is true for friends with benefits relationships, too.[8]

Another reason why partners might not talk about their friends with benefits relationships ahead of time is that, in most cases, they don't know it is going to happen. Again, some of Paul's recent data suggest that in many cases, friends don't go out to a bar or party with the intention of sleeping with their friend. First-time sex in a friends with benefits relationship isn't like a first date. Plans for first dates are most times made ahead of time and partners typically have a number of goals (i.e., outcomes such as testing the relational waters or having sex) that they want to reach by going on it. First-time sex in a friends with benefits relationship typically isn't like that. In many cases, partners don't know that they are going to have sex on a particular night, let alone sex with a particular friend. In these cases, it is nearly impossible to negotiate the friends with benefits relationship ahead of time because friends don't know that there is anything to negotiate.

The influence of alcohol is another reason why negotiating the meaning of sex might be difficult. Alcohol reduces inhibitions and causes people to focus on what makes their partner an attractive sexual partner instead of the damage that sexual activity might cause for the friendship. Therefore, while drunk, friends might initiate (perhaps unsafe) sexual activity with a friend that they wouldn't do when sober. Moreover, alcohol makes identifying the cause of the behavior more ambiguous (e.g., "I did it because I was really drunk" versus "I did it because I want something more from my friendship").

Once friends have sex the first time, there might be forces that keep them from directly negotiating the relationship. If partners have not discussed their friendship (including the meaning of the sexual behavior that occurs within it) beforehand, partners might be confused as to whether the sex is (using our distinction) casual or relational. In other words, friends may not know if the sex reflects a budding romantic interest or merely sexual desire that just happened to be directed toward the friend. If partners don't explicitly talk about the relationship (i.e., break the primary communicative taboo), partners appear to determine the meaning of the sexual interaction from other behaviors that partners either do (or do not) perform. For example, the meaning of the sex might be interpreted based on whether the friend calls or texts in the few days following the sex. Do friends engage in non-verbal behaviors that might reflect a romantic relationship (e.g., handholding), particularly in public? Do partners prearrange dyadic events that look like dates (e.g., going to a dinner, movie, or a sporting event)? How do partners act when they are both around other people? Under what conditions do they have sex again (e.g., after alcohol has been consumed)?

⁛ TIMOTHY R. LEVINE AND PAUL A. MONGEAU

Assuming that partners don't explicitly talk about the role of sex in their friendship, it is not surprising that high levels of uncertainty (and, potentially, discomfort) persist. The lack of explicit negotiation of the friends with benefits relationship, in many cases, is problematic. Across nearly all the relevant studies, there is a strong tendency for friends with benefits relationships to become problematic because one partner develops romantic feelings and a desire for romantic attachment, while the other does not. In such cases, the meanings associated with sex differ across partners. For one person, the sexual interaction reflects growing feelings toward the partner (i.e., it is romantic), but for the other friend, the sex remains casual (i.e., it is sexual gratification with no relational implications). Such a situation is likely to become increasingly distressing for both partners and is likely one of the causes why, in many cases, partners lose both the friends and the benefits in the relationship.

The Bottom Line

Friends with benefits relationships are not as simple as no strings attached sex with a friend. Thinking about friends with benefits relationships raises important questions about the meaning of friendship and sex, and of the moral implications of sex, alcohol consumption, and campus lifestyle issues. Perhaps the central issue is one's views on the idea of casual sex. The idea of sex outside romantic relationships is offensive to some and desirable to others. When moral choices are made while intoxicated, however, decisions are unlikely to be thoughtful.

NOTES

1 Kathleen A. Bogle, *Hooking Up: Sex, Dating, and Relationships on Campus* (New York: New York University Press, 2008).
2 Melissa A. Bisson and Timothy R. Levine, "Negotiating a Friends with Benefits Relationship," *Archives of Sexual Behavior* 38: 66–73; Paul A. Mongeau, J. Williams, C. Shaw, K. Knight, and A. Ramirez, Jr., "Definitions and Diversity of Friends with Benefits Relationships: A Two-Wave, Cross-Region, Study," unpublished manuscript (under review).
3 Bisson and Levine, "Negotiating a Friends with Benefits Relationship."
4 Ibid.

5 Ibid.
6 Ibid.
7 Leslie A. Baxter and William W. Wilmot, "Taboo Topics in Close Relationships," *Journal of Social and Personal Relationships* 2: 253–69.
8 Bisson and Levine, "Negotiating a Friends with Benefits Relationship."

KELLI JEAN K. SMITH AND KELLY MORRISON[1]

CHAPTER 8

THE PHILOSOPHY OF FRIENDS WITH BENEFITS

What College Students Think They Know

A Brave New (Sexual) World

Romantic and sexual relationships have been, and continue to be, a frequent focus of both the media and academic scholarship. In the 1970s, music lyrics pleaded "baby, please go all the way" (the Raspberries in 1971) and "I need somebody to love" (Queen in 1976), while currently, pop artist Kelly Clarkson informs listeners through her lyrics that "I do not hook up." A 1991 episode of the popular television sitcom *Seinfeld* portrayed the characters Jerry and Elaine attempting to negotiate a "this and that" deal by adding sex ("that") to their friendship ("this"). More recently, MTV's *True Life*, the television series *How I Met Your Mother*, and *True Blood* have all portrayed friends with benefits relationships, such as the one that Jerry and Elaine attempted to negotiate.

Similarly, the scholarly literature exhibits a wealth of research on romantic and sexual relationships. The phenomenon of friends with benefits relationships in particular has begun to attract the recent attention of the academic community. Several years ago, we noticed our students discussing and negotiating these types of relationships (with a variety of labels) and thus began an exploratory study on this phenomenon. We defined friends with benefits relationships as relationships that occur between cross-sex friends in which the friends engage in sexual activity, which can include sexual intercourse, but they do not define their relationship as romantic and do not define their friend as a boyfriend or girlfriend. This hybrid relationship combines the benefits of cross-sex friendship with the benefits of a sexual relationship, yet avoids the responsibilities and commitment that romantic sexual relationships typically entail. Additionally, friends with benefits relationships differ from "hook ups," sexual encounters between acquaintances or strangers usually lasting only one night, in that they are more stable. But are friends with benefits relationships really without their pitfalls? In this essay we review our research on friends with benefits relationships, report some of the unpublished data from the study, comment on current research in this area, and address the philosophical issues related to this phenomenon for contemporary college students.[2] We begin with a review of our earlier research.

The Original Study

We became interested in learning more about the phenomenon of friends with benefits relationships as experienced by college students after a particularly animated class discussion on the pros and cons of this type of relationship. We designed an exploratory study to gather information about multiple dimensions of friends with benefits relationships, including: how they emerge, the motivations, barriers and emotions related to them, the maintenance rules associated with them, the outcomes of these relationships, and how these relationships are discussed and supported by same-sex friend networks. Table 8.1 at the end of this chapter summarizes the results of this survey.

We surveyed 143 students enrolled in introductory communication courses at a large Midwestern university about their opposite sex friendships. The survey was eleven pages in length and included a variety of open-ended questions, the perceived same-sex network support scale (created by the authors for this study), and items assessing demographic information. A friends with benefits relationship was defined for participants as "an opposite sex friend that you have, who you also have sexual activity with (this can include sexual intercourse, but can also include other types of sexual activity). This is not someone you describe as your boyfriend/girlfriend." Participants who had experience with a friends with benefits relationship answered a series of questions describing their experiences, while participants with no experience with a friends with

𝄞   KELLI JEAN K. SMITH AND KELLY MORRISON

TABLE 8.1   Percentage of participants reporting multiple friends with benefits relationships

Number of FWBRs	Female	Male
0	47.4	43.2
1	14.4	11.4
2	18.6	20.5
3	12.4	13.6
4	4.1	2.3
5	2.1	2.3
6	1.0	4.5
7	0	2.3

N = 51 females reporting FWBRs from a sample of 97, and 25 males from a sample of 44.

benefits relationship skipped that section of the survey. The participants for this research were largely Caucasian (65 percent) and female (69 percent). Only heterosexual participants were included in the analyses, and this resulted in the elimination of one case.

We asked our sample of college students, "How many friends with benefits relationships have you had?" Seventy-nine out of the 143 participants had experience with at least one friends with benefits relationship (55 percent of the sample). Fifty-three percent of female participants reported experience with friends with benefits relationships, as did 57 percent of male participants. Furthermore, many participants stated that they had experienced more than one relationship. Analyses revealed that men were no more likely than women to have had friends with benefits relationships, and the number of relationships reported by men and women were similar.

"Let's get this party started": How Friends with Benefits Relationships Were Established

In response to the question, "How did you originally establish this relationship?" five different categories emerged from the data. The most frequently reported category was "it just happened," which was reported by 47 percent of the responses. The next most frequently reported categories

were that a "friends with benefits relationship previously had been discussed" (e.g., "we had talked about it before," 37 percent of the responses),
that they had "previously dated" (11 percent), that the friends with benefits relationship had been "indirectly established" (e.g., flirting, thought
about it, never directly discussed the arrangement, 13 percent), or
because "alcohol was involved" (9 percent).

"Is this a good idea?" Motivations and Barriers to Friends with Benefits Relationships

We asked participants who had participated in friends with benefits relationships to give their reasons for establishing their relationships, and the
data revealed five categories. The most frequently reported motivation
was "relationship avoidance," which included 40 percent of the responses
and described participants' desire to avoid being "tied down" to one
particular partner or preferring to be free to pursue another partner.
Twenty-eight percent of the responses were categorized as "wanted a
friends with benefits relationship," and included participants' descriptions about specifically wanting to have or try a friends with benefits
relationship. Not surprisingly, the simple "desire for sex," illustrated by
one participant's claim "sex is essential," was a common motivator.
Seventeen percent of the responses fell into this category. Another common motivator was "relationship simplicity" (17 percent of responses),
meaning that friends with benefits relationships were perceived as less
difficult to maintain than traditional romantic relationships. Participants
expressed the opinion that friends with benefits relationships "seemed to
be the best option to be together without being together." Finally, a small
number of responses (11 percent) indicated that a friends with benefits
relationship was established in order to feel an "emotional connection"
(e.g., "I missed the intimacy I had with my ex-boyfriend").

When asked to list the barriers to establishing friends with benefits relationships, the most frequently reported barrier was "relationship issues,"
reported by 73 percent of the responses. This category included concerns
about losing or ruining a good friendship, concerns about the relationship
becoming more difficult, and concerns that a friends with benefits relationship would prevent future relationships with other people. Another
barrier was the "emotional consequences" of a friends with benefits relationship, illustrated by 61 percent of the responses. This category consisted

of concerns about the relationship becoming more awkward, uncomfortable, or emotionally demanding. "Equity issues" were reported by 18 percent of the responses, and this entailed perceptions that conflict or misunderstandings could occur if one partner became more involved in the friends with benefits relationship than the other. "Moral reasons," such as ethics or religion, were reported by 12 percent of the responses; "self-presentational concerns" included reasons such as not wanting to be gossiped about or labeled "easy" or "a slut" (11 percent of the responses); and "physical consequences" included concerns such as catching an STD or having an unwanted pregnancy (9 percent of the responses.)

"How does it feel?" Emotions Associated with Friends with Benefits Relationships

When asked how the friends with benefits relationship made them feel, participants who had had friends with benefits relationships reported experiencing a range of emotions. Some of the emotions associated with friends with benefits relationships were positive. Many participants felt "happiness" (34 percent of responses) or satisfaction in what they perceived as a fun relationship. They reported feeling "comfortable" (8 percent of responses) and "laid back" in the relationship, which is consistent with the relationship simplicity motivation for engaging in friends with benefits relationships. In addition, participants enjoyed the "sexual accessibility" of their partners (8 percent of responses), knowing that they always had someone who would be there for them. Participants' "self-esteem" was positively affected (4 percent of responses) because their friends with benefits relationships made them feel wanted, needed, and desirable. Many participants also reported "falling in love" with their partners (19 percent of responses.)

Some participants also reported several negative feelings or emotions associated with friends with benefits relationships. "Negative uncertainty" referred to feelings of awkwardness or confusion over the relationship and was reported by 19 percent of the responses. Participants also experienced "anger" (18 percent of responses), "guilt or disgust" about feeling used (11 percent of responses), "jealousy" (5 percent of responses), and distress associated with the "inequity" of wanting more than a friends with benefits relationship (16 percent of responses.)

"Can we make this work?" Rules for Maintaining Friends with Benefits Relationships

The students in this study seemed well aware of the pros and cons of friends with benefits relationships. The idea of having sex without feeling "tied down" to any one person, and the belief that friends with benefits relationships were less complicated than romantic relationships, appealed to them. They did, however, have concerns about getting hurt and ruining their friendships, and several of the rules for maintaining friends with benefits relationships centered on minimizing these risks. The entire group of students was asked about rules that they thought could help maintain friends with benefits relationships. In other words, we wanted to know what students believed one should or should not do in order to keep the friendship satisfying once the sexual component was added. Their responses revealed seven categories of maintenance rules. The most frequently described were "emotional rules" (e.g., "don't fall in love," 56 percent), followed by "rules for communication" (e.g., discussion of honesty, calling, what topics they could discuss, 41 percent), and "rules for sex" (e.g., use of condoms, discussion of sex with other people, 33 percent). "Friendship rules" concerned placing higher importance on the friendship aspect of the friends with benefits relationship than on the sexual aspect of the friends with benefits relationship (23 percent), while "secrecy rules" described a need to keep other acquaintances from knowing about the friends with benefits relationship (22 percent), believing that it was nobody else's business. "Permanence rules" emphasized the temporary nature of the friends with benefits relationship and were reported by 17 percent, while the final category, "negotiate rules," demonstrated the importance participants placed on discussing maintenance rules at the beginning of the friends with benefits relationship so that people understood the nature of the relationship before proceeding with it (8 percent).

"Was it good for you?" Outcomes of Friends with Benefits Relationships

We also asked participants to describe the current status of their friends with benefits relationships. Their responses revealed that friends with benefits relationships do not always end badly. Six different categories of friends with benefits relationship outcomes emerged. Some participants reported that they were "still involved" in their friends with benefits relationships (30 percent). Others stated that they were still friends but "just friends," meaning that they were no longer engaging in a sexual relationship (38 percent), while others were "not friends" at all (25 percent). Twenty-five percent of the responses indicated that the friends with benefits relationships had "moved forward emotionally," describing that they felt closer to their partner, while 4 percent indicated that the friends with benefits relationships had "moved forward relationally," indicating that they had transitioned to a dating relationship. Finally, 13 percent of the responses categorized the outcome of their friends with benefits relationships as "worse."

"So, what do you think?" Friends' Reactions to Friends with Benefits Relationships

When asked whether or not they told any of their same-sex friends about their friends with benefits relationship, 84 percent of the friends with benefits relationship participants indicated that they had. This information was met by a variety of reactions from the same-sex friend; ranging from "approval" (38 percent) or "disapproval" (36 percent), to "silence" (25 percent), "surprise" (13 percent), or communicating their "shared experience" that they have also had a friends with benefits relationship (11 percent).

Participants' responses about their same-sex friends' reactions to being told about the friends with benefits relationship suggested that understanding, encouragement, and approval from same-sex friends affected the outcome of the relationship. Participants were more likely to still be involved in a friends with benefits relationship if they perceived support from their same-sex friends and less likely to be involved in a friends with benefits relationship if they did not perceive support.

Not everyone thought it was a good idea to tell their same-sex friends about their friends with benefits relationships. Participants' reasons for not telling their same-sex friends about the relationship fell into four different categories, including justifications that it was not their business to know, or "relevance" (47 percent), the concern that that they would suffer "personal embarrassment" (13 percent), or "network disapproval" (7 percent), and simply for reasons of "secrecy" (20 percent).

Friends with Benefits Relationships: The Good, the Bad, and the Ugly

Our college years are a time when we are likely to experience many cross-sex friendships. The information from our surveys indicated that friends with benefits relationships are one common approach to cross-sex friendships for college undergraduates, and one that is fraught with the dynamics, dilemmas, and emotions common to many romantic relationships. Broadly conceived, the experiences described by the participants in our study also suggest that college students may approach friends with benefits relationships pragmatically, thinking they know what to expect going into a friends with benefits relationship, only to discover that their knowledge base was flawed. Put differently, one doesn't truly "know" what it's like to be in a friends with benefits relationship, with all its consequences, until one experiences a friends with benefits relationship.

Over half of the participants reported experience with friends with benefits relationships, and furthermore, approximately half of those participants could report on more than one friends with benefits relationship. These findings are consistent with other research that has reported the prevalence of friends with benefits relationships on college campuses.[3] While the media and academic research may focus on the sexuality of these types of relationships, the responses from our participants indicated that relationship and emotional issues are just as relevant to these types of friendships.

Considering motivations for friends with benefits relationships first, we found that many participants were motivated to enter into their friends with benefits relationships because they specifically did not want romantic relationships, or for relationship avoidance. This finding is inconsistent with previous work on cross-sex friendships that suggested that the addition of sex to a friendship is a stepping stone to a romantic relationship.[4] This finding also goes against conventional stereotypes that suggest that men are the "players" and women are seeking commitment. Many participants assumed that friends with benefits relationships are easier because they don't require the maintenance work that committed relationships do. This finding may be a result of the age of our sample (i.e., college students). One female participant commented about wanting to have fun but not having enough time to devote to another person. She also mentioned the desire to "get some action" but also wanted to know who she was getting it from. These sentiments echo a pragmatic approach to relationships, time management, and sexuality.

Yet sex also was a popular motivation for friends with benefits relationships. As one female participant stated, "You get the buddy and the booty." Another commented that sex was a necessary part of life and they and their friends with benefits partner agreed that it would be better to do this than to sleep around. Beyond paralleling the pragmatic approaches described above, these statements highlight an additional gender issue. Our sample was largely female, and many of them described sex as necessary but that they wanted it without a commitment. Indeed, over half of the women in this sample could report on one friends with benefits relationship, and many could report on multiple relationships. This suggests that the idea that women associate sex with love may be outdated for contemporary college-aged women. Rather, it seems that some of the women in our sample took a functional, or pragmatic, approach to sex. Certainly, the idea that a friends with benefits relationship is justified because it actually can protect a woman's reputation is a rather contemporary and practical twist to sex and relationships. These sentiments also are consistent with what other authors describe as a "permissiveness-with-affection" attitude, or a more accepting attitude about sexuality outside of marriage but within the confines of a committed relationship. In this case, the committed relationship would be the cross-sex friendship.

In terms of emotional motivations, we found that 17 percent of the responses of participants with friends with benefits relationship experience indicated that these relationships were pursued because they were easier than romantic relationships, that is, they pursued them for relationship simplicity. In particular, several of these accounts described how it was emotionally easier because they didn't have to deal with jealousy, or they didn't have to worry about cheating or getting caught cheating. In contrast to the emotional vacation seemingly afforded by friends with benefits relationships were the accounts that described pursuing these relationships in order to feel wanted or connected to someone else. Thus, some participants specifically approached these relationships so that an emotional connection could be experienced. These findings highlight a limitation of this study, which was that the current romantic dating status of the participants was neglected. This issue should be explored in future research because it has implications for the emotional needs of individuals, as well as issues of fidelity.

The fact that a variety of motivations could be described regarding friends with benefits relationships is consistent with other researchers' conceptualizations of different types or "flavors" of friends with benefits relationships.[5] However, it also is possible that these differences in motivations (or flavors) are a product of the timing of the data collection. Specifically, people may experience different aspects of a friends with benefits relationship over the course of time during the relationship, especially if they are faced with issues they didn't expect to occur (such as "catching feelings" for their partner, as one of our participants stated.)

Regarding the perceived barriers to friends with benefits relationships, the data paralleled the motivation findings, with the top two most reported reasons for not having friends with benefits relationships being relational issues and emotional consequences. Despite the fact that many friends with benefits relationships begin in order to avoid relationship and commitment hassles, these same problems ultimately seem to emerge. Participants described the discomfort associated with getting too attached, feeling jealous, and the general awkwardness it brings to a friendship. Additionally, they described friendships being "destroyed," "ruined," or never being the same again.

Theoretically, our findings support and extend other researchers' work that suggests that sexual activity can be perceived as an expectancy violation in cross-sex friendships.[6] Our results suggest that the emotions aroused during the course of a friends with benefits relationship also may be perceived as a violation of expectations. In other words, while people entered friends with benefits relationships with the expectation that these relationships would be commitment-free and easier for them (compared to romantic relationships), many people who had experienced friends with benefits relationships reported falling in love with their friend, experiencing conflict due to the inequity of each other's feelings, and a host of negative emotions. Thus, one direction for future research on friends with benefits relationships would be to examine over a period time the expectancy violations that occur when these relationships originally are established, along with those that occur during the course of the relationship.

The outcome of friends with benefits relationships can also be expectancy violations. Several of the participants in this study expressed the belief that friends with benefits relationships are enjoyable while they last, but are destined to fail because one person inevitably develops romantic feelings for the other. Other participants entered friends with benefits relationships believing that they could maintain the relationship successfully, particularly if they established rules that are meant to

⁇   KELLI JEAN K. SMITH AND KELLY MORRISON

minimize the risks associated with this type of relationship. The data suggest that the outcomes of friends with benefits relationships are not always negative. Many participants remained friends after the sexual aspect of the relationship ended. Some reported feeling closer to their partners and some friends with benefits relationships even transitioned into romantic relationships. There were, of course, less positive outcomes as well. One quarter of the participants reported that they were no longer friends with their partners, and several stated that their relationships were worse. These findings suggest that while participants may think that they know what to expect if they establish a friends with benefits relationship, the outcomes do not always match their expectations. Future research should include an investigation of the impact of these expectancy violations as well.

The vast majority of participants reported that they had told their same-sex friends about their friends with benefits relationship. Several participants stated that their friends approved of the relationship, and some shared their own experiences with friends with benefits relationships. This suggests that one's social network may be a valuable source of information regarding what to expect and how to behave in this type of relationship. Friends who have experience with friends with benefits relationships may provide support and advice that help maintain these relationships. They can discuss the factors that made their relationships successful, as well as the factors that led to problems in the relationship. Friends who have gone through their own ups and downs in friends with benefits relationships may also be able to provide a sympathetic ear to a person who is having difficulties maintaining a friends with benefits relationship and give advice for how to cope with the challenges of maintaining this type of relationship. Our data revealed that network approval was positively correlated with continued involvement in friends with benefits relationships, so another avenue for future research is to explore the type of communication that occurs within social networks regarding friends with benefits relationships and to determine what role that communication has in the outcomes of these relationships. Including opposite-sex friends in the analysis of social networks may also reveal interesting information, as they can provide insight into the opposite sex's perspective.

In conclusion, the goal of this research was to further our understanding of friends with benefits relationships by exploring personal accounts that described the motivations, barriers, and emotions associated with these relationships. The data revealed the presence of relational, emotional, and sexual motivations and barriers, as well as a broad array of emotional responses, both positive and negative. The outcomes of these relationships also ranged from positive to negative. The support of their same-sex social network was associated with continued involvement in friends with benefits relationships. Friends with benefits relationships are a common dimension of cross-sex friendships, and are perceived in very similar ways between women and men. In particular, some college students seem to take a practical approach to these relationships, with their accounts indicating that this, indeed, is one of the things that friends are for.

NOTES

1 This essay is based, in part, on an article published in the *Western Journal of Communication*, 69 (January 2005).
2 A portion of the information summarized comes from the following two papers: Kelli Jean K. Asada, Mikayla Hughes, and Kelly Morrison, "Motivations and Barriers to Friends with Benefits Relationships," paper presented at the annual meeting of the International Communication Association, San Diego (May 2003); and Mikayla Hughes, Kelly Morrison, and Kelli Jean K. Asada, "What's Love Got To Do With It? Exploring the Maintenance Rules, Love Attitudes, and Network Support on Friends with Benefits Relationships," *Western Journal of Communication* 69 (2005): 49–66.
3 For example, see Melissa A. Bisson and Timothy R. Levine, "Negotiating a Friends with Benefits Relationship," *Archives of Sexual Behavior* 38 (2009): 66–73.
4 See Sandra J. Messman, Daniel J. Canary, and Kimberly S. Hause, "Motives to Remain Platonic, Equity, and the Use of Maintenance Strategies in Opposite-Sex Friendships," *Journal of Social and Personal Relationships* 17 (2000): 67–94.
5 See Jen Williams, Christina Shaw, Paul A. Mongeau, Kendra Knight, and Artemio Ramirez, "Peaches 'n' Cream to Rocky Road: Five Flavors of Friends with Benefits Relationships," paper presented at the annual meeting of the National Communication Association, Chicago (November 2007).
6 See Walid A. Afifi and Sandra L. Faulkner, "On Being Just Friends: The Frequency and Impact of Sexual Activity in Cross-Sex Friendships," *Journal of Social and Personal Relationships* 17 (2000): 205–22.

PART III

JUNIOR YEAR
Ethics of College Sex

CHAPTER 9

A HORNY DILEMMA

Sex and Friendship between Students and Professors

Pat and Sam

Few people would think it odd if they saw Pat, a philosophy professor at a small liberal arts college, having lunch in the dining hall with Sam, an undergraduate student in one of Pat's classes. Many might pause for thought, however, if they saw Pat and Sam having dinner at a fancy restaurant downtown. And if they found out the next day that the couple had gone back to Pat's place and made love all night long, most would be scandalized. To be told that it was not a one night stand, that Pat and Sam were in a long-term relationship, would do little to allay most people's concern. What is it, though, that people find scandalous about sexual relationships between professors and their students? Are these reasons good reasons, or merely prudish prejudice?

In this essay, I will argue that in confronting these issues we are faced with a dilemma. If we want to condemn sexual relationships between professors and students we must also condemn friendships between them. On the other hand, if we want to allow such friendships, we must condone (some) professor-student sexual relationships. I have two main reasons for this conclusion. The first reason is that the differences between close friendships and sexual relationships are more subtle than most people think – there is no clear boundary between the two. The second reason is that anything that would concern us about the latter should concern us about the former. I will argue, further, that though there may be reasons to avoid such relationships, there is nothing about the student-professor relationship in particular that should lead us to condemn all such relationships.

I should note that my interest here is primarily in the ethics of such relationships, in whether there is anything morally wrong about them. I will not discuss at all whether it is prudent to engage in such a relationship for the student or professor, and I touch only briefly at the end on the implications of the moral question for institutional policies.

Who Are We Talking About?

I will be talking only about relationships between undergraduate students and the faculty who teach them. I suspect that most people who find intimate student-professor relationships problematic find these ones most problematic, for reasons I will return to near the end of this essay. But it may well be that most of the reasons people give against such relationships have even more force in the graduate school setting, given the greater influence professors have over their graduate students' futures.

Unlike many people who have considered this topic, however, I will not restrict myself to relationships between male professors and female students. In her essay on this topic, Deirdre Golash notes that she adheres

> throughout to the male professor-female student example, not merely for simplicity but also because, as a result of social attitudes too well known to require recital, this is by far the most common occasion for a sexual offer. My observations would, I think, apply to other gender combinations, at least insofar as the same imbalance of power obtains.[1]

I do not adhere to this paradigm because I do not think that Golash's reasons support it. First, she explicitly mentions "sexual offers" here, but she discusses many other situations throughout her piece, such as friendships and loving sexual relationships, and it is not so obvious that all of these are most common between a male professor and female student. I am particularly interested here in comparing friendships and sexual relationships, so it is unnecessarily restrictive to consider only relationships between male professors and female students.

𝄞 ANDREW KANIA

Second, though it may be true that most intimate student-professor relationships are between female students and male professors, this might be for reasons other than those "too well known to require recital." For example, as a result of a pervasively sexist history, most college professors are men. Thus, there may be more male-professor–female-student relationships even if female professors are *more* likely than male professors to enter into relationships with their students. To discuss exclusively male-professor–female-student relationships for this reason is like exclusively using the masculine pronoun to refer to doctors, since most doctors are in fact male. This may reinforce sexism more than anything else.

Things That Are Just Plain Wrong

Some sexual relationships between students and professors are just plain wrong. A few examples will help illustrate what it is to consider the morality of student-professor relationships per se.[2]

If Pat and Sam enter into a consensual sexual relationship, but one of them thereby cheats on a spouse, the spouse has been betrayed. This betrayal, though, is no better or worse than that of any extramarital affair.

If Pat sexually assaults Sam, Pat is to be condemned, just as any sexual assailant is to be condemned. A professor may be open to greater censure than another sexual assailant if he or she uses his or her position of authority over a student to coerce the student's compliance, though the issues here are difficult since any assault implies coercion. But it is not obvious that the *academic* relationship between assailant and victim makes the assault worse than it would otherwise be.

Another kind of case that has been discussed by some philosophers is the "blatant sexual offer," that is, a professor suggesting sex to a student outside the context of even a friendship.[3] In such a case the power a professor has over a student will usually transform the "offer" into a case of coercion, but, again, the wrongness of the act does not depend on the fact that we're considering a student and professor, as opposed to an employer and employee, or any other two people on different sides of a power imbalance.

What I am considering here, then, is not cases like these, where the morality of the act would be unchanged whether or not the people involved were a student and professor. Rather, I am asking whether there is anything morally questionable about relationships between a professor and a student precisely because they are a professor and student.

A more specifically academic kind of case is what was called, when I was a student, "A's for lays" – the exchange of grades for sex. This is a case that relies on the people involved being a professor and student. Even if you have no moral objection to prostitution, you should condemn such arrangements, for grades are not like money or goods. They function as an objective measure of a student's academic abilities. To an extent, then, to offer grades for sex (or vice versa) is similar to selling an honor, such as an Academy Award. But given the role grades play in contemporary society, namely, significantly influencing people's early careers, such arrangements are even worse, since they constitute a serious injustice to other students.

I will not discuss any of these obvious moral wrongs here. Instead, I will investigate the morality of genuine friendships and loving sexual relationships between students and professors. This does raise the question of whether a student can freely enter into a friendship or sexual relationship with a professor. I believe the answer to this question is that a student can. How? The answer is the same as the punch line to the old joke about how two porcupines make love: very, very carefully. As several writers have pointed out, there are serious obstacles to clear and honest communication at every stage of the development of such a relationship; but those same writers agree that these obstacles can be overcome.[4] To the extent that these obstacles rely on a context in which "a trade [of sex for grades] is not seen as utterly fantastic,"[5] we might hope that as universities discuss these issues more openly, and become less sexist, some of these obstacles will be reduced.

Friendship and Sexual Relationships

Deirdre Golash has provided perhaps the best arguments that close friendships between students and professors are less morally problematic than sexual relationships.[6] A number of considerations lead her to this view. She argues for the following claims:

1. There is no clear line between being merely acquainted and being close friends.
2. There is a clear line between being close friends and being in a sexual relationship.
3. There are goods to be gained by both parties from a student-professor friendship that outweigh the possibility of resulting injustice.

👣 ANDREW KANIA

4. Any further goods to be gained by escalating such a friendship to a sexual level are outweighed by the possibility of resulting injustice.
5. Therefore, while student-professor friendships are acceptable, student-professor sexual relationships ought to be avoided.

I will argue that claims 1 and 2 cannot both be true. The degree of clarity of the lines between acquaintance and friendship, on the one hand, and friendship and a sexual relationship, on the other, is about the same, though it is unclear whether the lines are sharp or fuzzy. I will also argue that one cannot maintain both claims 3 and 4. Whatever dangers lurk in a sexual relationship between professor and student, they appear before the relationship becomes a sexual one; and those dangers do not seem to increase more than the value of the relationship as it is transformed from a friendship into a loving sexual relationship.

Most people think there's a clear line to be crossed between a non-sexual relationship and a sexual one. Golash doesn't say where she thinks that line lies, but one obvious possibility is that it's the line between *not* having had sex and *having* had sex. (For instance, at one point she asks the reader to "compare the feelings that one has for a lover before, as opposed to after, the first few sexual encounters.")[7] But where exactly is this line drawn? Perhaps the answer that comes first to mind for most people is "at the penetration of a vagina by a penis." But putting it this bluntly raises all sorts of concerns. For starters, this is clearly a heteronormative conception of sex. Neither two women nor two men can ever have sex according to this conception, and that's enough to reject it as obviously false. To retreat to a conception of having sex as the penetration of any one of some delimited set of bodily orifices by any one of some delimited set of bodily parts is more likely to promote ridicule than agreement. In her excellent essay on this topic, Greta Christina prompts us to test our intuitions about what counts as "having sex" against the following acts:[8]

- Penile-vaginal intercourse
- Penile-anal intercourse
- Oral sex (fellatio, cunnilingus)
- Digital/manual-vaginal/anal intercourse (fingering/fisting)
- Toy-vaginal/anal intercourse
- Manual genital stimulation (to orgasm?)
- Nipple stimulation (manual or oral)
- Kissing (with tongue?)

- Masturbating in one another's presence
- "Talking dirty"
- Participating in a sex party (in any of a number of capacities)
- Engaging in some of these activities without pursuing your own pleasure
- Engaging in some of these activities without anyone pursuing their own pleasure
- Engaging in some of these activities with a sleeping partner
- Sadomasochistic activity without genital contact
- Rape

One conclusion Christina draws from such considerations is that there is no clear line between having sex and not having sex. This does not mean there is *no* line. If you've had penile-vaginal intercourse, you've had sex, and if the only interaction you've ever had with someone is a brief kiss on the lips, then you haven't had sex with that person. But whatever the boundaries of the concept of "having sex" are, it seems clear that this is not the relevant concept for figuring out whether one is in a sexual relationship in the sense relevant to our topic. For if Sam and Pat spend office hours behind closed doors, kissing, talking dirty, and masturbating together, whatever concerns one has about the situation will be independent of whether one thinks any of this strictly counts as "having sex."

What we need, then, is a less stringent conception of being in a sexual relationship, one that is going to capture more of the cases that seem likely to worry those concerned about the ethics of student-professor sexual relationships. From now on, I will be using such a concept when I use the term "sexual relationship." I will not attempt to delineate this concept, since it is likely to be at least as vague as the concept of "having sex" (though it is not the same concept). Instead, I want to illustrate this vagueness in order to cast doubt on Golash's second claim: that there is a clear line between being in a close friendship and in a sexual relationship.

Recall the last time you entered into a loving sexual relationship. At some point you were not in the relationship – before you met the person, for instance. At some later point, you were in the relationship – the first time you were having sex with them, for instance. At what point did your relationship change from being non-sexual to being sexual? Even if you think that penile-vaginal intercourse is the only kind of sex there is, your relationship became sexual before the first penetration. When you were both undressing before the intercourse, for instance, your relationship had clearly entered the sexual stage. But it most likely entered that stage much earlier – perhaps with some earlier sexual acts, but before that with some kissing or hand-holding. What about *before* the first time you held hands, though? At any point when holding hands is a live possibility, it seems to me, you're in a relationship of the sort that we're interested in, that is, one that some people are uncomfortable about students and professors entering into. And this doesn't require having had any physical contact. In fact, it seems possible to enter into this kind of relationship *at first sight* (though that ain't love), given the right people and circumstances. Moreover, we usually hope that sexual relationships will develop out of close friendships, rather than being based purely on physical attraction, say.

If all this is right, then there are two ways Golash might go. She might withdraw the claim that there is a clear line between close friendship and a sexual relationship, but maintain that, nonetheless, sexual relationships between professors and students are wrong. If she goes this route, then it seems that she will have to disapprove of close friendships between professors and students, since they fall into a gray area where it is impossible to separate them from sexual relationships.

Alternatively, Golash might hold on to the idea that there is a clear line between a sexual and non-sexual relationship, claiming that the discussion above can help us to specify where that line falls, namely, much earlier in the development of a relationship than we might at first have thought. This route leads to the same practical consequences, though they follow from the classification of most cases as falling into the category of sexual relationships, rather than the gray area between close friendship and sexual relationship.

In fact, it seems that someone with either of these views cannot even encourage casual (non-close) student-professor friendships, since such friendships are likely in some cases to develop into close friendships (of the sort we have just seen they must condemn), and the line between the two kinds of friendship is at least as fuzzy as that between close friendships and sexual relationships. Furthermore, whichever response Golash gives, there will be some odd consequences. For if it's right that one can enter into the kind of relationship that concerns Golash *at first sight*, that is, without doing anything, then it is odd to condemn such relationships. The right response here seems to be that it is not *being in* such a relationship, but *acting on* the feelings one has, that is unacceptable. This will require quite a different argument, though, since it is precisely feelings rather than actions that are the basis of Golash's concerns about the consequences of such relationships, as we shall see below.

Harms and Benefits of Student-Professor Relationships

As I noted above, my interest here is in student-professor relationships per se. What kinds of harms or benefits can come from this specific kind of relationship? Two are discussed most frequently. First, there is the worry that there is an inherent imbalance of power in the relationship, and thus that the student may be coerced at some stage. As I argued above, though this is a serious concern, it is not something that distinguishes student-professor relationships from other relationships where there is a similar power imbalance. Second, there is the potential impact of such relationships on the academic careers of students.

Whether Pat and Sam are friends or lovers, it seems reasonable to expect, first, that Pat would spend more time discussing philosophy with Sam than with other students and, second, that Pat's assessment of Sam's work might be colored by their relationship (to Sam's advantage when the relationship is going well, or to Sam's disadvantage when it's going badly). On the positive side, some have argued that the benefits of the extra attention that Sam would receive are not unfair to other students. On the negative side are the potential or perceived injustice to other students of having their grades devalued by the illegitimate inflation of Sam's grades, and the potential effects a soured relationship could have on Sam.

Golash argues that there is more cause for concern in the case of sexual relationships, since the distorting feelings involved in such a relationship are much more powerful and harder to set aside than feelings of friendship (claim 4), and that the benefits of the friendship, but not the sexual relationship, outweigh the potential injustice resulting from the relationship (claim 3). I investigate these matters in the following three subsections.

Spending More Time

Is it a bad thing for Pat and Sam to spend more time discussing philosophy than they did before their relationship, or than Pat spends discussing philosophy with other students?[9] Golash argues that more time spent on one student does not necessarily come at the expense of time spent on another. Though this is strictly true, the time *may* come at the expense of

❙❚ ANDREW KANIA

another student, depending on what other demands there are on the professor's time. At some point, one's office hours run out, and one can see no more students, nor offer comments on any more drafts before the paper is due. But even in these cases, spending time with one student at the expense of another is not necessarily a bad thing. A student who spends more time discussing work with her professor because she seeks him out during office hours is not a recipient of favoritism. Nor is a student who ends up sitting next to his choir director on the plane during the choir's European tour, and ends up talking about the material in the music history course the director is teaching. It is not obvious that being in a relationship with a professor is any different in principle from the latter kind of example. The professor is available to talk with this particular student at additional times, and probably for much more time, than other students – for instance, at the pub or in bed. This might give the student an advantage, but – unlike unfair grading – it seems more like a lucky break than favoritism.

In short, there are many different reasons why a student might end up spending more time discussing academic matters with a professor, and such extra time does not automatically count as favoritism, even if it comes at the expense of time spent with another student. There are cases where such time *would* count as favoritism, for example, if one reserved one's office hours for one's friends, but it *need* not. Most important for my concerns here, though, is that these considerations apply equally to the time spent with a professor as a result of friendship or a sexual relationship.

Biased Assessment

Concerns about Pat grading Sam's work seem reasonable. There are two reasons I am skeptical of the claim that sexual relationships give *more* cause for concern here than close friendships, however. The first derives from the fuzzy border between these categories. One's feelings may be most powerful, most distracting, and so on, during the "high courting" period, when escalation to a sexual relationship is a clear possibility, but not a certainty. Whatever these distracting "sexual feelings" are, they don't necessarily depend on having had sex with the person, whatever that amounts to. The *desire* to have sex, and all that goes along with that, may just as easily influence one's judgment, and that desire can be at full strength before one has had sex. Indeed, again, it seems plausible that such desire can be pretty strong at first sight. Not everyone's emotions follow these patterns, of course, but they do not seem particularly uncommon, either.

The second reason I am skeptical of the greater power and tenacity of feelings in a sexual relationship as compared to a friendship is that it relies on a somewhat simplistic, and possibly sexist, view of emotions, including sexual feelings. The idea that emotions in general are to be sharply distinguished from reason, and cloud rather than aid one's deliberations, has a long history in Western philosophy, but, however strong Pat's feelings, it is implausible that Pat would be *unable* to assess clearly the merits of Sam's philosophy paper. This is not to say that Pat *will* assess the essay fairly, but the claim that Pat is (even probably) *incapable* of doing so may appeal to an illegitimate excuse grounded in a contingent history of disavowing control over one's passions. I think it helps to get a sense of the sexist roots of this idea to test one's intuitions against cases involving various permutations of the sex of the professor and student. Compare the case of a male professor and female student with that of a female professor and male student. Are you more likely to think that the professor's judgment will be colored in one case rather than the other? Is this because you think the professor in that case is really incapable of controlling his or her judgment, or for some other reason?

To return to the distinction between feelings and actions: if you think that a professor can resist the temptation to act on sexual feelings for a student, then you should think that a professor can assess the extent to which those feelings are affecting his or her assessment of a student's work. So it will be difficult to defend *both* the claim that friendships are acceptable but sexual relationships are to be avoided, *and* the claim that professors in love (or lust) are incapable of grading fairly. Furthermore, as we will soon see, there are steps that can be taken to eliminate grading bias.

The Benefits of Friendship

What of the potential benefits to the student of a friendship with a professor, which Golash argues outweigh the dangers of favoritism? She mentions only the good of friendship itself, which she claims is great and rare enough in the normal course of events that restricting one's range of possible friends even further "seems intolerable."[10] But most people would agree that if friendship is valuable and rare, loving sexual relationships are at least as valuable – and rarer. This, then, fails as an argument for allowing student-professor friendships on the one hand but rejecting sexual relationships on the other.

Avoiding Injustice

As several writers have noted, there are steps Pat can take to avoid the possibility of the kinds of injustice we have been considering. The grading of Sam's work can be checked, or simply performed, by someone else. Letters of recommendation standardly describe the writer's relationship with the student. Falsifications of this part of the letter, like any other, by act or omission, would be reprehensible, but there is nothing different here about friendship or a loving relationship. In fact, if anything, it may be that Sam will end up worse off as the result of an honest letter from Pat, since it would be difficult for any reader to assess the accuracy of the resulting evaluation. But students get letters of recommendation from more than one source, and the other letters should allow a prospective employer or graduate school admissions committee to contextualize the letter in question. Such measures should also eliminate the appearance of injustice, which some have given as a reason for prohibiting intimate faculty-student relationships.

One thing Sam can do is avoid taking classes with Pat. However, it is worth considering that those who find student-professor relationships scandalous are likely to find them so whether or not Sam is in one of Pat's classes. Why should this be? Two answers occur to me. The first is the power issue that has come up a couple of times already. To recap: though this is a cause for serious concern, it is not something unique to the student-professor relationship, nor is it an insurmountable obstacle to consensual relationships. (Anyway, professors have less power over other students at their institutions than those in their classes.)

The second is that students tend to be significantly younger than professors. This is overlooked surprisingly often in discussions of student-professor relationships, perhaps because it is not strictly a necessary feature of them. But imagine a world in which most people went to university only after ten or twenty years in the workforce. Even if this resulted in a correspondingly more aged faculty, I suspect that student-professor relationships would not be considered so scandalous in such a context. What this suggests is that it is the disparity in age between students and professors that is the source of a significant part of the concern about relationships between them. We may suspect that in such relationships the pure sexual attraction of the older partner to the younger is playing a disproportionate role in the relationship, mirrored, perhaps, in the attraction of the younger partner to a false sense of security the older partner may convey. We may also think that the older partner's greater experience with relationships gives that partner more power over the younger. But these features are common enough in relationships outside of academia. Like the power imbalance between professor and student, such factors may be cause for concern, but they are no reason to condemn professor-student relationships in particular.

Policing Pat and Sam

Where does all this leave us? I have argued that the fuzzy border between friendship and a loving sexual relationship, and the fact that we expect the latter (if it develops at all) to develop out of the former, suggest that whatever attitude we take towards the one, we ought also to take towards the other. In particular, it is difficult to see how we could clearly and consistently approve of the former while disapproving of the latter. Two questions follow: first, what attitude ought we in fact to take towards such relationships?; second, should we develop policies to deal with such relationships?

In answer to the first question, I think my discussion of the harms and benefits of student-professor relationships has demonstrated that we should not condemn such relationships simply on the basis that they are between a professor and a student. However, there can be bad relationships between students and professors, just as there can be between all sorts of people, and there is a significant number of "risk factors" present in the typical academic environment. Thus, when considering a relationship, either from a third-party perspective or, especially, as a student or professor contemplating entering such a relationship, one should pay heed to the imbalance of power between the parties, the role any age difference is playing in the relationship, and the potential for unjust treatment of the student involved and other students.

As for the second question, judgments about the need for a policy here, as often elsewhere, will come down to whether the severity and likelihood of harm to others outweighs the great good of freedom (in this case to decide what kinds of intimate relationships to enter into, and with whom). What follows here from the vague border between friendship and sexual relationships is that any such policies should be directed at both kinds of relationship. That said, there is a range of possible policies, from more stringent ones requiring professors to declare any relationships they enter into with students, and to follow certain procedures, such as reassigning grading, and so on, to less stringent ones, emphasizing the potential dangers of such relationships and recommending certain procedures, without requiring anything.

It seems to me that the less stringent approach is more justifiable for a couple of reasons. First, there is generally very little oversight of how faculty assess students, whether through grading or writing letters of recommendation. This is not necessarily a good thing, though it is too complicated an issue to address here. But if we want to ensure fairness in faculty assessment of students, we should ensure it across the board, not just in cases where a student-professor relationship is cause for concern. Faculty may be swayed just as easily, and more commonly, by sexism, racism, homophobia, favoritism, or overcompensation for any of these, as by being in a relationship with a student. To have a policy only about intimate relationships smacks of Puritanism. Second, as I mentioned above, problems arising from student-professor relationships can be in part the result of more systemic issues such as sexism or a distorted view of the nature of sexual relationships. Campus-wide dialogue and education is probably a more effective way of solving these problems at the root than instituting policies that attempt merely to suppress their symptoms.

NOTES

1 Deirdre Golash, "Power, Sex, and Friendship," in Alan Soble and Nicholas Power (eds.) *The Philosophy of Sex: Contemporary Readings*, 5th edn. (Lanham: Rowman and Littlefield, 2008), pp. 449–58, here p. 458 n. 2. Nicholas Dixon focuses on male-professor–female-student relationships for similar reasons in "The Morality of Intimate Faculty-Student Relationships," *The Monist* 79 (1996): 519–35.
2 Dixon makes a similar point in "The Morality of Intimate Faculty-Student Relationships," p. 521.
3 See, for example, Golash, "Power, Sex, and Friendship," pp. 450–2.
4 Golash, "Power, Sex, and Friendship," pp. 452–3; Dixon, "The Morality of Intimate Faculty-Student Relationships," pp. 522–5.
5 Golash, "Power, Sex, and Friendship," p. 452.

6   Edward Shils also defends this view in "The Academic Ethic," reprinted in *The Calling of Education: The Academic Ethic and Other Essays on Higher Education* (Chicago: University of Chicago Press, 1997), pp. 3–128, here pp. 58–9. Those who condemn both friendship and sexual relationships between faculty and students include Steven M. Cahn, *Saints and Scamps: Ethics in Academia* (Totowa: Rowman and Littlefield, 1986), pp. 35–6; Nicholas Dixon, "The Morality of Intimate Faculty-Student Relationships"; and Peter Markie, "Professors, Students, and Friendship," in Steven M. Cahn (ed.) *Morality, Responsibility, and the University: Studies in Academic Ethics* (Philadelphia: Temple University Press, 1990), pp. 134–49.

7   Golash, "Power, Sex, and Friendship," p. 454.

8   Greta Christina, "Are We Having Sex Now or What?" in Alan Soble and Nicholas Power (eds.) *The Philosophy of Sex: Contemporary Readings*, 5th edn. (Lanham: Rowman and Littlefield, 2008), pp. 23–9. Christina does not explicitly mention all of these acts, but she prompts thought about such a range.

9   Golash restricts her discussion at this point to graduate students, but the same issues seem to arise in connection with undergraduates, especially at small schools where faculty are expected to spend significant time with undergraduates on an individual basis.

10 Golash, "Power, Sex, and Friendship," p. 454.

CHAPTER 10

PHILOSOPHERS AND THE NOT SO PLATONIC STUDENT-TEACHER RELATIONSHIP

Higher Yearning 101

Sticky as the subject may be, everyone has an opinion about student-faculty sexual relationships. The commonplace image that comes to mind when we think of these affairs normally stars an aging, disenchanted male English professor, complete with leather elbow patches on his tweed jacket and an innocent drinking problem hidden in his office desk drawer. Most tend to picture him seducing and then exploiting young women by offering his attractive, but less than clever, students "extra assistance" while proceeding to teach them more than the poetry of Lowell or the narrative form of Hemingway.

Regardless of this standard pop-culture reference, for the most part, the academic discipline of philosophy has a much longer history of offering its students more than merely the "love of wisdom." Strikingly, this sexual tension between students and educators in the discipline of philosophy has ancient roots and can be traced all the way back to Socrates' desire for the young male philanthropist Alcibiades. Similarly, in twelfth-century France, the logician Peter Abelard infamously instructed his young student Heloise in much more than the standard *trivium* and *quadrivium* of medieval education. While more recently, Martin Heidegger's "private tutorials" with then 19-year-old Hannah Arendt raised a considerable number of eyebrows at the University of Marburg.

Clearly, some philosophers border on being promiscuously involved in the lives of their pupils and thus an examination of each of these affairs may help clarify some of the perennial issues facing student-faculty relationships on today's university campuses. In this essay, I discuss the possible naturalness and, perhaps, unavoidability of desire and intimacy in the classroom, alongside questioning the responsibility and possible exploitation or abuse of power that may occur when the usual boundaries between educators and students blur. To be clear, in no way will I condemn or condone such exploits between faculty and students, but merely hope to provoke some thought on the subject via narrating the affairs of a few unforgettable examples of higher yearning in higher learning.

Lesson 1: Socrates and Alcibiades on Stalking, Seduction, and Giving Birth

During Socrates' lifetime, classical Greek education or *paideia* dramatically differed from the contemporary university setting where students are expected to leave home and travel hundreds of miles to earn degrees in a variety of vocations. Rather, a class of self-professed intellectuals called the sophists traveled from city to city selling lessons concerning a variety of topics, most notably, political virtue and rhetoric, i.e., the art of public speaking. Like contemporary universities, these sophists charged heavy fees for their wares, but specialized in helping students recognize the precarious nature of traditional values by appealing to social relativism and relying on their ability to "argue on both sides" of a given issue. To be sure, many of the sophists also lectured on subjects like astronomy and mathematics but, ultimately, the ability to construct persuasive but often dissembling arguments appealed to the wealthy aristocratic youth who desired to acquire the skills necessary to appease and manipulate the masses. If one wished to excel in such studies, one need only memorize and regurgitate the speeches of these infamous public lecturers. Furthermore, these lessons occurred not in classrooms or formal lecture halls, but were often carried out in everyday arenas like the steps of the city market, the *agora*, or even the couches of drinking parties in symposia. While perhaps most importantly for the present purposes, *paiderasta*, or sex between the older wiser intellectual and his students,

❦❦   DANIELLE A. LAYNE

were not only conventionally accepted but lauded as a boon to the educational development of the young. In fact, in Plato's *Symposium* the character Pausanias spends a considerable amount of time explaining how such carnal pursuits help young men develop into mature adults and how, at the very least, such "extracurricular activities" demonstrated a student's noble and praiseworthy love of learning.

While markedly distancing himself from the practice of sophistry, the ancient philosopher Socrates hoped to inspire young men to the life of learning and inquiry by forcing them to examine their own lives and presuppositions. In this, he rarely conducted long didactic speeches but, oddly enough, would admit ignorance and ask his young companions to join him in a mutual search for wisdom and truth. Furthermore, while consistently disavowing knowledge of and the ability to teach moral virtue, Socrates provocatively admitted expertise in the ambiguous and messy subject of *eros*, or human desire and love, while confessing openly, e.g., in Plato's *Symposium* (177e) and *Lysis* (204b–c), his penchant for pursuing handsome and distinguished young boys who often became devoted students and disciples.[1]

The most noteworthy of Socrates' pursuits, of course, was his infamous seduction of the young Athenian Alcibiades. To understand Alcibiades' initial encounter with Socrates, it might do well to imagine that you are the most popular kid on your university campus (however difficult this may be for people reading a philosophy book). Not only are you physically attractive, athletic, and wealthy, but you are also president of several student clubs and the most eligible individual, fending off dozens of suitors a week. All in all, you are fairly confident that you can have anything you want and are set to live a remarkable life upon graduation. Now envision that in your senior year an older man begins to follow you around, gawking at you for long periods of time, never saying a word, merely noting all the classes that you attend and all the people you choose to date. Then imagine that when you finally confront this assuredly creepy stalker, he says he's a professor on campus and, unlike all your other lovers, he truly loves you, desiring only to assist you in obtaining the power over others you so desperately want. Remarkably, this is exactly how Socrates introduced himself to Alcibiades in Plato's *Alcibiades I* (103a–106b). Yet instead of running to the authorities as any student on a contemporary campus would do, this ambitious youth charges into discussion with Socrates and by the end of the dialogue appears to discard his youthful conceit by coming to admit his ignorance. Furthermore, after only a few hours, Alcibiades confesses that Socrates has become the object of his desire and thus the boy swears that "from this day onward it must be the case that I am your attendant, and you must have me always in attendance on you" (135d).

As most know, Alcibiades narrates the rest of the story in the *Symposium*, Plato's most impressive feast of speeches eulogizing the nature of Love or *eros*. Years after their first meeting, Socrates has moved on and has developed a new interest for the award-winning poet Agathon, conspicuously sitting next to him, and finally critiquing, in his usual manner, the young man's thoughts on love.[2] Unfortunately for Socrates, his ex-student/lover crashes the party and pushes himself on the sober circle of men. After his own drinking and revelry, the now prominent soldier and politician laments that he no longer has the heart of the puzzling philosopher and in order to warn Agathon against falling for his former teacher, Alcibiades makes a long, arduous speech describing what went wrong between them (215a–222a). First, waxing complimentary concerning Socrates' ability to make his heart pound and to reduce him to tears, Alcibiades confesses that he fell so in love with the philosopher that he, thinking that Socrates had a serious affection for his "youthful bloom," was ready to become teacher's pet by offering it to him the first chance that they were alone. Yet, upon securing a "private moment" with Socrates, the philosopher's behavior did not change. According to Alcibiades, Socrates continued to ask questions in the same manner as he always did, therein maintaining philosophic discourse. Frustrated, Alcibiades proposed that they go to the local gymnasium, an assured hot bed of sexual activity as both young and old trained in the nude, hoping that the sweaty exposed flesh and vigorous wrestling would encourage a consummation of their mutual love. Ashamed, Alcibiades admits to his drinking companions that even this had no effect on Socrates and, like before, the philosopher only wished to discuss and question the nature of virtue. Finally, resolved to have his conquest, Alcibiades confessed that in an attempt to loosen Socrates' inhibitions he invited him to dinner with the intent of getting him drunk. When even this proved futile, he took the direct route of simply stripping and cozying up under the philosopher's cloak while he slept (219b).

Curious for an ancient Greek, Socrates stoically ignored the randy student. As Alcibiades describes, "When I had done this he showed such superiority and contempt, laughing at my youthful charms to scorn, and flouting the very thing on which I prided myself ... that when I arose I had no more particular sense slept a night with Socrates than if it had been with my father or my elder brother" (219c). Ultimately, Alcibiades interpreted Socrates' chastity as a sign of his teacher's deceptive and untrustworthy behavior. He surprisingly felt victimized by Socrates "lofty disdain."

Regardless of his seeming disdain, Socrates confessed in several dialogues that he desired Alcibiades, but in a far different sense than Alcibiades had hoped.[3] Rather, as dialogues like the *Phaedrus* and the *Symposium* indicate, love between him and his disciples, along with all other forms of desire, potentially opens the doors to a higher form of intimacy, an intimacy fostered by intellectual conversation and a love not of one's physical charms but of one's soul. Similarly, in the *Charmides*, Socrates notably lusts after the boy he plans to converse with and, when the young boy enters the setting, Socrates' surreptitious glimpse under Charmides' cloak reveals, so to speak, all the boy's school supplies. Due to this, Socrates confesses that the sight inflamed his body and frustrated his tongue (155d). Yet, after a moment's pause, Socrates redirects this longing and proceeds gracefully to question the boy's opinion of temperance. Ultimately, Socrates shows how, far from lacking any physical desire for his students, he drowns in it. Yet regardless of this, Socrates tempers his physical aching with the recognition of his responsibility, his duty to care not for his own carnal interests but his companion's well-being and development.

Furthermore, in the *Symposium*, Socrates suggests that love or *eros* naturally arises in all settings where human beings pursue wisdom and, thus, shows how such desires may necessarily exist between students and teachers in contemporary classrooms. As Socrates' own teacher on love, Diotima, demanded, "Love must needs be a friend of wisdom" (204a). Put in to the context of the university, Diotima's speech on Love indicates that when a professor enters a classroom, she should not merely impart or distribute knowledge like a doctor passing out medicine to patients. Rather, Diotima uses overt sexual language to insist that the young, teeming and pregnant with vague ideas, should search out teachers who recognize their potential, since a coupling with these desired and resourceful individuals would allow them to "bring forth," or birth, their long-felt conceptions (208e–212a). With both student and teacher, or as the *Theaetetus* explicitly suggests, the pregnant and the midwife, incept a partnership that transcends a mere physical union or a simple friendship because through their love and desire, they encounter and bear timeless wisdom they have brought forth traces of immortal beauty (150b–151a).

For Socrates, there was no such thing as a detached, dispassionate pedagogy. As Diotima argued, all learning arises from some sort of need, a recognition of lack, and thus we learn that the best teachers take risks, dismiss the pretense to knowledge, and in contrast expose themselves and flaunt their love of learning for the sake of inspiring the young to do the same. In other words, Socratic philosophy suggests that educators recognize the swarm of desires fluttering in the classroom and the volatility of situations when human beings become vulnerable and come together for the sake of overcoming their lack and their ignorance. Most importantly, Socrates' and Alcibiades' relationship shows how student-teacher affairs, which begin with a mutual interest in the subject matter, can explode, as Alcibiades' case neatly evidenced, into an obsessive physical desire for the other.

In the *Phaedrus*, Socrates describes how love directed towards true beauty and wisdom is by nature passionate, copious, and overflowing. In fact, Socrates acknowledges that this "waterfall" of desire is capricious and can lead many lovers to recognize that "they are in love" but know not with what, i.e., lovers easily transfer their love for true beauty onto the physical beauty of the other. Think here of the enthusiasm or pleasure both students and teachers feel when the course material stimulates heated discussion and/or restless questioning outside the classroom. In these moments, both students and teachers have been seized by the natural and unavoidable longing for knowledge. Problems arise, however, if and when this initial love for the course material overflows and transforms into physical desire. In this case, Socrates would contend that such a relationship arises through ignorance of what should truly be loved, the pursuit of wisdom, rather than mere sexual satisfaction.[4]

Committed to his own promiscuous passion for inquiry, Socrates remained keenly aware of the responsibility emerging from such desire, insisting all the while that lovers transfer their vulgar hankerings for physical union into a divinely inspired pursuit for the good. For Socrates, educators should avoid at all costs embracing the pleasure of the moment or the mere gratification of physical longing, as this is merely an unimaginative manifestation of love, by contrastingly committing themselves to aiding students in their search for wisdom, the highest expression of love between two people. In this, educators nurture the seed of transcendence in their students by acting not as cold, informational conduits, but as inflamed role models or, as Socrates called himself, "paradigms for the examined life," inspiring students to become lifelong learners.

DANIELLE A. LAYNE

Lesson 2: Peter Abelard and Heloise on Fondling and Losing "Tenure"

Fast-forward now to the infancy of the university under the tutelage of the Catholic Church where students, regardless of religious intentions, were expected to attend classes in clerical habits. Here we meet an educator not unlike Socrates, who disdained those teachers, or "masters," who taught the young only by offering pedantic, long-winded speeches. Instead, Peter Abelard rose to fame by practicing dialectic, or the art of questioning and answering, in the classroom. In early twelfth-century France, Abelard, like Socrates before him, helped transform medieval education and notably founded the school which would later become the University of Paris during a period in which scholars, like the ancient sophists, wandered from city to city and from school to school until they amassed a loyal following of students. Despite becoming enemies with the philosopher Anselm of Loan and the cleric Bernard of Clairvaux, among others church clerics, Abelard's fame grew and Paris began to bubble over with students eager to learn from the logician. Yet, regardless of his ability to educate and inflame the love of learning in his students, Abelard would ultimately fail to live up to the code of conduct first set by Socrates between students and educators.

With his reputation as the greatest master in France secure, Abelard's mind began to wonder from logical to carnal pursuits. As he writes, "I began to think myself the only philosopher in the world, with nothing to fear from anyone, and so I yielded to the lusts of the flesh."[5] Thus, due to boredom, Abelard sought for a student who could, in several senses of the word, "stimulate" him. In this he looked to a girl whose fame, like his own, was renowned in France: a young woman named Heloise, niece of the prominent canon Fulbert. In the *Historia Calamitatum*, or *The History of My Misfortunes*, Abelard notes that while Heloise was not the prettiest of young things, she was the cleverest because her uncle saw to it that, unlike most women, she was well educated. Always measured and calculating, Abelard convinced Fulbert that his niece needed his tutelage while suggesting that, due to his own financial burden, he could more easily assess Heloise's progress by living in her home and acting as not only her instructor but her caretaker.

With Heloise's uncle toeing the line and acquiescing to Abelard's demands, one of the most famous affairs between a student and teacher began. Yet, despite the constant attempts to idealize this famous affair between a teacher and student in movies, books, and even scholarly articles, it is evident that Abelard epitomizes and parallels the stereotype of the lecherous professor preying on a young woman. As Abelard himself admits when discussing Fulbert's decision to let him care for Heloise's education, "I was amazed by his simplicity – if he had entrusted a tender lamb to a ravening wolf it would not have surprised me more."[6] Realizing that he wielded a great power over his apparently naïve student, Abelard makes it clear that, unlike Socrates, he was far less concerned with leading Heloise to the life of inquiry than to the bed. As Abelard describes, "We were united, first under one roof, then in heart; and so with our lessons as a pretext we abandoned ourselves entirely to love."[7] Abelard haughtily admits that while their books were open and the lessons planned, nothing but romance passed between them. He confesses that, "more words of love than our reading passed between us, and more kissing than teaching," and famously concludes that his "hands strayed oftener to her bosom than to the pages."[8] Furthermore, like professors trying to avoid the admonishing eyes of university administration, Abelard spent a considerable amount of time trying to dissuade Heloise's uncle Fulbert from suspecting their affair. In this, Abelard avoided the appearance of favoritism by making it look like he was harder on his beloved pupil. Yet, unlike a contemporary academic, instead of merely insulting his favorite in public lectures or giving her lower grades, Abelard preferred to beat Heloise. He explains though that "these blows were prompted by love and tender feeling rather than anger and irritation."[9]

Despite these "heroic" attempts at hiding their affair, eventually Heloise's uncle discovered the couple. Strikingly, Fulbert did not immediately seek vengeance, as Abelard quickly decried his actions and offered to marry the girl. Yet – here's the rub – Abelard wanted to keep the marriage a secret, since anyone who hoped to advance in the world of education administered by the Church had to uphold the pretense of chastity. Here, we recognize that Abelard, like most contemporary professors, had to secure a praiseworthy reputation beyond his scholarly activities and that, like university professors trying to achieve tenure, having relations with a student, regardless of whether they were being validated by marriage, would damage his career. Moreover, his obsessive care for his reputation, rather than a genuine concern for Heloise's wellbeing, strikes a considerably more sober tone when we turn to Heloise's response to the idea of their marriage. So devoted to Abelard's success, and so seduced by the image of him as a great philosopher, Heloise adamantly disfavored their union and famously declared that she would rather be her teacher's whore than the wife of an emperor.[10] She decisively cared not for her own reputation, but only for his.

In the end, the couple were wed, but despite Heloise's and Abelard's demand, Fulbert did not keep the marriage secret and when Heloise refused to admit her marriage to others, her uncle, like her teacher before him, beat her.[11] In the guise of protecting Heloise from such a hot-tempered man, Abelard sent his beloved to a convent, disguising her in religious dress. Outraged by this seeming attempt to get rid of the girl, Fulbert took it upon himself to teach his employee an unforgettable lesson. In the middle of the night Fulbert had his henchmen sneak into Abelard's bedroom and castrate him, thus effectively punishing him for his earlier transgressions and assuredly preventing him from ever playing such reindeer games again.

Strikingly, this horrific picture of retribution has an odd parallel to the contemporary university. Consider the fact that despite only being her uncle, Fulbert, believing, as many colleges do, that he had the right to act *in loco parentis*, or in the stead of a parent, takes it upon himself to meddle in his niece's adult decisions and in this neglects to account for her active role in the affair. For Fulbert, like universities who draft sexual harassment policies denying consensual affairs between faculty and students, Heloise was merely a victim who was too young to grasp the consequences of her actions, too innocent to have had any real ability to say no to such a big bad wolf like Abelard. In other words, many universities rely on the premise that the nature of the student-teacher relationship is asymmetrical because the power that professors wield is too great to confer legitimately upon students an equal responsibility for these affairs. Put otherwise, Fulbert denies Heloise her dignity, her freedom to choose, and thus punishes only Abelard. In so doing, he displays how university administrators in similar positions exercise a far greater authority over the outcome of such affairs. While playing the self-appointed judge and jury of such relations, many universities try to nip this supposed problem in the bud by first implementing sexual harassment policies that discourage all forms of social contact, therein "purifying" the classroom from the dangers of erotic desire, while also rebuffing a group of adults, however young, their right to consent. In the end, these so-called objective arbitrators often deny some professors their tenure when they transgress the acceptable boundaries between students and teachers – perhaps a less sanguinary punishment than gelding, but a penalty that can ultimately destroy, as it did for Abelard, one's entire academic career.

To be sure, universities, and even Fulbert, act out of concern for the young in their charge and, in the case of Heloise, Fulbert seems to have appropriately recognized Abelard's insidious ability to manipulate his student, an ability that was not much deterred even after his loss of "tenure." Soon after receiving his punishment, Abelard, hoping to repair the damage done to his reputation, quickly joined a monastery. Yet, more regrettably, Abelard did not advise his former student/lover/wife to move on, but, in stark contrast to her uncle's hopes, he demanded that she too take religious vows and turn what was originally a mere disguise into the authentic dress of a nun. In this he secured a lifelong hold over her, becoming her only source for guidance and comfort in a world in which she never felt she belonged. His dominant presence even infiltrated her thoughts during mass, leading her to replace prayer with "wanton" fantasy. As she admits to Abelard years after their affair, "It was not any sense of vocation which brought me as a young girl to accept the austerities of the cloister, but your bidding alone," as "it was not [her] pleasure and wishes [she] sought to gratify," but Abelard's.[12] Thus, regrettably, and regardless of her accomplishments later in life, Heloise becomes the paradigm for the devoted student victimized by the myopic desires of a self-serving master.

Lesson 3: Heidegger and Arendt on Concealed Unconcealment

On the surface, Martin Heidegger and Hannah Arendt's affair in early twentieth-century Germany looks like another case of the lecherous professor syndrome, as Heidegger's behavior toward then 19-year-old Arendt seems equally suspect. As her instructor at the University of Marburg, he went to great lengths to keep their affair a secret from his colleagues, wife, and children, which forced Arendt to submit to his schedule and proclivity for cooking up clandestine rendezvous. When the relationship became untenable for Arendt, she, clearly heartbroken, transferred to another university on the other side of Germany. Yet regardless of this self-imposed distance, like Heloise with Abelard, Heidegger continued to brandish a pervasive emotional grip on Arendt as even on the eve of her wedding to another man she wrote a letter to her former professor and lover confessing that their relationship was "the blessing of [her] life," insisting that he never forget her, as she would never forget him.[13] Eventually losing all contact with her, Heidegger most markedly ignored her internment in a

❬❭ DANIELLE A. LAYNE

holding camp during World War II. In the end, he only appears to rekindle interest in his former Jewish student once she had gained her own prominence in the States and could be of some use in cleaning up the stain that his undeniable association with Nazism had done to his career.

Yet despite this persistent and deplorable picture of the philosopher's behavior toward Arendt, when one takes a closer look at Heidegger's philosophy of education as well as his early letters to Arendt it becomes undeniably evident that the relationship cannot be so easily compartmentalized into the pigeonhole of the lecherous professor stereotype. First, it should be mentioned that, like Socrates and Abelard, Heidegger also desired radical reformulation of the standard practices in higher education. Throughout his letters and early work, Heidegger repeatedly expressed his general distaste of the contemporary German university, where learning was divorced from everyday life, where programs carved up thinking into a multiplicity of abstract disciplines, where so-called teachers merely lectured on topics dispassionately and with little concern for their impact on human activity. This form of ossified or "sterilized" teaching characterized for Heidegger the "general stagnation" of the modern university. In contrast, he believed that the university should be a site of "genuine scientific consciousness and life-relationships" where radical inquiry must always merge with one's contemplation on the perplexities of human existence.[14] Thus, he writes to Arendt that he desired "to teach young ones" and to take risks in the classroom for the sake of stimulating philosophic investigation rather than "pulling students along and drumming something into them."[15] Completely uninterested in producing scholars, Heidegger hoped his classrooms would open a space were "thinking could be made possible again."[16]

It should also be noted that Arendt, more than Heidegger, seems to have been the acting catalyst in their break-up and her subsequent transfer to Jaspers' tutelage in 1926. In fact, Heidegger notably did not take Arendt's decision well, but constantly sought Jaspers out to find out how she was doing.[17] Finally, after some time, he accepted her decision and wrote that perhaps her transfer was the best thing for her education, while also deeming it a sign of her "freedom of instincts" that evidenced how, apart from all his other students, i.e., the "Heidegger disciples," she had allowed herself to grow.[18]

Finally, in many of his letters to Arendt, Heidegger expresses something that is conspicuously absent in his magnum opus *Being and Time*: his thoughts on the nature of love, thoughts which suggest that the asymmetrical relationships between teachers and students merely mirror all human relationships, thus making issues of power between students and teachers, beloved and lover, man and woman, entirely irrelevant. Rather, for Heidegger, the context of the relationship, i.e., the fact that he was a teacher and she was his student, was merely the condition in which they found themselves, a condition that must be overcome if they ever wished to nurture an authentic dialogue. In other words, like his philosophy, which asserts that truth is not a mere correspondence to facts but a process of *unconcealment* or constant disclosure, Heidegger thought their relationship allowed for an honest and pure dialogue that would allow for a dynamic show of themselves where neither had to conceal anything from the other. He writes: "Dear Miss Arendt! I must come see you this evening and speak to your heart. Everything should be simple and pure between us. Only then will we be worthy of having been allowed to meet. You are my pupil and I your teacher, but this is only the occasion for what has happened to us."[19] Further along in this letter, Heidegger describes how he understands that she will never be his, he will never possess her as a mere object to appease his desire, but that her presence in his life will instigate a memorable and lasting growth in both of them. While alluding to the power of amorous relationships, Heidegger explicitly praises the mystery of love: "Dear Hannah! Why is love rich beyond all other possible human experiences and a sweet burden to those seized in its grasp? Because we become what we love and yet remain ourselves.... That is how love steadily intensifies its inner-most secret."[20] For Heidegger, unlike Abelard's mere bodily lust for Heloise, his affair with his young student created an intimacy that "opened up" a "great distance" between the "other" that allows the "other" a chance to "break into our life," while also claiming that through love "a human fate gives itself over to another human fate, and the duty of pure love is to keep this giving as alive as it was on the first day."[21] For Heidegger, love was "to be forced into one's innermost existence," and quoting Augustine, the sub-ject of Arendt's dissertation, "*Amo: volo ut sis,*...: I love you – I want you to be what you are."[22] In one letter, Heidegger explicitly analyzes the nature of love while suggesting how their affair has less to do with an asymmetrical power play than with a mutual care where each player takes a risk, learns to trust, and ultimately discovers themself in union with the other. He writes:

> To belong in the life of the other – this is genuine union. And only such a union can be the source and guiding light for a truly joyous closeness....When I say my joy in you is great and growing, that means I have faith in everything that is your story. I am not erecting an ideal – still less would I ever be tempted to educate you, or anything resembling that. Rather, you – just as you are and will remain with your story – that's how I love you. Only then is love strong for

the future, and not just a moment's fleeting pleasure – only then is the potential of the other also moved and strengthened for the crises and struggles that never fail to arise. But such faith is also kept from misusing the other's trust in love. Love that can be happy into the future has taken root.[23]

In these brief but assuredly philosophically loaded discussions of the nature and intent of his feelings for Arendt, Heidegger shows how, in tune with Socratic values, "love must needs be a friend of wisdom." Unlike the ancient philosopher, however, who avoided all sexual dealings with his disciples, Heidegger repeatedly intimates that his affair with Arendt did not hinder his or her work but aided it, and that regardless of his administrative power over her she wielded a remarkable sway over him that she, rather than he, never relinquished. He confesses to Arendt in a handwritten dedication to her in his manuscript *Existence and Temporality*, "You came straight from the center of your existence to be close to me and you have become a force that will influence my life forever. Fragmentation and despair will never yield anything like your supportive love in my work."[24]

Ultimately, Arendt continued to influence Heidegger as even after their ten-year break in correspondence, he in his "autumn years" continued to write her poetry and repeatedly risked sparking the jealousy of his wife to remain in contact with his former pupil. To be sure, what Heidegger and Arendt illustrate in their affair is not a simple picture of the manipulative lecherous professor, but an image of how some affairs between students and their professors cannot be so easily condemned. In other words, Heidegger and Arendt's affair demonstrates how the consequences of student-faculty relationships are not always dire, the role of power is not always clear, and that intimacy created in such relationships might not always be something to be avoided.

"So I'll see you after class ..."

In the end, instead of offering a platitude directly summing up the nature of student-faculty relationships, I thought it best to close with a joke neatly mocking Socrates, Abelard, and Heidegger's exploits. Three leading professors at a university, notably, a stalker, a eunuch, and a national socialist, walk into a freshman orientation. The eunuch turns to the stalker and asks him "What do you see in this mass of young men and women?" The stalker succinctly says, "The potential for the good. Why, what do you see?" The eunuch, staring at the scantily clad students, says, "I perceive trouble that only God can save me from." Finally, both the stalker and the eunuch turn to the national socialist and ask what he thinks. The national socialist gazes at a particularly attractive young freshman bending over to pick up books and smiles as he says, "I like to focus on the possibility of unconcealment."

NOTES

1   See Plato, *Charmides* 153d; *Theaetatus* 143d; *Lysis* 204b–c; and *Symposium* 177e. For all works by Plato cited in this essay, see John M. Cooper (ed.) *Plato: Complete Works* (Indianapolis: Hackett, 1997).
2   See Plato, *Symposium* 199a–201c.
3   See Plato, *Protagoras* 309a–b.
4   Cf. Plato, *Phaedrus* 255c–d.
5   Peter Abelard, *Historia Calamitatum*, p. 65. All references to Abelard throughout this section are to Betty Radice, *The Letters of Abelard and Heloise* (London: Penguin Classics, 1974), p. 65.
6   Ibid., p. 67.
7   Ibid.
8   Ibid.
9   Ibid.
10   Ibid., p. 70.
11   Ibid., p. 74.
12   Ibid., pp. 116–17.
13   Ursula Ludz (ed.) *Letters 1925–1975: Hannah Arendt and Martin Heidegger* (Orlando: Harcourt Books, 2004), pp. 50–1.
14   See Martin Heidegger, *Zur Bestimmung der Philosophie, Gesamtausgabe*, Vols. 56/57 (1987), p. 4, cited in and translated by Alan Milchman and Alan Rosenburg, "Martin Heidegger and the University as a Site for the Transformation of Human Existence," *Review of Politics* 59, 1 (1997): 82.
15   Ludz, *Letters*, p. 8.
16   Ibid., p. 151.
17   Ibid., p. 45.
18   Ibid., p. 45.
19   Ibid., p. 25.
20   Ibid., pp. 4–5.
21   Ibid., p. 5.
22   Ibid., p. 21.
23   Ibid., p. 25.
24   Ibid., pp. 16–17.

CHAPTER 11

THINKING ABOUT THINKING ABOUT SEX

Goldilocks Epistemology: Not Too Soft, Not Too Firm, but *Just Right*

As I recall it, on the 1980s television show *Murphy Brown*, the title character told a young colleague that sex is better in your 40s. Among other things, she said, you reach "the Big O" every time. "Every time?" the young woman asked, somewhat wistfully. "Every time," Murphy asserted smugly.

She over generalized, of course, but now that I'm in *my* 40s, and so are most of my friends, I think I understand what Murphy was getting at. Furthermore, I have a good theory about achieving better sex. I'm an epistemologist – I study knowledge, belief, reasoning, and thinking – so I see a crucial connection: better sex comes largely from better thinking and knowing.

My aim in this essay is to lay out some views, concepts, and tools from epistemology that can help people think more clearly and effectively about sex. The focus is on college students because their circumstances, sexually and epistemically, are distinctive. To put it briefly, college changes everything, and sex is a big part of everything (especially in college). Students have virtually their whole sexual lives ahead of them, and it's a time when they can get a good start toward healthy, enjoyable, wise, fulfilling sex – or a bad start.

I'm interested in students getting a good start. Therefore, this essay is aimed primarily at them, or those who care about them, rather than people interested in thinking about the issue in the abstract. I'll necessarily gloss over or leave out details important to philosophers, just as a physicist would in a paper about college, sex, and physics (which strikes me as an entertaining idea, by the way).

Before we get down and dirty with epistemology, I should clarify a couple of other things. To make general points, I'll illustrate using specific genders, sexual orientations, religions, or levels of sexual activity. However, the ideas apply to sexual beings in all their marvelous variety, and to all kinds of relationships, genders, and choices to engage or not engage in various sexual activities. Most of the philosophical views here aren't even limited to sexual matters, much less to specific sexual circumstances, but I'll focus on ones I consider especially useful in improving our thinking and knowing as sexual beings. If I don't explicitly articulate the tie to sexuality, you can play the old fortune cookie game of adding "in bed" to anything I say that's epistemological.

So here's my theory: if college students are to have healthy and good sex lives – in any of the many forms those can take – they must improve themselves epistemologically. To do that, an excellent source of advice is philosophical epistemology.

What is epistemology? It's the philosophical field that examines the nature of knowledge, its presumptions and foundations, and the extent of its validity. I think of its primary question as "What is it to believe well?" This is a *philosophical* field, so we're not giving empirical descriptions of things like the psychological mechanisms involved in belief formation, what people claim to know, or how a culture defines knowledge. We reason about the deeper meaning of knowledge and belief.

I'm going to be using "know" in a particular way, although there are other uses in ordinary speech. Sometimes when people talk about knowing, they mean knowing with absolute certainty. This is philosophically interesting but too strict as a requirement for ordinary, everyday knowledge. I'll talk about the kind of knowledge we mean when we say we know that some people are homosexual, and that men and women are biologically different. My representation of ordinary knowledge as opposed to absolutely certain knowledge is to use "know" as we do with "like" in "Of course you like him, but do you *like* him?"

On the other end of the spectrum, people commonly use the word "know" in a relativistic way that corresponds to the phrase "true for," as

ASHLEY MCDOWELL

in "Joe knows that Jill wasn't faking her orgasm – that's what's true for him." The problem is that its being "true for" him doesn't make it so. In the sense of "know" I'll use here, if Jill (as a matter of fact) really was faking it, we can't say that Joe knows that she really had an orgasm. There's an actuality about whether Jill was faking or not, just like there are facts about whether condoms help prevent STDs (yes, although with some important exceptions), whether losing weight makes a man's penis bigger (no), and whether things can get lost in a woman's vagina (no). The epistemological "know" counts only for actually true propositions.

The best way to channel our "true for" impulse is to recognize that we can judge beliefs differently than believers. We can call people's beliefs and rationales understandable and even internally consistent given circumstances like their cultural background or psychology.[1] Then we can hold the person blameless in holding the belief, although the belief itself isn't true, known, or well founded.[2] Something "true for" an individual can be epistemically problematic even if we're not judging her for believing it.

These concepts (strict certainty at one extreme, knowledge is in the eye of the beholder at the other, and ordinary knowing in between) all have a place in our thinking, but also underlie many people's epistemological confusions and weaknesses. Our language doesn't delineate clearly the differences between them, and it's tricky to place beliefs along what turns out to be a complex spectrum of epistemological classes. Part of epistemology's usefulness is in clarifying otherwise vague and imprecise ideas like these.

To be known, a belief has to be what epistemologists call justified as well as being true. "Epistemic justification" means something like reasonableness or being well founded. Beliefs can have varying amounts of justification. To see this, think of friends talking about whether one of their professors is gay. Each has a different basis for belief, and some are better – and more convincing – than others. Some beliefs have characteristics that make them better representations of reality; they have a better chance of getting things right.

So like Goldilocks all grown up and discovering sex off at college, you ought to pursue the kind of knowledge and justification that's just right. You don't need to know absolutely, or to be justified 100 percent (using rigid standards). On the other hand, you should expect more than just finding what's "true for you" or has scant justification (being too soft on yourself and others).

Sex Talk: You Should Know Better

You want your sex-related beliefs to be justified, and preferably known, if only because such beliefs can prevent harm and lead to benefits ("… in bed." See how well that works?). Let's look at the importance of epistemic merit in one area of sex-related knowledge.

Many people don't know much about sexual communication, and many of those who do have good beliefs about it don't know how to act on what they know. Although most would acknowledge good sexual communication as a means of improving sex, people really struggle with it. Why should it be so hard to say something like, "I need you to move up a couple of inches and touch me like this"? You wouldn't hesitate to say it if your partner were giving you a foot massage or scratching your back.

Even the names of important body parts are hard for us to articulate with our partners. In the sexuality section of the online health Q&A site "Go Ask Alice!" someone asks, "What are some respectful names for genitalia that are also 'hot'?" Alice suggests slang terms from other languages, such as the Japanese *chinchin* and the Portuguese *verga* for penis; famous landmarks, such as the Eiffel Tower and Big Ben; food items like fish taco or fur-burger for female genitalia; and rather silly names like doodle-dandy and the winking eye.[3] The convolutions involved in using such (apparently respectful and "hot") terms show how inexplicably uncomfortable sex talk can be.

In 1993, Antioch College instituted a famous – or infamous – Sexual Offense Policy requiring that "Verbal consent should be obtained with each new level of physical and/or sexual contact/conduct."[4] It is certainly hard to imagine an Antioch-policy-sanctioned sexual encounter, with partners asking things like "May I kiss your mouth?" "Is it all right if I touch your breast?" and "Can I fellate you?" But why should it be so hard to imagine using, during sex, the form of communication arguably most, well, communicative?

However difficult and uncomfortable, though, improving one's knowledge of sexual communication (what, when, why, and how) is surely among the most important ways to make sex better. Such communication doesn't have to be verbal, but it should be good, as in informative, effective, and candid. If you don't know enough about sex talk, you can be stuck using mysterious, indecipherable attempts to communicate, like subtly edging your body in the direction you want your partner to move, or using a moan-to-pleasure classification method that seems obvious to *you*. Meanwhile, you're wondering, with disappointment, why your partner just doesn't get it. For the Murphy Browns of the world, a fully satisfying sex life didn't just happen. They have, among other things, gained knowledge and wisdom about getting and sending the right messages.

Epistemology Helps You Be More You (… in bed)

For anything you want, you need justified beliefs to help you succeed in getting it. One of the things you should want most is to maximize your autonomy. You are, at your best, a self-directing person with unique preferences, values, and projects. To be autonomous is to have your integrity in these terms cultivated and protected, so that you have the power to promote your special goals and aims.

Your autonomy is impaired when you base your actions on problematic or false information, since you are blocked from engaging in informed self-direction. If someone lies to you about having been HIV tested, or about loving you, she steals your autonomy: you might make commitments and engage in acts that you never would if you were in possession of the truth.[5] You also deprive yourself of autonomy when you deprive yourself of knowledge. You're most likely to have a rewarding sex life (which spills over into a rewarding life in general) if you learn about your distinct sexual preferences, projects, goals, and aims, so that you can increase your autonomous ability to promote them.

Our thinking ranges from low-level (basic and specific) to high-level (complex and wide ranging).[6] Justified beliefs at any level can be beneficial. For instance, "An uninformed pre-orgasmic" asks Alice a pretty low-level question, limited to a basic factual issue:

I was wondering if it were possible for a man to tell if a woman has had an orgasm. If so, how noticeable is it to a man and is there a substantial amount of fluid involved in a woman's orgasm?[7]

Getting an answer does give her more to work with in making autonomous decisions. However, she – and you – can gain knowledge at increasingly high levels of complexity and magnitude. Each upward step expands your awareness and gives you more power to guide your life through informed choice. For instance, you could seek (and gain) justified beliefs in response to each of the following, increasingly high-level, questions:

- Why is "an uninformed pre-orgasmic" person asking this question? Is she wondering how easily she can get away with faking an orgasm?
- Why would a young woman *want* to know how to fake an orgasm?
- What harm might come to a woman from setting up her sexual life in a way like this?
- What cultural influences might shape and restrict people's approaches to sex?
- How might my own culture have influenced my approach to sex?
- How might I change in response to what I've learned about all of this?

Justified beliefs at higher levels are like increasingly powerful intellectual climaxes, and they're a good way to reach better climaxes elsewhere: they help you discover your best desires, get rid of misconceptions and impediments, and learn to get what you want in the most meaningful and profound ways.

How To Get Better Sex From Epistemologists

Knowledge, justified belief, and epistemic effort are good for you: not just good for your knowledge base, but good for *you*, including the sexual you. My research project is to find ways to expand people's ability to evaluate and question themselves epistemically, take on an active, self-directed role, and become conscious authors of their epistemic selves. The authority I invoke as an epistemologist comes from our disciplinary expertise on knowledge and justification, not our more esoteric scholarly disputes. We have determined particularly plausible distinctions, conceptual frameworks, definitions, views, and intuitions. These include not only ideas within our broad shared knowledge base, on which we've been focusing, but also particular epistemologists' valuable and effective works and innovations. It's a crying shame that the great insights of those whose expertise is on thinking and knowledge almost never directly reach the vast majority of thinkers and knowers. Let's go through some helpful work from a few of them. I think these are especially relevant to thinking about sexual matters, and I'll give examples to illustrate.

Hilary Kornblith's work on rationalization is a good instance of a useful epistemological view.[8] One ought first to accumulate evidence and reasons and think about them, and then form an appropriate belief. One rationalizes, on Kornblith's account, when he starts with a belief and produces reasons that would support it. Take Todd, who needs, psychologically, to believe he's good in bed. He sincerely thinks he's looking at all the evidence and reasonably deciding what it indicates. Without even realizing it, though, he starts off believing he's good in bed, and then he picks and chooses the evidence and reasons substantiating that belief. He thinks, "She'd say something if she weren't enjoying it," and selectively focuses on times partners have complimented his performance. An especially insidious factor is that Todd gets the illusion of being a responsible thinker, because he does reflect on reasons – just not with the right motivation.

Once Kornblith gives us a name and description for this phenomenon, we realize it makes a lot of sense of our experiences. This can provide insight into when and why it happens, and what makes it hard to recognize rationalization happening in oneself. We end up with more resources to notice and correct for rationalizing in ourselves and others.

Another helpful concept is what Jennifer Church calls "taking it to heart."[9] Knowledge goes beyond merely possessing true information and having a surface ability to "regurgitate," she says: truly known beliefs involve more depth of understanding.

Here's an illustration. In the *New Yorker* article "Red Sex, Blue Sex," Margaret Talbot explores evangelical Christians' lack of dismay at Sarah Palin's daughter Bristol's teenage unwed pregnancy. Talbot reports that such pregnancies are not at all unusual among evangelicals. She cites studies finding that although 74 percent of white evangelical adolescents say they believe in abstaining from sex before marriage (as compared to half of mainline Protestants and 25 percent of Jews), they are more sexually active than Mormons, mainline Protestants, and Jews. She adds, "On average, white evangelical Protestants make their 'sexual debut' – to use the festive term of social-science researchers – shortly after turning sixteen. Among major religious groups, only black Protestants begin having sex earlier."[10]

Such teens might affirm a belief in abstinence, and even take pledges of abstinence, yet the belief somehow doesn't really sink in. This illustrates Church's contention that a person might acknowledge a proposition as true, build theories and plans around it – and yet not take it to heart.

Here's another example. Jane accepts, when she thinks about it, that it's wrong to invoke a double standard for men and women in using labels like "slutty," but privately she continues to hold on to the double standard. A belief taken to heart guides one's automatic thoughts, feelings, and actions, whereas a belief not taken to heart seems more like "a mere phrase on a page or in someone's mouth, the implications of which must be worked out deliberately and laboriously."[11] In her unguarded moments, Jane says her friend Li Mai "sleeps around" and looks "easy" to men, whereas in her more mindful and careful moments she can – not quite consciously – work out and say what follows from the less prejudiced view.

Church holds that we can affect what we take to heart by making certain choices, so we are responsible for our deeply held commitments. Jane could change the way she thinks about more promiscuous women: she could choose a metaphor of "adventurers" rather than "tramps," remind herself to think of a sexually active male friend whenever she catches herself using the double standard, and work to associate images invoking empowerment, choice, and independence with such women.

Recognizing Church's distinction allows us to look at our own and others' beliefs in terms of a scale from accepted only on the surface to deeply taken to heart. This invites us to explore implications and responsibilities, and it provides us with a tool for doing so.

Although we should try to scrutinize and evaluate certain of our deeply rooted commitments, we should recognize that in most cases it's advantageous to have beliefs so firmly entrenched and automatic that we don't have to make a conscious effort to form other beliefs on their basis. Kent Bach develops this notion when he talks about "jumping to conclusions" – unconsciously, automatically drawing inferences from beliefs and experiences. If we always had to stop and think through beliefs like whether the couch would be a soft place to make out, we couldn't function. To make beliefs justified, though, the default automatic processes must recognize and respond to the real situation, not continue on "autopilot" when that's inappropriate.[12]

Antoine and Erika have made love every Saturday during the two years they've been dating. They no longer have to even mention it – Saturday night is a ritual both cherish. One Saturday, however, they have a huge argument, and then Erika is uncharacteristically withdrawn and even somewhat hostile, and is avoiding casual physical contact with Antoine. Normally, there's no reason Antoine should go through a step-by-step set of inferences to form the belief that Erika is willing and eager to make love on a Saturday – it's epistemically okay for him to assume it, and consciously going through a reasoning process would just waste his time and mental resources. Tonight, though, he should notice that there's a relevant difference in the situation, and his normal default reasoning should be interrupted. Not having taken into account the different factors in the situation, Antoine jumps straight into foreplay at bedtime, blithely assuming Erika is as willing and eager as always. Bach contends that we're justified in making snap judgments and automatic inferences, but only if we're reliable enough at detecting exceptions.

Bach himself isn't discussing how his insights might be used to help people improve their reasoning, but my approach would explore such a use. I advocate finding opportunities to formulate epistemic guidance from epistemological research even when that was not the epistemologist's original intention – as I will do with the next view, as well.

Richard Foley argues that it's epistemically best for one to be internally consistent. We should "have beliefs that are to our own deep satisfaction – ones that do not merely satisfy us in a superficial way but would do so even with the deepest reflection."[13] If one could really examine herself and apply her own intellectual standards to her thinking – without allowing herself to rationalize or hide anything – the rational beliefs would be those she wouldn't criticize herself for having. Antoine ought to believe as he would if he could step back and see that he is unintentionally failing to live up to his normal standards of belief formation.

Using Foley's model, we can recognize that there's a core set of epistemological principles within each of us, whether we realize it or not, and that we are at our most rational when we believe consistently with those principles. Taking this idea further, we can try to figure out how this can be helpful, rather than just descriptive. As with most epistemic self-examination and improvement, it might be hard to identify those principles and decide whether you're meeting them, but it's worth trying, to the best of your ability.

Leslie Stevenson pursues this concept quite explicitly, arguing that we have a responsibility to try to increase our awareness of the features that might make our beliefs more or less justified, and to at least be able, in principle, to articulate the basis of a belief.[14] He proposes that epistemically responsible people use the method philosophers call "wide reflective equilibrium." This is a state of balance or coherence among a set of beliefs, arrived at by deliberately making adjustments among one's general principles and particular judgments. Ideally, our beliefs about particular cases or in particular situations match our general principles. With wide reflective equilibrium we should reflectively increase this matching, or balance, using all of our information and reasoning strength.

Consider the following example. Randy is an evangelical college student who considers himself a believer in abstinence before marriage. If asked, he would affirm this view, and criticize those who believe otherwise. He would draw support from the views of his religion, family, and community. However, Randy, like so many evangelical young men, has impregnated his girlfriend. He formed beliefs along the way contrary to his general principle, as when he decided to have intercourse with his girlfriend. Randy, like Jane and Antoine, has beliefs and principles in a state of disequilibrium; they all have beliefs in "tension" with one another – beliefs that are conflicting or inconsistent.

To increase equilibrium, the first step is to try to detect tensions in your belief system. This involves, first and foremost, a willingness to accept responsibility for your beliefs and principles, and work toward changing them. To detect tensions, you must learn about yourself and your belief system. You can do this by introspection, observation of your actions, perhaps asking others for their observations and insights, and – I hope – using some epistemological concepts and ideas.

Once you detect what seems to be a tension, you have several options (I'll italicize them for ease of use). First, I suppose, you could *do nothing*. However, ignoring the problem doesn't often make things better: it just reduces the likelihood of getting what you want and preserving your own and others' autonomy.

Second, you could *drop* one or more of the beliefs or principles. For instance, Jane could let go of her particular belief that Li Mai is a slut. If Randy has straightforwardly conflicting beliefs ("Those who have premarital sex are sinners," "I engaged in premarital sex," and "I am not a sinner"), he can decide which to keep. If "an uninformed pre-orgasmic" person holds the principle that faking orgasms is okay, but would be upset if her partner faked orgasm, she could rid herself of the general pro-faking principle. It's harder to drop a general principle than a specific belief, but it does reduce the tension, and can be preferable. Consider Richard, who holds the tenet, "All homosexuals are evil pedophiles." Richard could drop particular beliefs – like his judgment that his gay brother is not an evil pedophile – or he could get rid of the general principle. In Richard's case, difficult as it may be, the latter choice is better.

Another approach is to *modify* one or more of the beliefs or principles. Randy might modify his original principle by toning it down: "Premarital sex is usually wrong but is permissible when a couple intends to marry." Richard could modify his particular judgment by using a distinction many have invoked, between orientation and behavior: "All homosexuals are evil pedophiles, but my brother isn't. He doesn't act on his preferences, so he isn't a homosexual." Jane could modify her principle ("The double standard is wrong, but promiscuous people are sluts") as well as her particular judgments ("Not only is Li Mai a slut, so is Luke").

Finally, a means to resolve tensions and increase reflective equilibrium is to *dissolve* the apparent tension, figuring out that the tension was merely apparent, as revealed by more careful self-examination and clarification. An "uninformed pre-orgasmic" person might take time to discover that the apparent disequilibrium was just a result of an ambiguity, so the two weren't really in conflict. The "okay" in her pro-faking principle meant okay from the faker's perspective, and the "not okay" in her anti-faking judgment regarding her partner meant not okay from the fakee's perspective, if you will. Randy might figure out that his anti-premarital sex principle never was as strong as he was thinking it was – it must not have been, because he was accepting of Bristol Palin's pregnancy.

The beliefs and principles involved in wide reflective equilibrium include, importantly, those you've gotten from sources outside of yourself. If you learned somewhere that most campus rapes occur after alcohol use,[15] it's internally inconsistent to form beliefs that don't take that knowledge into account. You also have some responsibility to seek out information relevant to your beliefs – for instance, about safer sex, signs of abusive relationships, and cultural influences affecting you. In addition, you can be negligent in avoiding evidence available to you – as in Todd's selective attention to the evidence of how good he is in bed, and Antoine's failure to notice Erika's signals.

John Heil gives us one more way of thinking about changing ourselves epistemically for the better. He argues that purposeful, intelligent activity can have an influence on how you perceive the world, which affects what you believe. You can explore, investigate, and manipulate your environment; keep your eyes open for things that could override or contradict your beliefs; and notice when you should examine evidence extra-cautiously. You may not be able to simply decide to believe something and immediately believe it, but Heil and others argue that you can engage in long-term activities to change your mind (literally).[16]

The View from Here

We've now looked at epistemological ideas, clarifications, theories, and distinctions that, in an ideal world, all college students would study. What I find most remarkable about the college years is their nearly entire focus on personal transformation. In college, you change and grow by gaining information, discovering alternative perspectives, developing an identity as an ongoing autonomous being, and building a foundation of abilities. Research has found that few college students learn to evaluate critically and transform their beliefs and ways of thinking.[17] My vision is for students who may never have considered their own thinking about sex to gain resources for a lifelong process of guiding and developing their personal approaches to sex and sexuality. Philosophical epistemology is an ideal resource of this kind.

Stevenson declares, "One must in the end make up one's mind for oneself," since to do anything less is "to be less than what one can and should be as a rational being."[18] I would add that to do anything less is to be less than what one can and should be as a *sexual* being, as well.

NOTES

1   Alvin Goldman, "Strong and Weak Justification," *Philosophical Perspectives* 2 (1988): 51–69; and William Alston, *Epistemic Justification: Essays in the Theory of Knowledge* (Ithaca: Cornell University Press, 1989).
2   Kent Bach, "A Rationale for Reliabilism," *The Monist* 68 (1985): 246–63.
3   The Trustees of Columbia University, "Go Ask Alice! Nice Names for Naughty Bits," available online at www.goaskalice.columbia.edu/5887.html (accessed July 20, 2009).
4   See discussion in David S. Hall, "Consent for Sexual Behavior in a College Student Population, Appendix A: The Antioch College Sexual Offense Policy," *Electronic Journal of Human Sexuality* 1 (1998), available online at www.ejhs. org/volume1/conseapa.htm (accessed August 20, 2009).
5   Charles Fried makes this argument well in a section entitled "The Evil of Lying" in *Right and Wrong* (Cambridge, MA: Harvard University Press, 1978), pp. 59–69.
6   Some good psychological sources clarifying and defending a range of intellectual development include the following: William Perry, *Forms of Intellectual and Ethical Development in the College Years: A Scheme* (Cambridge, MA: Harvard University Bureau of Study Counsel/Holt, Rinehart and Winston, 1970); and Barbara K. Hofer and Paul R. Pintrich (eds.) *Personal Epistemology: The Psychology of Beliefs about Knowledge and Knowing* (Mahwah: Lawrence Erlbaum, 2008).
7   The Trustees of Columbia University, "Go Ask Alice! Can a Man Tell if a Woman Orgasms?" available online at www.goaskalice.columbia.edu/1413. html (accessed July 20, 2009).
8   Hilary Kornblith, "Distrusting Reason," *Midwest Studies in Philosophy* 23 (1999): 181–96.

9   Jennifer Church, "Taking It to Heart: What Choice Do We Have?" *The Monist* 85 (2002): 361–80.
10 Margaret Talbot, "Dept. of Disputation: Red Sex, Blue Sex," *New Yorker* (November 2008), available online at www.newyorker.com/reporting/2008/11/03/081103fa_fact_talbot?currentPage=1 (accessed August 2, 2009).
11 Church, "Taking It to Heart," p. 367.
12 Bach, "A Rationale for Reliabilism."
13 Richard Foley, "Skepticism and Rationality," in M. D. Roth and G. Ross (eds.) *Doubting: Contemporary Perspectives on Skepticism* (Dordrecht: Kluwer Academic Publishers, 1989).
14 Leslie Stevenson, "First Person Epistemology," *Philosophy* 74 (1999): 475–97.
15 See Carleton College Wellness Center, "Alcohol and Sex," available online at http://apps.carleton.edu/campus/wellness/info/alcohol/sex/ (accessed August 20, 2009).
16 For instance, see John Heil, "Doxastic Agency," *Philosophical Studies* 43 (1983): 355–64; Church, "Taking It to Heart"; and David Christensen, *Putting Logic in Its Place* (Oxford: Oxford University Press, 2004).
17 Marcia Baxter Magolda, *Knowing and Reasoning in College: Gender-Related Patterns in Students' Intellectual Development* (San Francisco: Jossey-Bass, 1992).
18 Stevenson, "First Person Epistemology," p. 497.

CHAPTER 12

EXPLORING THE ASSOCIATION BETWEEN LOVE AND SEX

Romeo and Juliet Talking about Sex and Love

We may imagine a modern day Juliet and Romeo walking in a romantic landscape, maybe the historic main street of St. Charles, surrounded by modest galleries, inviting small cafés, and glimpses of the slow lazy Missouri river nearby (one may imagine one's own preferred romantic landscape). Our contemporary Romeo and Juliet are not lovers but rather undergraduate college students and good friends who enjoy discussing their thoughts openly. Romeo is talking excitingly about a one night stand he had. He is describing the mutually lusty gazes, the harmonious movements, and the extreme bliss he felt. Juliet, who is a romantic person (or a conservative one; it depends on your point of view), is waiting for some ending where both "fall in love"; however, nothing like this has happened. Romeo is describing it as "a perfect hot and lusty one night stand, not a love story." Juliet cannot understand this. She feels that something is missing, and she believes that sex that doesn't have any association to love is superficial and meaningless. Once she even tried it – attempting to relax and enjoy the moment, to be light as a breeze – but she couldn't. The feeling of actually "making love" without feeling real emotion, the empty caresses, the hot but tasteless kisses and the intimate closeness of a stranger, all seemed absurd to her. She cannot understand Romeo's use of the phrase "a wonderful one night stand."

Romeo respects Juliet's feelings; however, he wonders whether they cover up something else. Maybe Juliet sincerely believes that she is a free and liberal person, but in fact she's got some semi-unconscious prejudice against sex. Maybe, she assumes that sex is low and animalistic (even immoral in some sense) and that it is, somehow, purified by connecting it to a "noble" emotion of love. Juliet, however, reassures Romeo, that neither of these is true. She does not judge that sex without love is immoral or perverted in any sense, nor is her approach aesthetic (i.e., a view that might say sex without love is ugly). But she keeps feeling that "something is missing in sex without love." She believes that it is limited and even vain.

I believe that Romeo and Juliet's disagreement reflects different notions of sex. On the one hand, Romeo's approach reflects a notion of sex as an activity in which one derives pleasure from physical contact with another person. On the other hand, Juliet assumes that there is an inherently unavoidable interpersonal aspect to sex. First, I will develop Romeo's notion of plain sex. Then I will explore whether there is an interpersonal aspect to sex and whether this aspect constitutes an association between sex and love.

Plain Sex

One may suggest that "sexual desire is desire for contact with another person's body and for the pleasure which such contact produces; sexual activity is activity which tends to fulfill such desire of an agent."[1] This analysis defines sex as an act in which a pleasure is derived by having a physical contact with another person. This is a rough definition. It leaves open various questions, for example, whether *any* pleasure that is derived by a physical contact with another person is a sexual pleasure.

For our purpose, the notion of plain sex is important because it suggests an alternative to a "means-end analysis" of sex, that is, sex conceived as a mere instrument for some end. Traditionally, the analysis of sex as a mere instrument for reproduction was dominant. That is, reproduction was considered as the natural function of sex; accordingly, sexual activity that deviated from it was considered as perverse and even immoral (e.g., oral sex, homosexual intercourse).[2] However, "the development of contraception rendered the connection weaker."[3] (Moreover, reproduction might be considered as "nature's role" for sex, but often the individual's motive is different.) According to the notion of plain sex, a conception of sex as an activity that expresses love is correspondingly mistaken. Sex is not an act that intends to achieve some function or express anything. Sex's solitary inherent result is sexual satisfaction. Other "purposes of sex" are contingent. In other words, of course, sex may answer various needs and may communicate various feelings such as attraction, tenderness and trust, domination, and passivity; however, sex does not inherently communicate feelings (the act by itself does not express anything; it is not supposed to). Moreover, love might be better expressed by activities that are focused only in the receiver's profit, such as helping your beloved with writing her term paper; however, in sex both of the parties intend to enjoy.

To recapitulate, one may maintain that the sexual act does not express anything all; it is just a plain pleasurable physical act (i.e., a strong position of plain sex). Alternatively, one may hold a moderate position: sex may express love, but it may express other feelings, or not express anything at all (i.e., a moderate position of plain sex). The bottom line is that even if sex may express love in some cases (which is controversial) there is neither a natural connection nor a normative one between love and sex; sex and love are different, not necessarily related phenomena. Therefore, nothing is missing or wrong with sex without love.

Moreover, it seems that a central motivation for denying the notion of plain sex is the supposition that plain sex is immoral since it implies that sexual desire is directed towards the body itself; and, viewing another person or being treated only as a physical body (i.e., as an object) is humiliating and even immoral. For example, in *Lectures on Ethics* the philosopher Immanuel Kant (1724–1804) writes:

> There is no way in which a human being can be made an Object of indulgence for another except through sexual impulse.... Sexual love makes of the loved person an Object of appetite.... Sexual love ... by itself and for itself ... is nothing more than appetite. Taken by itself it is a derogation of human nature.... As an Object of appetite for another person becomes a thing.[4]

Supporters of the notion of plain sex hold, like Kant, that sexual desire and sexual activity are directed only to the partner's body, but deny the negative connotations that are related to this approach. That is, according to the positive approach to plain sex, sex is indeed directed towards the body alone. It is pleasurable, exciting, and might lead to a rich and complex experience, and of course is moral and respectful. Moreover, sex between lovers is also directed towards the body alone; beyond the legitimizing veils of love and marriage, it is the same sexual act – an activity in which one derives pleasure from a physical contact with another person, that is, sex by its nature is plain sex. Thus, an association of love shouldn't change one's evaluation of sex; one should have a positive or negative evaluation of sex irrespective to the question whether it is done between lovers.

Loving Sex between Non-Lovers

In order to reply, Juliet has to sharpen her position. She has to distinguish her position from the vague position that sexual activity expresses (or ought to express) love. Juliet may suggest that even if one does not assume that a sexual act expresses love, there is still some association between love and sex. However, she has to explain of what this association consists.

Juliet may maintain that the strong emotional bond of love makes a difference, since "sex with love … is deeply personal. One forms a unity not only with body, but also with all the other aspects of what constitute a complete experience: the mental, emotional, and spiritual."[5]

In response, Romeo may differentiate the characterization of sex from the characterization of the relationship between the partners: non-lovers may have "loving sex," that is, sex with mutual care, sex in which each one of the participants relates and appreciates her partner's special qualities, and sex which constitutes a warm and complex experience. At this point, Romeo may relate again to an experience he had at the end of the semester. After an exhausting period of classes, tests, and papers to submit (a period in which one doesn't have any time to attend to one's personal life, and even less time to be involved in a romantic relationship), he went out to a pub and there he noticed her. He couldn't avoid staring at her; she seemed adorable to him. He sent her a glass of white wine, and then their eyes met. The evening they had spent together was "an evening of sensuous eroticism that continued for hours and included all the foreplay, kisses, and caresses that actual lovers enjoy, perhaps done simply out of mutual admiration for each other's sensuous qualities and out of gratitude for having been chosen by the other for such an evening. Yet, because of inability (or will) to maintain a serious relationship, the pair went their separate ways in the morning; they never saw each other again."[6] The vulgar image, according to which sex without love is impersonal, selfish, cold, and mechanical, is baseless.

I doubt whether the notions of loving sex and plain sex are compatible. After all, the notion of loving sex relates to an emotional component that is over and above the pleasure that is derived by the physical contact itself (which characterizes the notion of plain sex). Introducing Thomas Nagel's philosophical analysis of sex may help reveal the stress in Romeo's position (i.e., assuming both the notion of plain sex and the notion of loving sex). In the next section, I will introduce Nagel's position and show how it sheds light on this issue.

Being Embodied

Nagel's analysis combines the embodiment ingredient of sex (which Romeo assumes) and the interpersonal ingredient of sex (which Juliet assumes).[7] That is, his analysis acknowledges the centrality of the body in sex without neglecting the interpersonal element. Nagel portrays a process of mutual perception and arousal of sexual desire: the self is sexually aroused by the other's presence; the self's arousal is perceived by (and arouses) the other; then, the perception of the other being aroused by the self's arousal contributes to the self's arousal, and vice versa; the arousal-loop may extend repetitively.

This multilevel, interpersonal arousal involves a process of mutual embodiment in which "one's body actions are taken over by the body; ideally, deliberate control is needed only to guide the expression of those impulses."[8] That is, deliberate control is narrowed to a minimum; the body, which knows how to "fit into the complex of mutual perceptions,"[9] takes control. Nagel describes a development of such a process:

> Hunger leads to spontaneous interactions with food; sexual desire leads to spontaneous interactions with other persons, whose bodies are asserting their sovereignty in the same way, producing involuntary reactions and spontaneous impulses in them. These reactions are perceived, and that perception in turn perceived; at each step the domination of the person by his body is reinforced, and the sexual partner becomes more possessible by physical contact, penetration, and envelopment.[10]

Nagel's analysis has pointed out essential characterizations of sexual activity: it involves an interpersonal interaction that happens in an

⁙ GUY PINKU

embodied mode. One of Russell Vannoy's criticisms of Nagel's analysis is directed to this point:

> This inner complex of thought, emotion, lust and fantasy is miles removed from some kind of neo-primitivistic state of merely "becoming one's body" or being in a state of sheer lust. Once again, therefore, Nagel's two concepts of mutual perceptual feedback and sheer embodiment seem to work against each other, and it is not clear how the former state is going to produce the latter.[11]

Vannoy has suggested that there is a conflict between being in an embodiment mode and interpersonal communication. I believe that this conflict is false; however, its falsity is not trivial. Explaining this falsity may assist us in clarifying the special characteristics of the interpersonal ingredient in sex.

A Primary Emotional Awareness

Psychologists maintain that interpersonal interaction between adult human beings requires a sophisticated cognitive ability that enables a conception of other minds. That is, an ability to attribute mental states (such as beliefs, desires, and hopes) to other persons, and to differentiate another person's mental states from one's own mental states.[12] Moreover, an embodiment (a mode in which "one's body actions are taken over by the body")[13] has something in common with an automatic mode of action (such as driving, typing, or reading); similarly, in an embodiment mode one "flows" with action. That is, the agent does not have to set up a goal and evaluate each action or step that she takes (the agent may set up her action at the upper level of activity and perform the subordinate activities in automatic mode).[14] The seemingly incompatible characterization of a highly complicated "multilevel interpersonal awareness"[15] within an embodiment mode strengthens the doubt concerning Nagel's analysis; it seems to be a typical case in which a philosopher has theorized over and above a real phenomenon.

I believe that Nagel is right in that some interpersonal, complicated interactions are performed by an agent in habitual ways according to norms, without a need to comprehend the other participants' mental states. For example, ordering meals in cafeterias is such a routine situation that one need only identify the person standing beyond the counter as the cashier. That is, identifying the participant's social role (i.e., "a cashier") enables the interaction to take place. In this circumstance, thinking about the cashier's mental states is redundant.[16]

A critic, however, may respond that this is a Pyrrhic victory, that it comes at a great cost. If the interpersonal component in sexual relationships is similar to the interpersonal relation between a client in a cafeteria and a cashier, then indeed Nagel is wrong; such patterns of "interpersonal interaction" are extremely dull and routine – unlike the multilevel interpersonal awareness that Nagel has assumed (I can imagine Juliet nodding her head disappointingly to the comparison of making love to ordering a dish in a cafeteria). But I think that Nagel's analysis is adequate to a different realm of interpersonal relationship: a realm that was described by psychologist Ulric Neisser by the notion of an "interpersonal self." As Neisser notes, "The interpersonal self is the self as engaged in immediate unreflective social interaction with another person."[17] The essence of this notion is self-awareness of the emotional changes which are created (in the self) by the perception of another agent and the interaction with her (including her response to the self). To illustrate the primacy of the interpersonal self, Neisser references a notion introduced by Charles Darwin:

> As Darwin put it, "when two young dogs in play are growling and biting each other's faces and legs, it is obvious that they understand each other's gestures and manners" ... Darwin's use of the term 'understand' in this context should not be misunderstood. He does not claim (or at least I do not claim) that puppies have an intellectual understanding of each other's behavior.... What is going on between them is sometimes called 'nonverbal communication,' but even that term can be misleading; it tends to suggest that each participant is somehow telling the other about his/her own mental states. If that were true, the achievement of intersubjectivity would depend on the accuracy with which we attribute thoughts and feelings to other people. While we do sometimes attempt such attributions in adult life, they can hardly be the basis of the smooth and immediate interpersonal coordination I am considering here.[18]

The same applies to sexual activity: it is a smooth and immediate interpersonal interaction that is performed without attribution of thoughts and feelings. However, it does include a sort of (mutual) awareness of the partner's feelings. This is a primary awareness of an interpersonal interaction. It is mediated by emotional changes in the self. In other words, the primary awareness of an interpersonal interaction is emotionally experienced; one may feel oneself good or bad, secure or anxious, relaxed or nervous, delighted or annoyed, or happy or sad within an interaction with others. These feelings, to a large extent, reflect the quality of the interpersonal interaction. Thus, in this respect, they constitute a primary emotional awareness of the interpersonal accommodation.

Neisser has also discussed studies of the communicative aspect of baby-caregiver interaction (e.g., what is called affect attunement). It has been shown that these communicative interactions have a potent emotional effect on the caregiver and the baby; disturbances in their content may lead to an extreme mutual emotional distress. Nagel's analysis of sexual activity relates it to the realm of primary emotional awareness of interpersonal interaction. And accordingly, this characterization of sexual activity may explain (at least partly) the powerful emotional influence that sex has. In this regard sex is similar to dancing, being an audience in a live performance, or having a fight with someone. All these activities involve a very powerful emotional interpersonal interaction. However, it seems that besides infant-caregiver interaction, there is no other activity that involves such an extended and potent primary interpersonal interaction (adequately, in response to the notion of plain sex, one could have paraphrased: "it's not the orgasm, stupid!").[19]

Back to Romeo and Juliet: A Variety of Attitudes towards Sex without Love

So, where does the suggested analysis leave us in regard to Romeo and Juliet's debate? It seems that both Romeo and Juliet are right (and wrong) to some extent. I believe that Juliet can establish an association between sex and a primary emotional awareness of interpersonal interaction. Juliet's sexual desire has an interpersonal ingredient; she desires a sexual experience that includes emotionally positive interaction with another person, and this desire is often identified as a (desire for) a feeling of bonding and intimacy within sex (in contrast to mere appetite for the other's person body, similar to an appetite for food). However, some people (on some occasions) may feel exactly a desire for this – a yearning for the flesh alone. The difference between sexual desire that includes an interpersonal ingredient and a sexual desire for the body alone might be captured by James Barrel's description of two attitudes towards the partner's body. The first description is when we feel tenderness we "look at the other's body as a whole"; in contrast, the second, objectifying attitude views the other "as an object separate from and not embedded in the world."[20]

The second kind of attitude, i.e., what Barrel calls the "objectness position," is typical to the view of the body in pornography, to a relation of a client to a prostitute, and to sexual acts that are done out of "sheer lust" in order to discharge a sexual tension, e.g., a sailor on a short vacation with the one thought, *woman*, rattling in his head, desiring to have sex in a club's restroom or an orgy. Thus, Juliet may maintain that these kind of sexual desires and activities are limited because they do not include an interpersonal ingredient. Therefore, she feels that something is missing in sex without love.

Romeo, however, may respond that sex without love might be a loving, intimate, and tender act as well. Romeo's response is justified only on pain of holding a distinction between feelings of love that are limited to the sexual activity alone (i.e., a sexual love, which is related to the realm of primary emotional awareness of interpersonal interaction) and love that is typical to long-term relationships (i.e., a long-term love). A prominent difference between these sorts of love is their maintenance: sexual love is limited to the time of the sexual interaction – it is the feeling of "love to be with" one's partner for sex, which disappears a short time afterwards. This is in contrast to "love as a long-term, deep, emotional relationship, between two individuals. As in this type of relationship, love is permanent at least in intent, and more or less exclusive."[21] More particularly, long-term love assumes conceiving of, and taking care for, the spouse as a person; that is, directing one's interest and caring of the spouse's thoughts and emotions independently of a specific context or interaction. This assumes an advanced process of attributing mental states to another person. In contrast, sexual love is limited to a narrow context: the emotional state during a specific sexual interaction without an explicit consideration of the partner's thoughts and emotions. According to this distinction, Romeo acknowledges that sex without sexual love (i.e., a loveless sexual act) might be experienced as limited, but maintains that this has nothing to do with love in the regular sense of the term "love." That is, one may have loving sex only in the sense of sexual love. Thus, Juliet's assumption that something is missing in sex with a non-lover might be regarded as adolescent confusion between a sexual love and a long-term love.

We can imagine two sorts of responses: Juliet may deny Romeo's distinction and argue that long-term love and sexual love are empirically mingled (i.e., Romeo's distinction is conceptual, at best). However, this reaction is not convincing; Juliet's inability to distinguish long-term love and sexual love might be related to her lack of experience or to emotional immaturity. An alternative, more modest response might be to acknowledge the distinction between long-term love and limited sexual love, but to insist that these sorts of love have some association; accordingly, sexual love is often mingled with long-term love, e.g., sexual love often leads to long-term love. Due to the association between long-term love and short-term love, Juliet (and some other persons) finds it difficult to feel sexual love and intimacy without feeling (or intending to feel) long-term love. The knowledge that the love is limited to the sexual act alone violates Juliet's ability to feel love at all (even a limited sexual love). Juliet may mention three difficulties: first, a difficulty to "jump" into sexual love from a previous state of lack of love; second, during the sexual act itself she may find it strange to feel emotional accommodation (e.g., intimacy and tenderness) to a person with whom she soon won't have any contact; therefore, she experiences her feelings during the sexual act as limited and even artificial; and third, after the sexual act she may feel depressed because of the immediate transformation from a feeling of emotional accommodation to an absence of any feeling. Juliet longs for harmony in her feelings; a fragmentation of her emotion makes it difficult for her to have any emotion at all.

At this point Romeo and Juliet, acknowledging the personal and probably the gender differences between them, find nothing to say anymore; so they may immerse themselves in the delightful landscape of the historic main street of St. Charles, embodied in the experience of enjoying it together. And what about us? In order to maintain our integrity we may have to clarify whether (and when) we are more like Juliet and whether (and when) we are more like Romeo. What do we really want to achieve from our sexual life? Do we want to – are we able to – distinguish between short-term sexual love and a long-term bond of love?

NOTES

1 Alan Goldman, "Plain Sex," *Philosophy and Public Affairs* 6 (1977): 268.
2 Nowadays this approach is still identified with a religious approach. For example, Pope Paul VI, "Humanae Vitae" in R. Baker and F. Elliston (eds.) *Philosophy and Sex*, 2nd edn. (Buffalo: Prometheus, 1984 [1968]), pp. 167–83.
3 Goldman, "Plain Sex," p. 271.

4 Immanuel Kant, *Lectures on Ethics*, trans. L. Infield (New York: Harper and Row, 1963), p. 168; cited in Alan Soble, *The Philosophy of Sex and Love* (Minnesota: Paragon House, 1998), p. 51.

5 Russell Vannoy, *Sex without Love: A Philosophical Exploration* (Buffalo: Prometheus, 1980), p. 13.

6 Based (with some adaptations) on Vannoy, *Sex without Love*, p. 26.

7 Thomas Nagel, "Sexual Perversion," in Alan Soble (ed.) *The Philosophy of Sex*, 2nd edn. (Savage: Rowman and Littlefield, 1991 [1969]).

8 Ibid., p. 47.

9 Ibid.

10 Ibid.

11 Vannoy, *Sex without Love*, p. 66.

12 John Barresi and Chris Moore, "Intentional Relations and Social Understanding," *Behavioral and Brain Sciences* 19, 1 (1996): 107–54.

13 Nagel, "Sexual Perversion," p. 47.

14 Josef Tzelgov, "Specifying the Relations between Automaticity and Consciousness: A Theoretical Note," *Consciousness and Cognition* 6 (1997): 441–51.

15 Nagel, "Sexual Perversion," p. 49.

16 Based on Bermúdez José Luis, *Philosophy of Psychology: A Contemporary Introduction* (London: Routledge, 2005), p. 203.

17 Ulric Neisser, "Five Kinds of Self," *Philosophical Psychology* 1 (1988): 35–59, here p. 41.

18 Ibid., p. 42.

19 Sexual activity between persons is far more satisfying than masturbation. However, according to the notion of sex as pure physical enjoyment, the orgasm itself (i.e., the highest physical pleasure) should be regarded as the main concern of sexual activity. Based on Solomon Robert, "Sexual Paradigms," in Alan Soble (ed.) *The Philosophy of Sex*, 2nd edn. (Savage: Rowman and Littlefield, 1991 [1974]), pp. 39–52.

20 James Barrel, "Sexual Arousal in Objectifying Attitude," *Review of Existential Psychology and Psychiatry* 13, 1 (1974): 98.

21 Goldman, "Plain Sex," p. 273.

CHAPTER 13

SEX FOR A COLLEGE EDUCATION

Degradation for a Degree: A Tragic Paradox

Natalie Dylan, a 22-year-old college student, is auctioning off her virginity to afford her education. John Gechter, also 22 and a former college student, became a gay porn actor so that he could manage to pay tuition. The "girls" of VoyeurDorm.com are 13 students who allow themselves to be broadcast over the Internet so that they can meet college expenses. College students are turning toward sex exploitation as college expenses become unattainable. Is college tuition so high now that our youth have to prostitute themselves in order to pay for it?

In this essay, I explore a contemporary paradox confronting many college students: that to become autonomous through higher education, they must subjugate themselves, sexually, to afford it. Higher education increases one's autonomy, cultivates individual flourishing, and affords graduates greater opportunity. Paradoxically, the expense of a college education often coerces students to engage in sexual enterprises that betray a lack of autonomy, inhibit flourishing, and often result in personal degradation. Though there are many manifestations of sexual exploitation, I will focus primarily on two: prostitution and webcam pornography.

The purpose of this essay is to investigate forms of sex exploitation among college students that are circumstantially coerced by the increasing expense of college. The arguments should not be mistaken as a sermon against prostitution, pornography, or casual sex. I accept the possibility that prostitution could be ethically acceptable, if in idealized non-sexist, non-coercive circumstances. Unfortunately, these are not the circumstances in which prostitution typically occurs, and it is not under these "ideal conditions" that college students are used, sexually, for money. My examples focus mostly on women, as they tend to be the first subjects of exploitation; however, I will discuss cases of male sex exploitation as well.

Prostitution for Higher Learning

Avia Dylan was 19 years old when she financed her education by working as a prostitute for Nevada's Moonlite Bunny Ranch.[1] She worked three weeks and earned several thousand dollars. Her sister, Natalie, is currently auctioning off her virginity: the bids had reached $3.8 million dollars as of January 15, 2009.

Both of these sisters claim that their respective decisions to prostitute themselves were rational, free, and voluntary. Natalie attests that her sister didn't pressure her into auctioning off her virginity, and says that her own decision to auction off her virginity is actually empowering:

> Deflowering is historically oppressive.... When I learned of this, it became apparent to me that idealized virginity is just a tool to keep women in their place. But then I realized something else: if virginity is considered that valuable, what's to stop me from benefiting from that?[2]

Natalie, a former women's studies graduate from Sacramento State University, plans to use the money to pay for a master's degree in marriage and family therapy. She reasons, "We live in a capitalist society.... Why shouldn't I be allowed to capitalize on my virginity?"[3] Natalie's statements deserve philosophical examination. Namely, they introduce us to two moral controversies: commodification and consent.

Commodification: Using Oneself as a Mere Means

Students are increasingly viewing their own bodies as tools that they can exploit in order to gain much needed cash. The sharp line between the intrinsic versus instrumental value of the individual has become blurred.

MATTHEW BROPHY

Legally, commodification of a person is illegal: one cannot, for instance, sell one's kidney for profit. Presumably, the law recognizes the intrinsic dignity of the human body, so it prevents the human body from being exploited.

A fertile woman, however, can sell her ova for implantation into another woman. The money gained – up to $10,000 – is supposed to be "compensation" and should not be motivating her to donate an egg if she wouldn't otherwise have done so. This veneer of compensation is translucent, especially when one Los Angeles company advertised for egg donors simply: "Pay your tuition with eggs."[4]

The sexual exploitation of college students increases yearly, and it has been changing the way that such students view themselves. The advent of the Internet is one main catalyst for this change. Internet media teem with advertisements about "barely legal" pornography of supposed sorority girls performing X-rated acts, and "webcams" where a consumer can pay to watch a woman behave sexually while gratifying himself. Inundated with such marketing messages, college women cannot help but view themselves as potential sexual commodities to a vast sex market.

Human beings, however, possess intrinsic and unconditional value. This is the view presented by Immanuel Kant (1724–1804) in his seminal book, *Groundwork of the Metaphysic of Morals*.[5] Kant states in his "second formulation" that one ought not treat another or oneself as a mere means to an end, since doing so would be contrary to the recognition of this intrinsic and unconditional value. Humans are not objects to be used; they are subjects to be respected. Any action that treats a human being as a mere tool or object rather than as a person, who is worthy of respect and consideration, is an immoral action. For this reason, Kant condemns casual sex as an act in which an individual objectifies not only the other person as a tool for his own sexual gratification, but moreover as an act in which he uses himself as a mere tool to satiate his lower-minded lusts. Religious morality echoes Kant's sentiments, for many of the same reasons. Engaging in promiscuous, recreational sex can be fun for awhile, but it allegedly debases the dignity of the individuals involved.

While we might reject Kant's condemnation of casual sex, his second formulation seems apt concerning prostitution. The prostitute rents out his body in a way that is not fully voluntary, and in a way that disrespects his intrinsic value and dignity as a person. A college student who prostitutes herself to afford college is denying her intrinsic worth: allowing her own body to be used as a mere tool by a stranger. Human beings are not tools, however, and so should not be treated as mere objects for another person's use. The intrinsic and unconditional value of human beings cannot be captured in terms of dollars and cents. While student prostitutes have a noble end in mind – to better themselves by earning a college degree – their means of getting there deeply violate their own integrity and value.

Deflowering is Empowering: Feminism or False Consciousness?

Natalie Dylan has put her virginity up on the auction block, claiming it as research for her upcoming master's thesis in marriage and family therapy on the value of virginity. She assures a curious public that "my study is completely authentic in that I am truly auctioning off my virginity but I am not being sold into this. I'm not being taken advantage of in any way."[6] Rather, Natalie contends that her actions "flip the equation, and turn my virginity into something that allows me to gain power and opportunity from men."[7]

Natalie, an intelligent and educated graduate of Sacramento State University where she majored in women's studies, insists that her auction-deflowering is empowering. She denies that her proposed prostitution is exploitative; rather, she asserts that she is turning female-oppressing capitalism on its head – using her virginity as a tool for her liberation.

Further exploration in women's studies might provide Natalie reasons counter to her prostitution-as-liberation thesis. One might question whether her justifications may be representative of a "false consciousness." In Marxist theory, false consciousness is defined as "a failure to recognize the instruments of one's oppression or exploitation as one's own creation, as when members of an oppressed class unwittingly adopt views of the oppressor class."[8]

One mundane example of false consciousness is when women elect to wear high heel shoes. Many women want to buy and wear high heels, even though these shoes are often designed contrary to function and comfort. This desire to wear high heels stems from a male-dominated society that promotes women as sex objects: high heels are a soft-core version of the archaic Chinese foot-binding tradition that subjugated women. Chinese women would endorse having their feet bound, as it made them more attractive to men: it made women valuable commodities to be married off in arranged matrimony. High heels have the same function, a feminist might extrapolate, as foot-binding did: to make women valuable as

⚥   MATTHEW BROPHY

commodities to men. Women, however, have internalized this oppression and have adopted the views of the androcentric society, freely subjugating themselves, and even spending their hard-earned money, to fill their bedroom closets with instruments of oppression.

Prostitution, of course, is far more severe than wearing high heel shoes – an example which seems trivial by comparison. Prostitution represents the commodification of a person's entire body in a complete, intimate, and violating way. To assert that prostitution is a path to liberation, a celebration and furtherance of pro-choice values, seems to beg some thoughtful reconsideration.

One might consider why Natalie, an attractive 22-year-old woman, who reports having had several boyfriends in her life, never engaged in sexual intercourse itself, though expressing that she has engaged in other sexual activities with these partners. Perhaps a reasonable conjecture is that, at that time, Natalie viewed sexual intercourse as an intimate experience that was not to be casually regarded. If so, it appears she has changed her mind, or has sufficiently rationalized that prostituting herself to a stranger for money is a triumph for women's liberation. It seems dubious that most feminists would agree.

Agreeing to Be Exploited

Imagine a woman named Helena who lives in Singapore, where there are few employment opportunities – especially for women. When Helena turns 18, she can legally become a prostitute. Prostitution is one of the few jobs available to women that pays a living wage. Helena realizes the associated dangers with prostitution: physical violence, disease, emotional trauma, bodily ill-health, and so forth. Nevertheless, knowing that she has no comparable options, Helena elects to become a prostitute. Sadly, there are many women in impoverished nations that have stories just like Helena's, though their stories are typically worse. We might characterize Helena's decision to become a prostitute as a "free" decision, but is it truly? It seems, rather, that Helena is coerced by her circumstances to exploit herself in order to survive. True consent requires that Helena had other reasonable alternatives available to her.

Contrast this example with Ashley Dupré: the prostitute at the Emperor's Club in New York who had several sexual rendezvous with former New York Governor Elliot Spitzer. Dupré moved to New York

City to pursue her dream of becoming a singer. She explains the reasoning behind her high-end escort prostitution: "I really didn't see the difference between going on a date with someone in New York, taking you to dinner and expecting something in return ... whereas, you know, being an escort, it was a formal transaction."[9] After the media exposure of their affair, Dupré received several lucrative offers, including $1 million to pose in *Hustler* magazine, but she turned them all down, explaining, "You stop and think, but that's not who I am."[10]

We might question if Dupré's casual attitude toward her prostitution is indicative of false consciousness. Is she rationalizing her oppression into her own internal desires? In her defense, it does appear that she draws a line, albeit an odd one, respective of her identity: she will not pose for *Hustler* or participate in a reality show because it's not authentic to who she is as a person. The fact that she turned down $1 million for a nude photo shoot suggests that Dupré feels as if she has reasonable alternatives available to her, and that she needn't cross any lines that are untrue to her integrity and commitments intimate to her identity.

Helena and Dupré's decisions to prostitute themselves might both be characterized as consensual. Helena's decision, though, seems less free than Dupré's decision – and more ethically troubling. Any perspective that regards both women's decisions as *equally* free seems to suffer moral myopia: a blindness to differences we recognize as morally relevant.

Our case of college prostitution lies somewhere between the two cases: more circumstantially coercive than Dupré's but less than Helena's. I proffer that the degree of our moral concern should be proportionate to the degree of circumstantial coercion that motivates the prostitution. Venerable feminists make similar points: sexual intercourse is rape to the degree that it occurs in a context that is not truly consensual.[11] Our legal system tends to recognize that context can diminish or undermine consent. For instance, a licensed psychologist is prohibited from having sexual relations with an adult patient who has been under his care, as such sexual relations can never be purely consensual. There is such an imbalance of power between psychologist and patient, that there can be no such thing as patient consent – even if patients attest that they are consenting.

College students who prostitute themselves are not patients, of course, but they do exist in an imbalanced power relationship in a similar way to Helena (though not to the same degree). They have a bleak choice: struggle through life with limited opportunities or sexually exploit themselves in order to afford college.

Higher Education: A High Personal Cost

A paradox confronts college students of today and tomorrow: the path to liberation first demands their exploitation. A higher education affords the student greater knowledge, wisdom, and training. It imbues them with a greater autonomy: the ability to rationally and successfully direct their own lives. Graduates are empowered to thrive in careers that fulfill them and enable them to gain greater economic stability. The growing irony, however, is that to achieve this flourishing, autonomy, and empowerment, many students are discovering that the only way to achieve these mantles is to sexually exploit themselves.

In today's economy, a college education is necessary to achieving economic freedom and stability. As of 1999, young women with a college degree earned 91 percent more than young women with no more than a high-school degree or GED.[12] According to a 1997 study, the lifetime income of families headed by an individual with a bachelor's degree will be about $1.6 million more than those headed by just a high-school diploma or GED.[13]

College has become unaffordable for many young Americans. From 1982 to 2007, college tuition and fees increased 439 percent, while the median income of families only rose 147 percent.[14] In 2008 the net cost of attending a four-year public university was 28 percent of median family income; it was 76 percent to attend a four-year private university.[15] Student loans have more than doubled in the past decade, and students from lower-income families tend to receive smaller grants, on average, than students from more affluent families. Many students do not receive much, if any, financial support from their families. If tuition increases at the current rate, we can expect that sex exploitation will increase with it.

Prostitution as Voluntary Slavery

The skyrocketing costs of college are increasingly impelling students to sell themselves sexually. Prostitution is a form of voluntary slavery – even if temporarily. And selling oneself into slavery is both illegal and immoral in that it is irrational.

Legally, the Supreme Court concluded in Paris *Adult Theatre I v. Slaton* (1973) that while "most exercises of free choice ... are explicitly protected by the Constitution," there are some disallowances. Some laws protect "the weak, the uninformed, the unsuspecting, and the gullible from the exercise of their own volition." For instance, one cannot legally sell oneself into slavery as it violates one's own *inalienable* right to liberty: "inalienable" means that no one is to alienate you from that natural and inviolable right – including yourself.

Predating these formal legal arguments, eighteenth-century philosopher Jean-Jacques Rousseau (1712–78) argued that "to alienate another's liberty is contrary to the natural order."[16] Further, Rousseau denies the validity of any contract that creates a master and a slave, for initial fairness must not exist for the individual to consent to becoming a slave. In essence, Rousseau states that "to renounce one's liberty is to renounce being a man, to surrender the rights of humanity and even its duties ... such renunciation is incompatible with man's nature; to remove all liberty from his will is to remove all morality from his acts."[17] For voluntary slavery "there is no possible compensation"[18] – even for a limited time. In *On Liberty*, John Stuart Mill (1806–73) joins Rousseau's denouncement of slavery as illogical: "The principle of freedom cannot require that he [the voluntary slave] should be free not to be free. It is not freedom to be allowed to alienate his freedom."[19]

Sacrificing One's Identity for Higher Education

Sex exploitation extends beyond commodification and coercion and corrodes personal identity. Rosie Reid, an 18-year-old college student, is a lesbian who auctioned off her virginity to a 44-year-old man, via the Internet, so that she could pay for her college education. She received £8,400 (approximately US$15,525) for her deflowering from this mid-40s engineer, with whom she had sex in a hotel room. Reid reports: "It was horrible ... I felt nervous and scared."[20] Reid's partner, Jess Cameron, stayed in the same hotel in a show of support. Reid told the *News of the World*: "I felt obliged ... to please him as he had just paid all this money."[21] After the affair, Reid and her partner met up and "just cried and cried."[22] Reid cites her motivation as an attempt to avoid years of relative poverty. She had been working extensively so she could pay tuition and living expenses and found herself without sufficient time to study. Her partner, who was supportive of Reid's decision, states: "I feel angry that Rosie has to be in this position at all."[23]

❨❩   MATTHEW BROPHY

Rosie Reid's torment contrasts with that of Ashley Dupré, previously mentioned, who did not seem to be coerced by desperation and did not appear to be sacrificing her identity in her high-end escort occupation. Dupré resisted the financial allures of *Hustler* magazine and other lucrative offers after the story broke in the press, citing that these offers wouldn't be true to herself: authentic to her identity and integrity.

Reid's experience, however, did violate her personal identity and integrity. This deep violation resonates in Reid's report of her experience as sexual trauma: "It didn't feel like it was happening to me. I felt like I was watching it happen to someone else."[24] This description matches a typical symptom of sexual trauma called disassociation: an extreme coping mechanism where the traumatized subject retreats from what is occurring to them in the present, until the traumatic experience passes. Of course, one never quite gets over such an experience. Reid compromised the integrity of her identity in this desperate and miserable experience, but faced with college costs, she found herself with little choice. The words of Reid's father probably echo with her today: he told her she was "selling her soul."

Religious identity can also be compromised by the sex exploitation that high college costs induce. John Gechter attended Grove City College, a Christian liberal arts college in Pennsylvania, where students commit themselves to attending a minimum of 16 services in the college chapel each semester. Though Gechter hasn't publically made statements regarding his faith, it seems clear that he is a Christian, and he attests that he never sought to become an actor in gay pornography.

Gechter states that he nonetheless engaged in the enterprise in order to finance his education: "Instead of working 40 hours a week as a busboy or waiter, you do a scene and then you have time to concentrate on your schoolwork." Gechter had tried working in low-wage jobs – a deskclerk, a cook, a waiter – and became too "burned out" given the full-time hours.

John Gechter's part-time porn-acting career was cut short when emails circulated around Grove City College with photographic evidence of his extracurricular career and was indefinitely suspended for acting contrary to the stated values of the Christian college. Like Reid, though perhaps to a lesser degree, Gechter contravened his values – religious in nature – in order to finance his way to a higher education. Before he left the university, he was the target of both ridicule and hate mail.

Prostitution Meets Internet: A Global Crisis

The media spotlight shines brightly on controversial stories like those of Natalie Dylan, Rosie Reid, and John Gechter, yet its glare distracts us from the shadows where most college prostitution is occurring: via free classifieds websites such as craigslist, backpage, and redbook, as well as via webcam and other discretion-enabling technologies. Such college student prostitution spans the US, France, and Britain, among other nations.

Laura D. was a 19-year-old college student in France when she eased into prostitution via the Internet. While browsing the Internet, she encountered a personal ad that stated: "Young man aged 50 looking for occasional massage. Students welcome." The man paid her 250 euros (about US$359). Laura recounts her tales of a college student prostitute in her memoir *Mes chères études*.[25] Laura claims that her college student status was a "selling point" to potential clients, as it fed into a "Lolita" type of fantasy these older men seemed to have. Laura reports that some of these men were violent with her, but that they rationalized their abuse by the fact they were helping a poor college student pay for her education.

Laura's memoir is intended not only as an informative recounting of her experiences but also as a warning to other college students who may be tempted down the same path of Internet-facilitated prostitution. Laura states that while Internet negotiations with clients afforded a feeling of safety, it also may have made her especially vulnerable to abuse: "I felt safe behind the screen … but it was a lure, because at the meeting [with the client], I was alone and no one could help me."[26] Meanwhile, Laura D. has given up prostitution, stating: "I'm still a student and I have a hard time living," but noting that prostitution was not the answer: "It's really hard to find yourself in front of a 50-year-old man, naked, and to become an object of fantasy."[27]

To shine a spotlight on the Internet-fueled explosion of college-student prostitution, Eva Clouet, a 23-year-old master's student in sociology at a university in France, wrote a book on the subject.[28] Instead of needing to peddle sex on the streets, college students can discreetly serve as an "erotic escort" or "erotic masseuse." Estimates by a student union reports that as many as 40,000 French students resort to prostitution to meet college costs.[29] Research from Kingston University in 2006 estimates that the number of students there who resort to prostitution increased by 50 percent between 1999 and 2005, due to a sharp rise in tuition across universities.[30]

The case of Laura D. provides us with reason to suspect that statistics underestimate prostitution's prevalence among college students: "There are a huge number of girls like me who do not talk about it, even with their friends. It's hard to talk about, so it stays secret and taboo."[31] As tuition rates rise worldwide, we can extrapolate that this crisis of college-student prostitution will proportionately increase, as well as other forms of sexual exploitation.

The Dorm Porn Industry

"Peep shows" are an American standard in the pornography industry. With the rise of webcams in the Internet age, a troubling number of young women and men are engaging in webcam "peep shows" in order to afford college expenses. VoyeurDorm, CocoDorm, and DancerDorm are three such websites based on a simple premise: wire a private dormitory with webcams and charge viewers to watch. The first two boast of their college student residents, the last of its "hot" dancers, struggling to make a living.

VoyeurDorm's website advertises "the girls of Voyeur Dorm are fresh, naturally erotic and as young as 18. Catch them in the most intimate acts of youthful indiscretion."[32] Subscribers can watch the college students as they walk around naked, shower, party, dance, masturbate, have sex, and urinate. CocoDorm is the gay male version of VoyeurDorm, and DudeDorm is a mix of heterosexual and gay college students from the University of Southern Florida. Both sites promise similar sexually voyeuristic viewing as VoyeurDorm. And all three sites pay the students' college expenses, and even a bit more: the six male USF students receive free tuition, free rent, and a salary of between $500 and $600 a week.[33]

VoyeurDorm's web-broadcast "sex shows" can be one-on-one, or to audiences of multiple viewers. Over 80,000 web peeping-toms subscribe to VoyeurDorm at $34.95 monthly. Nearly 40 percent of these toms pony up an additional $16 a month for the ability to chat one-on-one with the female residents. VoyeurDorm takes in $40 million annually.[34]

In-the-flesh prostitution seems more violating of college students' integrity than sex exploitation via webcam. Nonetheless, webcam exploitation can be thought of as a soft form of prostitution: college students are allowing images of their bodies to be used for gratification, and will often actively engage in sexual acts for their audience, all to raise money for college.

Large dorm-porn operations, such as these, number a handful. More prevalent are webcam sites which employ "camgirls" – women who put on sex shows for subscribers. Also common are the independent web-cams run by a college student herself, where she will perform sex shows to viewers for a fee. And if viewers have a webcam as well, they can often pay extra to "interact" with the camgirl, masturbating while she performs sexual acts by herself or with others.

With the safe, reliable, and anonymous middleman of PayPal, "cam-girls" and "camboys" can collect their fees from cyber-peepers safely and without much chance of legal action: zoning laws may differ from county, state, and country. Furthermore, all a college woman needs to broadcast her own sex show for money is a webcam, a PayPal account, and the willingness to engage in sexual acts for strangers. Of course, such "will-ingness" is usually one of desperation when it concerns college women trying to find a way to afford college. Despite what the ads promote, the college women who work as camgirls are not as "eager to please" as web-site banners suggest to potential subscribers. Of course, some of the sex-cam businesses trade on the allure of sexual exploitation, enticing cyber-peeping-toms with ads such as "18yo college student fucking to pay her tuition." The very real desperation of some of these women feeds into the rape fantasies that many of the cyber-toms have.

DormPorn and other peep shows not only sexually exploit college stu-dents, but they provide an all-too-perfect gateway to in-the-flesh prostitu-tion. Interactive webcam shows with cyber-toms can lead to the tom propositioning the camgirl to go one step further: meet them for real-life sex. Oftentimes, the tom will be willing to pay for the travel expenses, if necessary, in addition to a large pay-out for services rendered. Such propo-sitions go so far as to include requests that the camgirl or boy become a temporary sex slave. On a counseling website, one college student asks Dr. Joseph M. Carver, an online clinical psychologist, whether or not she should agree to become a sex slave to a couple for whom she had been performing webcam sex shows: "They wanted to pay me a lot of money – more than my psychology degree will cost me – if I would not only have sex with them.... They wanted to tie me up, and more [graphic details omitted]."[35] She inti-mates that she is torn between her desperation to pay her college expenses and her fear of suffering physical and emotional damage.

While such sexual slavery cases may prove rare, the downward path of exploitation from webcam sex show to real-life prostitution is an easy one to descend, and financial desperation pressures many college students to walk it. The descent is especially tempting for many camgirls who feel they have some familiarity with the cyber-toms that are "regulars" to their sites, which can provide camgirls with a modicum of comfort and safety, though often illusory.

Future Consequences of Exploitation

Younger college students may not be able to fully appreciate the future consequences of allowing themselves to be exploited. Egg donation, as previously mentioned, is one example of a choice that may haunt some female donors later in life. Though the women being targeted by egg donation companies are legal adults, they might not be mature enough to fully appreciate the gravity of their decision. How can any of us know how we will feel decades into the future? Our identities change drastically: our values, our roles, our life aspirations.

Sex exploitation carries similar consequences, both internally and externally to the person. Internally, an individual may suffer emotional distress from their subjugation. Externally, evidence of their sexual exploitation may follow them, as in the case of Rosie Reid, Natalie and Avia Dylan, and John Gechter, among too many others. Laura D., for instance, now working in a Paris restaurant, expresses regret over her life as a college student prostitute: "It is difficult now with boys. I hope never to go back to it. It is very violent. It's a money relationship and there is financial domination. It is very difficult to rebuild oneself afterwards."[36]

These young adults will never be free of their past, where the quip "I was young: I needed the money!" doesn't seem so funny. Beyond the emotional trauma of prostitution lies the specter of their self-exploitative decisions rematerializing. An 18-year-old female college student, for instance, may come to regret having served as a webcam girl, if video of her masturbating comes back one day to haunt her as a mother, as a wife, as a more discreet person who might be mortified by such footage. Even the webcam captives of VoyeurDorm, as well as other camgirls, may be forever haunted by the fact that their sexual exploitation is saved on hard disk somewhere and may later rear its ugly and shameful head.

A college education aims to empower young persons to flourish personally and financially. Unfortunately, the skyrocketing cost of tuition carries a hidden human cost: the sexual exploitation of college students who cannot otherwise afford it. No longer is college education necessarily affordable through the traditional means of part-time work and financial aid. And no longer is college unnecessary to achieving a comfortable standard of living.

College is essential to young adults flourishing, achieving, and empowering themselves: it must also be essential that a higher education is affordable. Otherwise, exorbitant expenses of a higher education will exact a high price on our youth. It will undermine our young students' identity, autonomy, and wellbeing. They will have sold their soul for a degree, struggling to reach the American Dream – now beyond their reach.

NOTES

1 Catey Hill, "Student Natalie Dylan from San Diego Auctions Her Virginity, Reportedly Got Bids up to $3.7 Million," *NY Daily News*, January 13, 2009. To protect their privacy, both sisters have elected to use pseudonyms, which I will use throughout.
2 Carey Polis, "Now Up for Auction: One Virginity," *Huffington Post*, January 26, 2009.
3 Belinda Goldsmith, "Student Auctions Virginity, Sparks Online Debate," *Reuters*, September 11, 2008.
4 David Cohen, "'Pay Your Tuition with Eggs' Students Urged," *Guardian*, May 29, 2001, available online at www.guardian.co.uk/education/2001/may/29/internationaleducationnews.highereducation (accessed August 6, 2009).
5 Immanuel Kant, *Groundwork of the Metaphysic of Morals*, trans. H. J. Paton (New York: Harper and Row, 1964).
6 Natalie Dylan, "Why I'm Selling My Virginity," *Daily Beast*, January 23, 2009.
7 Ibid.
8 "False Concsiousness," Dictionary.com, available online at www.dictionary. reference.com/browse/false%20consciousness (accessed August 6, 2009).
9 Kimberly Launier and Katie Escherich, "Ashley Dupré Exclusive: My Side of the Story," *20/20: ABC News*, November 19, 2008, available online at www.abcnews.go.com/2020/story?id=6280407&page=1 (accessed August 6, 2009).
10 Ibid.
11 Catharine MacKinnon, in her book *Women's Lives, Men's Laws* (Cambridge, MA: Harvard University Press, 2005), claims that "force" relating to sex should include hierarchies of power, where, presumably, a woman is *de facto* punished by not allowing herself to be employed as a sex object by her hierarchical superior/s.
12 Katharine Hansen, "What is a College Education Good for Anyway?" *Career Source Magazine*, March 13, 2007.

13   Ibid.

14   Tamar Lewin, "College May Become Unaffordable for Most in US," *New York Times*, December 3, 2008.

15   Ibid.

16   Jean-Jacques Rousseau, *The Social Contract*, ed. Lee A. Jacobus (Boston: Bedford/St. Martins Press, 2006), section 1.2.3.

17   Ibid., section 1.4.3.

18   Ibid., section 1.4.6.

19   John Stuart Mill, *On Liberty* (Oxford: Clarendon Press, 1980), p. 158.

20   No Author, "Student 'Sells Virginity' via Web," *BBC News*, March 21, 2004, available online at www.news.bbc.co.uk/2/hi/uk_news/england/bristol/somer set/3554121.stm (accessed August 6, 2009).

21   Ibid.

22   Ibid.

23   Ibid.

24   Ibid.

25   Laura D., *Mes chères études* [My Dear Studies] (Paris: Max Milo, 2008).

26   Lisa [No Last Name Given], "Seeking Lolita: Student Prostitution in France," *French News for Anglophones Blog*, January 30, 2008, available online at www.frenchnewsforanglophones.blogspot.com/2008/01/seeking-lolita-student-prostitution-in.html (accessed August 6, 2009).

27   Ibid.

28   Eva Clouet, *La Prostitution étudiante à l'heure des nouvelles technologies de communication* [Student Prostitution in a Time of New Communication Technologies] (Paris: Max Milo, 2008).

29   See the SUD Education web page at www.sudeducation.org/ (accessed August 6, 2009).

30   Jonathan Milne, "Female Students Turn to Prostitution to Pay Fees," *Times Online*, October 6, 2008, available online at www.timesonline.co.uk/tol/news/uk/article665019.ece (accessed August 6, 2009).

31   Charles Bremner, "Confessions of a Student Who Sold Sex to Live and Learn," *Times Online*, January 18, 2009.

32   VoyeurDorm website, www.voyeurdorm.com (accessed August 6, 2009).

33   Steve Huettel, "Where the Dudes Are: Pinellas Park," *St. Petersburg Times*, February 3, 2000.

34   Perdue Lewis, *EroticaBiz: How Sex Shaped the Internet* (Sonoma: Harper Collins, 2002).

35   Joseph M. Carver, "College Student Asks: Should I Take a Job as a Sex Slave?" *Counseling Resource*, December 4, 2008, available at www.counsellingresource.com/ask-the-psychologist/2008/12/04/job-as-sex-slave/ (accessed August 6, 2009). Graphic details omitted in the original text.

36   Bremner, "Confessions of a Student Who Sold Sex to Live and Learn."

SENIOR YEAR
Sex and Self-Respect

CHAPTER 14

MEANINGFUL SEX
AND MORAL RESPECT

College Sex Today

In the title essay of his book *Hooking Up* and his novel *I Am Charlotte Simmons*, Tom Wolfe presents a dismaying picture of American college students' sexual attitudes and practices.[1] Wolfe's essay and subsequent novel provide a portrait of college sexuality largely consistent with recent empirical accounts. Indeed, they are based on first-hand research that the author undertook on the campuses of several major American universities, living with students, attending social events, and interviewing many people directly familiar with current college mores. Many freshmen at these institutions are on their own for the first time, confronted with important choices in a permissive environment that provides opportunities for sexual adventure well beyond what they might have had in high school. The decisions young adults make at this stage can have consequences for the rest of their lives. Wolfe's novel presents these choices in a way that is arguably more vivid and compelling than any non-fiction work. Love and the strengthening of a long-term commitment are no longer part of most sexual liaisons on most college campuses. Experimentation and status-seeking – apart from mere physical pleasure and release – are now the major motivations for sexual relations.

The overall impression that Wolfe creates is that sexuality has become coarsened and cheapened, rendered ugly and substantially empty among the current generation of college students. This is by no means, of course, a sudden development, but one that has taken place over several decades; nor is it unique to college students, for it begins in earlier grades and represents a broader societal trend in countries such as ours. But the special circumstances and privileged status of most students at the more prestigious colleges and universities, Wolfe suggests, appear to facilitate what more conservative Americans would consider widespread immorality and a loss of self-respect among many of these students, the elite opinion leaders of the future. A "brave new world" in which sexual activities have little more meaning than do athletic activities looms on the horizon.

These two alleged aspects of casual sexuality – its devaluing of sexual experience to the point of virtual meaninglessness and lack of respect for self and others – will be the focus of this essay. That the practice of hooking up can often be self-destructive and abusive of others should be nearly as obvious as that it violates the standards of Judeo-Christian morality. But for the many who reject traditional sexual ethics, and so tend to discount the possible detrimental effects of these casual attitudes about sex, some other kind of ethical case must be made against such attitudes. Broadly stated, the idea that the ethos of hooking up robs the sexual experience of most of its potential value and the participants of much of their dignity is what we will examine, beginning with the claim of meaninglessness.

Meaning and Sexuality

This will require, as a preliminary, a broader account of the relevant idea of meaning and its relationship to our sexuality in general. What gives sexual experiences and relationships meaning, and how is meaning to be explicated in a sexual context? Is this kind of meaning objective or subjective? Is it absolute or relative? How might it increase the value, i.e., the moral value or value of some other kind, of sexual activity? Is it a matter of sexual engagement serving some external purpose, or a question of the intrinsic qualities of the experience? What sorts of purposes, or which intrinsic qualities, might these be? Could purposes such as obtaining or giving sexual pleasure, or developing or displaying sexual skills, give meaning? Might experimentation and exploration, self-discovery, and even esteem or acceptance be reasons for sexual involvement that provide

⚑ ROBERT M. STEWART

meaning, or do they possibly give it value in some other way? Could it be that love and perhaps procreation are, as widely believed, the only things that give sex genuine meaning, in the final analysis? Or might it even be that the sense of meaningfulness in sexual relations (and possibly all other human activities) is essentially an illusion?

Implicit in these questions is a distinction between meaning and value.[2] While these terms are sometimes used interchangeably – and there is no reason to deny that, in one of its many senses, "meaning" is indeed the equivalent to "value" or "worth" – it is useful to contrast "value" with (other kinds or senses of) "meaning" in the present discussion. Something has value or worth, at least of the kind that concerns us here, if and to the extent that it contributes to human wellbeing, flourishing, happiness, or fulfillment. Meaning may thus be one source of value. What, then, is meaning? There are several senses of "meaning" that are relevant here. First, there is the idea of importance, significance, or what matters; this also concerns value – having a high degree of worth. Second is the idea of portending, the meaning of something is what it leads to, presumably a consequence of positive or negative importance, i.e., what something is a sign of. This relates to a third sense, meaning as purpose: what important aim or outcome activities and events might somehow be directed toward, often on a grand or even cosmic scale, perhaps as a result of collective choice or as a matter of fate, destiny, divine plan, or at least natural teleology (purpose or end). The idea of having a place or a role in, of connecting to something greater, e.g., than oneself, is implicit in this sense. And fourth, there is the notion of meaning as representation – what something signifies, expresses, or stands for. Texts, works of art and music, occurrences, actions, and even human lives might have a meaning in this fourth sense; in the latter case, biographical narrative involving an account of personal growth or decline, redemption or fall, "what a life is about," can be given, again relating to purpose and intentionality.

All of these senses of "meaning" arise in contexts of questions about meaning in life, and all involve a notion of signifying or significance, as well as the idea of some connection, typically intentional, to things of substantial value. In these senses of the term, "meaning" is not itself value but a relationship of some kind connecting with value, causal or intentional. Meanings may be either objective in the sense of involving connections that exist apart from individual ascriptions, interpretations, or intent; or subjective in that they do not have reality independent of a person's intentions or way of looking at things. All meanings are relative to some structure: any meaning presupposes a context of intentionality or causality within which it is possible. These contexts may be theoretical, linguistic, conventional, or perhaps natural, at least if we interpret nature as purposive or normative. Value judgments implicit in such structures may themselves be either objective or subjective, i.e., factually independent of the opinions of an individual or just expressive of his personal attitudes. Moreover, meanings are relative insofar as things have meaning to or for people, for some but perhaps not all.

If finding meaning thus involves interpreting natural or human events, actions, activities, and practices as intentionally or otherwise causally connected to values, then the objectivity of meaning depends on the reality of such patterns of connection. If meanings instead are the mere projections of our creative imagination – ways of seeing things devoid of factual basis – then they are to be classified as subjective. Of course, this is a simplification that ignores the various forms and different degrees of subjectivity and objectivity, but it suffices for present purposes.

Work and sexual activity are useful examples of human endeavors that can have or lack meaning. An objective meaning that work might have could consist in its contribution to some larger purpose of value to the community or to one's own personal development; sex can have meaning objectively given certain assumptions about its natural purpose or religious role. Most of the meanings ascribed to our experiences and activities are socially evolved or individually attributed, however, with no reality apart from humanly created structures. One's work can be viewed as having or lacking meaning from a personal point of view, at least for oneself, quite apart from whatever institutional good or societal benefit it might provide. Having a subjective meaning is not distinguishable from believing something meaningful, and the subjective meanings we attach to our work and other activities are often far removed from reality.

Sexual activity, as all human activities, has no given meaning in itself; rather, whatever meanings attach to it are due to the network of intentions, practices, and other cultural systems within which it occurs. Individual intent is widely variant here – sex can serve many different aims, a large subset of which could be construed as meaning-giving. Only connections of certain kinds to values of significance can provide meaning, not just any sort of connection or any possible purpose. That purposes of limited or relatively trivial sorts do not imbue activities with meaning should be apparent. We see things as meaningful only to the degree they are related to values that are important, deep, or profound. An experience might be worth having or an activity be of some value, yet not be really meaningful.

But what can be said about the character of the connection(s) giving meaning to what we do and what we experience? A detailed attempt at an answer is well beyond the scope of this essay, and it would certainly involve a very complex explanation. But one thing that seems essential is this: whether an intentional relation or some other kind of causal connection, it would appear to be one that brings us in contact with a deeper level of value in such a way that the meaningful event, activity, or experience is endowed with a greater significance than it would have had otherwise, and in such a way that the more profound value seems as if it is one of its intrinsic features. Something that might or might not have value in itself – be worth having or doing – becomes meaningful to us when we see it as connected to a realm of higher values, thereby connecting us to what is important. We tend to experience this meaning connection emotionally as well as in a cognitive capacity. Of course, something may have an objective meaning for us, but not one that we perceive or understand.

Sexual acts that lack meaning are often gratifying but not fulfilling. A feeling of emptiness and pointlessness can follow, no matter how physically satisfying as well as technically satisfactory they can be; a mere handshake could have more meaning despite being less satisfying. A meaningless sexual experience is at best like a good massage or a fine but lonely meal that has no social aspect, no sharing of love or even friendship.

We should not forget, however, that human activities can have meaning of a negative sort when what may be perceived subjectively as a connection to higher values is in fact related to things that are objectively lacking in value, even disvalues, as when perverted or otherwise unhealthy or immoral experiences and practices give a disordered individual a false sense of fulfillment. We can be mistaken about what has genuine value or meaning, just as we can be proud of shameful things. In the former case, we fail to understand what is ultimately best for human beings; in the latter, what is truly excellent. A narcissist, for instance, whose sense of superiority and entitlement is in constant need of support from others via praise, awards, admiration, and fame might feel his life to be meaningful when "enough" of these recognitions are accorded him (as if there ever can be enough). But if these forms of positive recognition are unmerited, he possesses only a pseudo self-esteem, for they hardly warrant his distorted idea of personal greatness. His sense of meaning based on such esteem would be just as false, however subjectively perceived.

Sexual practices and preferences motivated by or rooted in needs for things that are of little value, e.g., scoring and conquest, that are pursued to an extent out of proportion to their value and perhaps at great cost, or for the sake of things that cannot generally be obtained through those sorts of sexual pursuits, are likewise lacking in objective meaning, whatever one may subjectively think or feel. The perverse and unhealthy reasons for which some human beings engage in certain kinds of sexual habits and practices are varied and often complex. And there are also motivations not abnormal in themselves but taken to undue lengths and involving exaggerated desires and needs. Consider, again, a narcissist whose sexual satisfactions are based on needing to be worshipped rather than truly loved, to dominate and subordinate others, and to be constantly reassured of her attractiveness and desirability. As with a craving for repeated novelty and excitement, when taken beyond reason, these motivations cannot be a basis for meaningful sexual experience.

Meaning requires deeper relationships, which in turn demand time, energy, consideration, appreciative awareness, and, to some degree at least, emotional investment. The widespread pursuit of hook ups on college campuses today appears of a piece with other social trends toward superficiality: the diminishing level of appreciation of higher culture and scholarship even among the educated, the decline in the number of avid readers and the quality of what is read, even among students, and the "dumbing down" and vulgarizing of most things other than the scientific or technical, especially entertainment, celebrity worship, and public discourse. Much of the sexual involvement on campuses nowadays, if Wolfe is accurate, represents a fast-food standard of human interaction: we are in an age of junk sex. As physical activities go, sex has become less like yoga, with its many possibilities for spiritual meaning and higher-level consciousness, e.g., tantra, and more akin to weight-lifting. How one looks and performs are the ultimate criteria of good sexual experience. All of these developments have a common feature – the devaluation of the intellect and the spirit.

What gives human beings our special moral status among creatures is our capacity for higher-level experiences and activities. It is the source of human dignity, the basis for morality, and the *sine qua non* of meaning. The cheapening and devaluing of what can and arguably would best be experienced at higher levels – at least if it becomes the norm – degrades those who engage in the lower-level pursuit. (Compare the way in which popular versions of the classics demean both the audience and the arrangers.) But suppose one is convinced of this point – that experiences and activities that omit intellect and higher sensibilities are devoid of meaning and of less objective value – so usually to be disdained when something better is open to us. Is this any reason to condemn morally or even to avoid absolutely the lower pursuits and forms of experience?

Not by itself, perhaps, but insofar as lower-quality, less meaningful, or meaningless activities corrupt or stunt us, undermining or even destroying our capacity to enjoy the higher forms of human experience, then we have a good reason to eschew them, e.g., if our preferences for the finer and more elevated will not develop otherwise, or if we will lose our preferences for them, as drug addicts often do. Meaningless pursuits are sometimes worse than a waste of time and energy, a squandering of potential. They can dull our minds, coarsen our tastes, and make us emotionally insensitive, like the animalistic frat boys and callous jocks in Wolfe's novel. Should we indulge in them beyond a certain point, they can trivialize our lives. Obsessive devotion to making more and more money as an end in itself, acquiring greater and greater fame (or notoriety), larger and larger muscles, or higher and higher numbers in the competition of sexual scoring, ignoring the costs, are common examples of the increasingly quantitative way in which many people, oblivious to quality, spend their lives. While this is not to say that meaningless sorts of game-like endeavors should take up none of our time, at least they should not be predominant, and one ought to avoid them if there is a real chance of our (to use a much-misused word) addiction.

Meaning and Morality

This brings us to the remaining question: Is there a moral reason to prefer, in general, the meaningful things to the relatively meaningless? The philosopher John Stuart Mill (1806–73) made a famous argument in chapter II of *Utilitarianism*[3] for the rationality of generally preferring higher pleasures over lower ones on the basis of their quality – the argument being that this would be the preference of most if not all competent judges. This could also be interpreted as a case for preferring meaningful experiences over the meaningless, simply as such, in most situations. But the difficulties and shortcomings of Mill's argument are equally well known. Even assuming that competent judges would have such a preference, why does this give all of us conclusive reason to share their priorities, especially if we are not likely to become competent judges, i.e., higher, more experienced, refined, and sensitive beings ourselves? Granting that higher pleasures will be more satisfying or fulfilling to a higher being, why become one?

And were we to concede that Mill's idea of happiness, as opposed to mere contentment, represents the best in human life, the utilitarian standard of morality is not the happiness of the individual but rather the maximization of social utility. Adapting this criterion to present purposes, there is little plausibility in the notion that moral rightness is a function of the amount of meaningful experience that we directly or indirectly bring about in society.

Immanuel Kant (1724–1804), the other most influential moral philosopher of the modern period, fails in his argument against the moral acceptability of sexual acts aimed solely at one's own physical gratification, done outside the context of a loving marriage and without the intent of procreation. The categorical imperative, in its second formulation, forbids acts that do not respect all persons – oneself and others – as ends in themselves, including those that treat humans as mere means to one's own subjective ends. The very idea that there are moral duties to oneself may strike us as unacceptable, and it is doubtful that sexual acts motivated only by lower pleasure are never autonomously chosen. The assertion that such sexual acts violate the requirement to respect others similarly lacks plausibility in those instances when no one is forced, misled, or in some way emotionally manipulated into becoming a sexual partner. The possibility of giving free and rational consent to a sexual encounter that has physical pleasure as its sole reason must be admitted.[4]

But perhaps there is a different way in which sex for physical gratification alone is disrespectful to self and possibly others as well, a kind of disrespect which has no particular reference to autonomy. Wolfe's character Charlotte Simmons, a girl from a conservative rural family in the South, is crudely seduced by handsome Hoyt Thorpe; she feels complete shame and humiliation in consequence, a total worthlessness resulting from a failure to live up to her own standards and leading to a serious depression. Arguably, she was manipulated and misled by his false gestures of kindness and attention, of love and devotion, thinking he worshipped her as if she were the meaning of his life. Suppose, then, that instead she had merely been overtaken by the moment, by physical lust. Would this have been a moral failing on her part, and perhaps his as well? Or would it have been merely imprudent, a case of miscalculation and poor judgment at worst, not to be interpreted in ethical terms? This is how her friend Laurie would see it – in a more positive vein, taking a chance and learning from experience – as opposed to a reason for guilt and remorse, which only serves to amplify the badness of the situation. Attaching a moral meaning to virginity and its loss, another aspect of the religious morality with which she was raised, is at least part of the cause of the problem.

One can, however, lower oneself or another person without anyone being "used" in the usual moral sense. It undermines not only self-esteem but also self-respect if we allow ourselves to sink to certain kinds of sexual acts with unworthy partners, and it shows a lack of respect for those whom we entice. This need have nothing to do with autonomy; rather, it expresses a lack of respect for humans as capable of higher-quality, more meaningful experiences, and more importantly, may disregard that some people are better than others, or that not just anyone should be given the gift of our physical intimacy, however pleasurable it might be for a time. We need not say that sex of this sort is morally wrong in the sense of being unjust, violating a right, or failing to carry out a duty. But it is a serious failure of character and judgment evincing a lack of concern for excellence and value.

A broader, eudaimonistic (happiness or flourishing) conception of the ethical as found in Aristotle's (384–322 BC) theory and Friedrich Nietzsche's (1844–1900) philosophy of value, in contrast to more Judeo-Christian notions of morality's object and scope as expressed in either the principle of utility by Mill or the categorical imperative by Kant, allows for a better account of moral reasons for avoiding some kinds of sexual activities and strongly preferring others. This is not about the meaning of "moral reason" so much as what amounts to a rationally compelling reason, one with considerable weight. And what could be a stronger, more important reason than that a kind of activity connects to, or fails to support, or worse, undermines, our pursuit of higher values? The virtues as understood by the Greeks, such as Aristotle, are traits of the body, intellect, or (moral) character that tend, at least under normal conditions, to benefit those who exemplify them. They are among the most excellent things in life, essential to living happily. These excellences relate to higher values – particularly the virtues of mind – and so have aspects of meaning.

Respect and Higher Value

Respect is a matter of how people are regarded or treated by others or by themselves. Self-esteem amounts to confidence based on our accurate judgments about our excellence or worth in various dimensions of comparison (e.g., as professionals, as parents, as friends, as drivers, and many others), including these two forms of respect. When we lose the respect of others, often our self-respect, and in turn, our self-esteem, suffers. Recall how Charlotte Simmons feels herself worthless after succumbing to Hoyt; though understandable, her loss is out of proportion to what actually happened. Losing the respect or the esteem of ignorant or worthless people is not such a terrible thing unless they have some other ability to harm us. Nevertheless, it is often difficult to ignore, if only because it can lead us to question the accuracy of our own judgments of our worth – is our self-esteem too high or false? – and even the need to respect ourselves. (This is, of course, one of the reasons we need true friends, who can offer us legitimate assessments of our good and bad traits and acts, based on their knowledge, shared proper standards, and common basic interests.)

Normally, to degrade, demean, or abuse others, especially in the intimate context of sexual relations, is to inflict on them a considerable injury. The degradation of others (including taking advantage of those on their own downward spiral), then, is something we morally ought to avoid out of a respect for their potential as well as a regard for our own dignity. We need not love or befriend or even like or admire others – let alone believe in equality of human potential – to have moral respect.

There is, further, the matter of respecting the higher values themselves, as things we should want to have and to appreciate in ourselves and in our lives. We must not denigrate them as human ideals. Yet we often do so when we reject them in favor of pursuing things that are less valuable and less meaningful. The assumption that there are higher values cannot be justified here, if in fact a defense is either necessary or possible. There is also some room for disagreement about exactly what values are higher and so potentially bestow objective meaning. By and large, however, reflective and intelligent people with experience of life tend to agree, at least when dubious religious or metaphysical convictions do not factor into the discussion.

Making Love Meaningfully

Returning to the central topic of sexuality, we should be able to agree that mere physical pleasure and tension release, though desirable in itself, is not a higher value that can give meaning, nor in general is a display of skill, power, or domination in this context. Procreation could in general give meaning to sexual intercourse, but only if we make optimistic assumptions about the value of our species continuing into the future

‡‡ ROBERT M. STEWART

and of the life offspring are likely to lead. Sexperimentation might or might not involve higher values, depending on the knowledge one seeks; self-knowledge of a deeper kind could certainly be a higher value. Raising one's own self-esteem or expressing esteem for another through sexual contact could relate to higher values, since these aims concern self-love and love of another person; it is a matter of the details. Social acceptance or gaining the esteem of others per se is not usually a motive relating to higher values, at least not directly or necessarily. Wolfe's novel offers painful illustrations of how nothing more than a false, subjective meaning could come from what is merely a boost in false self-esteem from hooking up with the "right" partners in the estimation of those with corrupt values. Love, provided that it is healthy and grounded in accurate assessment, is not the only value that can give true (objective) meaning to sexual relations, but it is surely the most significant.

Finally, if having meaning in what we do and experience is a matter of leading to and/or expressing higher values, as argued, it should be clear on reflection that it does not depend on human life as a whole having meaning. Parts of a larger whole may be meaningful even though the whole has no meaning itself. This is something to keep in mind when purveyors of religious or "spiritual" (e.g., New Age) or messianic political doctrines tell us that without belief in their system there is nothing for which to live. At least for the more fortunate among us, there is considerable meaning to be found in our lives quite apart from any cosmic purpose or possible future existence, if we are wise enough not to sacrifice higher values for the lower ones.

NOTES

1 Tom Wolfe, *Hooking Up* (New York: Picador, 2001) and *I Am Charlotte Simmons: A Novel* (New York: Picador, 2005).
2 My account has been influenced by the work of H. P. Grice on meaning, beginning with his seminal article "Meaning," *Philosophical Review* 66 (1957): 377–88; also by Robert Nozick's account of meaning in his books *Philosophical Explanations* (New York: Basic Books, 1983) and *The Examined Life* (New York: Simon and Schuster, 1990).
3 John Stuart Mill, *Utilitarianism* (Indianapolis: Hackett, 2002), p. 6.
4 See Kant's *Groundwork of the Metaphysics of Morals*, trans. Mary Gregor (Cambridge: Cambridge University Press, 1998), and *Lectures on Ethics*, trans. Peter Heath (Cambridge: Cambridge University Press, 1997).

CHAPTER 15

CAN GIRLS GO WILD WITH SELF-RESPECT?[1]

Naked Women and Cheering Men

In her recent book *Female Chauvinist Pigs: Women and the Rise of Raunch Culture*, Ariel Levy describes the multitude of women willing to bare their breasts, drop their pants, and simulate sex with other women on camera for a "Girls Gone Wild" T-shirt and a few moments of fame.[2] One participant explains, "The body is such a beautiful thing ... if a woman's got a pretty body and she likes her body, let her show it off! It exudes confidence when people wear little clothes."[3] Even so, it seems worth noting that this form of free expression is typically accompanied by shouts of "show your tits," "show your ass," and "take it off." At risk of sounding uptight, I find this behavior troubling. Let me be clear. The body *is* a beautiful thing, and there's nothing inherently wrong with nudity (even public nudity). Since women are capable of making their own decisions, they should be allowed to expose themselves to other adults if they like. But going wild for the camera threatens to undercut a woman's self-respect.

Consider another illustration. Meghan Daum writes that "the raunchy contests and general debauchery [of Spring Break in Cancun] were something that these women had prepared for, almost as though for a final exam. They'd logged hours at the gym, in tanning booths and at body wax salons. They'd saved up money for breast implants and then timed the surgery so they'd be healed by spring break."[4] Whatever else might be said of them, these women are motivated. They want a particular type of body and the popularity that goes along with it. At one level, it even makes sense. Who doesn't want to look good in a swimsuit? But while I admire their discipline, I worry that these women lack an important aspect of self-respect. It is unclear, for example, whether they (or the men cheering them on) have thought about whether they ought to endorse social norms that valorize hyper-sexualized debauchery. Moreover, I'm concerned that some of these women derive their sense of self-worth from these displays and as a result they are selling themselves short.

This essay explores several forms of sexual expression and what they might tell us about self-respect in the developing and transitional lives of college students. I should caution, however, that there's little consensus in the philosophical literature on the nature of self-respect. Robin Dillon, for example, argues:

> There's good reason for the absence of settled opinion about something so widely regarded as morally quite important. For what makes self-respect a theoretically useful concept is also what makes it hard to pin down: it is embedded in a nexus of such profound and profoundly problematic concepts as personhood, rights, equality, justice, agency, autonomy, character, integrity, identity, and the good life.[5]

My goal is to motivate the importance of several features of self-respect and use these to help us understand what might be troublesome about young women going wild.

Self-Respect and Self-Conscious Reflection

Thomas Hill captures one powerful argument for the importance of self-respect.[6] He argues that our value as persons is grounded in our ability to organize our lives in meaningful ways. A person should be allowed to decide whether to go to school, join the army, start a family, or spend her nights hooking up with random strangers. Our worth as persons stems from our ability to give our lives some shape and direction. There is something intuitively troubling about a person not recognizing this fact. Hill illustrates with reference to a deferential housewife willing to acquiesce to her husband's every wish. As Hill describes her:

She buys the clothes *he* prefers, invites the guests *he* wants to entertain, and makes love whenever *he* is in the mood. She willingly moves to a new city in order for him to have a more attractive job, counting her own friendships and geographical preferences insignificant by comparison. She does not simply defer to her husband in certain spheres as a trade-off for his deference in other spheres. On the contrary, she tends not to form her own interests, values, and ideals; and, when she does, she counts them as less important than her husband's.[7]

Hill is careful to distinguish between a woman who self-consciously decides to stay with a domineering man (say, because she calculates that life will be better for her children if she does) from someone who always defers to her husband without knowing why or because she's internalized a set of values that diminishes the status of women. Hill's deferential housewife falls into the latter category. She is not utterly unreflective. She has given thought to how best to prepare the food her husband likes, satisfy him sexually, and raise their children according to his standards. As Hill describes the case, however, the deferential housewife does not have values, interests, and ideals of her own. She has not considered, for example, how to construct a relationship that satisfies her sexual needs or even whether a healthy sexual life is something that she ought to want. More generally, she lacks self-respect because she does not recognize her ability to organize her life and make it meaningful.

We can glean the following lessons from Hill's account. First, if a person is to acknowledge her worth as a person, then she must seek to organize her life in meaningful ways. Second, self-respect requires reflecting on one's life in a way that allows one to take ownership over one's "values, interests, and ideals." This is more than mere practical reasoning concerning how to obtain what she thinks she wants, but it also requires reflecting upon whether these are things that she ought to want. Hill's deferential housewife fails to meet these conditions, perhaps because women's lives have historically been scripted in such a way that becoming subservient to men may seem like a foregone conclusion. A woman may decide to devote her life to her family and she may even choose to favor her husband's sexual interests over her own, but if she is to have self-respect, then she must take ownership over these "values, interests, and ideals" through self-conscious reflection. Harry Frankfurt sums up the challenge this way:

Taking ourselves seriously means that we are not prepared to accept ourselves just as we come. We want our thoughts, our feelings, our choices, and our behavior to make sense. We are not satisfied to think that our ideas are formed haphazardly, or that our actions are driven by transient and opaque impulses or mindless decisions. We need to direct ourselves – or at any rate *believe* that we are directing ourselves – in thoughtful conformity to stable and appropriate norms. We want to get things right.[8]

Taking ourselves seriously (or having respect for our self-worth) requires not simply doing what others are doing because they are doing it or living according to whatever values are in the air because they happen to be in the air. A self-respecting person should be able to look in the mirror and say, "This is not just some life that I happen to be living, it is *my* life." People aren't expected to start from scratch. It is quite natural that they will draw on an existing stock of norms. However, a person's life is made meaningful when she decides whether or not to endorse these values as her own and incorporate them into her own self-conception.

Reasons and Self-Conceptions

College is typically seen as a time for soul searching and forming one's own identity. Students come to campus already shaped by their upbringing. Their choices in fashion and music, for example, are informed by their background. Yet, becoming one's own person requires crafting one's own sense of style. Coming from a "buttoned up" family with restrictive views about nudity may explain why someone is reluctant to go skinny dipping in a lake, but students need not continue to share their parents' values. Upon reflection, a student may decide that there's nothing wrong with ditching her clothes and swimming out to the middle of the lake by moonlight. Her parents would disapprove, but it might nonetheless be fun, refreshing, and even liberating. In forming her own self-conception, she ought to decide for herself whether this is something that she ought to do. Not every action can or should be meticulously considered, but a person should take owner-ship of her life by reflecting on what she values and why.

While college is a time for self-creation, it is also often seen as an oppor-tunity to drink one's self silly. At many schools, a student's BAC (blood alcohol content) is at least as important as her GPA. Students have been known to spend a good deal of time thinking about what sort of alcohol to buy, how to pay for it, and what sort of drink will give the biggest buzz in the shortest amount of time and at the lowest cost. Many students also hope for the notoriety that comes from being able to drink their friends under the table. To be successful, students will need to consider how best to achieve this goal. However, this form of reflection differs from considering whether being the last drunk standing is actually worth striving for.

Given that binge drinking has historically been part and parcel of the college experience, many students may not think to question the wisdom of this activity. As we've seen, however, a self-respecting person does not mindlessly internalize existing norms, but reflects upon whether they are worth endorsing. Such a person might consider the various pitfalls associated with binge drinking. These could range from the embarrassment that comes from finding drunken pictures floating in cyberspace to the much more serious dangers of drunk driving. There is nothing inherently wrong with drinking and surely people can learn to drink responsibly. Far from haphazardly internalizing a collegiate norm, a self-reflective student might consider how drinking figures into his life and conclude that drinking is worth doing while remaining mindful of both the dangers and the need to carefully balance his drinking with his other pursuits. This discussion points to a third feature of self-respect, namely, responsiveness to reasons. In deciding which values to endorse and which actions to pursue, he will weigh the advantages and disadvantages of each. When the evidence is in, he will evaluate his behavior accordingly.

Standards and the Freedom to be Foolish

Not everyone will consider the consequences of their actions or listen to the reasons favoring one course of action over another. There's even something perversely admirable about a person willing to do anything on a dare (e.g., chugging all of last night's half-empty beer cups, running completely naked across a football field, or performing sexual favors for the next person coming through a door). While different people will draw different lines in different places, we should be concerned about a person who is unwilling to draw any lines at all. It seems unlikely that such a person has developed a consistent set of values or core sense of self. Like Hill's deferential housewife, she seems willing to take her direction from others. The self-respecting person, by contrast, has given some thought to the course of her life and the values that underwrite its meaning. When a particular course of action conflicts with one of her core values, she is prepared to say, "There are just some things that I won't do."[9] This discussion points to a fourth feature of self-respect, namely, forming and adhering to one's personal standards.

In "Self-Respect Reconsidered," Hill argues that even a self-reflective person can lose his self-respect if he fails to maintain high standards.[10] He illustrates this point with reference to a waitress willing to become a prostitute in order to pursue other ends. Unlike the deferential housewife, the waitress-turned-prostitute reflects on and organizes the details of her life, but Hill suggests that she lacks self-respect because she's sold herself short. She may be attempting to make the best of a bad situation. Because of enormous debt or her desire to succeed in school, she may decide to accept pay for sex. In deciding to lower her standards, however, she also accepts a situation in which she risks serious bodily injury, risks damaging her future sexual relationships, and allows her body to be seen as a mere tool for male sexual gratification. There may be nothing inherently wrong with prostitution. The waitress-turned-prostitute may have reflectively considered whether this is something that she ought to want, but Hill believes that she has mistakenly allowed her standards to fall too low.

Consider another illustration. Imagine a young college freshman coming to campus full of enthusiasm. He wants to set the world on fire or at least to learn a language, travel the world, write a novel, and find the time to prepare for medical school with the eventual goal of caring for the urban poor. It is probably the case that his goals are a bit lofty and unlikely to be fulfilled in four years. Upon reflection, he may decide to change his views and lower his standards in light of the need to find part-time employment and succeed in the rigors of college life. He hasn't sold himself short. Rather, he has revised his expectations in light of the available evidence. He need not give up his other goals, but he may decide that preparing for medical school is his top priority and consequently devotes himself to spending time in the library. Now suppose that our aspiring medical student decides to take a break from his studies to spend some time drinking with his friends. This is a perfectly reasonable thing to do. But if he starts drinking the night before a big exam, then we might begin to question his judgment or perhaps his commitment to his studies. After a semester or two of falling grades, we can imagine a close friend pulling him aside to say, "I remember when you were a freshman. All you talked about was going to medical school. Your teachers said you were really talented, but now you never go to class. What do you think you're doing?"

Friends can help us make sense of our lives by holding up the mirror of self-reflection. They can give voice to what we often fail to see in ourselves, namely, that we've allowed our standards to fall too low. They can remind us of our values, interests, and ideals. Our aspiring medical student may have been systematically deceiving himself about his situation or he may have lacked the wherewithal to live according to his professed goals. It is also possible that after careful reflection, he decides to give up his former ideals and embrace the life of a barfly. However, like Hill's waitress-turned-prostitute, he is capable of a great deal more and has sold himself short. His friends speak out because they know he is walking down a foolish path. Once a friend has said her piece, however, there may be little more that she can do. Sometimes we choose wisely and sometimes we don't. Since friends cannot live our lives for us, they must stand back and watch us make our own mistakes (even foolish ones). Respecting a person's ability to give her life shape and meaning can sometimes require respecting her freedom to be foolish. This discussion points to the fifth feature of self-respect, the willingness to accept the possibility of error and the corresponding willingness to live with the consequences.

Can Girls Go Wild With Self-Respect?

There seem to be plenty of women willing to take it all off for strange men and engage in the raunchy displays captured on "Girls Gone Wild" videos and jumbo screens in Cancun. There's nothing inherently wrong with public nudity or women deciding to perform for men. Under the right conditions, women could do either of these with self-respect. I worry, however, that some of these women are going wild without considering whether pandering to hollering crowds is something that they ought to want. There is some concern that they have internalized unhealthy expectations and unconsciously tied their sense of self-worth to fulfilling them. Mistakes happen, but if they have failed to reflect or respond to available reasons, then they have sold themselves short. But what's so troubling about women going wild?

First, the producers of "Girls Gone Wild" videos and organizers of spring break festivities give the impression that they are documenting ordinary women feeling the urge to be spontaneous. It is true that the behavior depicted isn't strictly scripted, but the displays fall into highly predictable patterns. Moreover, the level of cheering, baiting, and cajoling suggests that this is more than ordinary women deciding to be playful on a whim. There is some degree of manipulation at work.

Second, DVDs and cell phone videos serve as a visual record of a woman's decision to go wild. Women should be concerned that these will be found by parents, potential employers, or even grandchildren.

Of course, if "she's got a pretty body," then she might be able to look back on them with some satisfaction. It is less clear whether the same can be said of the ever-escalating displays of lewdness. Video evidence reminds us that these activities come at some cost. Like the dangers associated with binge drinking, they are costs that ought to be counted.

Third, producers give the impression that the women on display are eye candy to be consumed. I worry that this feeds into sexist stereotypes suggesting that a woman's worth lies in how she looks. In its strongest form, the criticism suggests that the women depicted in these videos are being treated as mere commodities that are useful only insofar as they have the power to satisfy male sexual desires. The philosopher Immanuel Kant (1724–1804), for example, distinguishes between dignity and price.[11] The latter value applies to items that can be bought, sold, traded, and thrown away when they are no longer useful. The former value applies to human beings, which, unlike commodities, are inherently valuable and beyond compare. The strong criticism suggests that the hyper-sexualization of women has contributed to the perception that they are merely objects to be used and then discarded. This perception and the actions that flow from it are wrong because they fail to respect the basic dignity of women.

In a weaker form, the criticism suggests the characterization of women in these videos is too one-dimensional. Women are not depicted as fun-loving people who also have intense interests in poetry, engineering, and intricate public policy questions. It is their sexuality, and only their sexuality, that is on display. While there is nothing wrong with being sexual or being seen as sexual, there's cause for concern when a woman's sexuality eclipses her other noteworthy features. The concern is not that women are sexual creatures, but that they have sold themselves short if they fail to appreciate the many other things they have to offer. The same can be said of men who have mindlessly internalized a one-dimensional view of a woman's worth and seem all too eager to encourage its propagation.

Fourth, the "Girls Gone Wild" culture promotes a shallow conception of feminine beauty. Consider the narrow range of body types on display. It is not as if ordinary women of all shapes and sizes are flashing their natural endowments. Rather, the producers are "looking for tens.... You know, 100 to 110 pounds, big boobs, blonde, blue eyes, ideally no piercing or tattoos."[12] They are tapping into a set of cultural norms that promote an unrealistic and consequently unhealthy standard of beauty. Because not everyone can conform, many women will enter the arms race of diets, beauty products, and plastic surgery. Because no woman can maintain this body type forever, she will eventually fail to measure up. This would be far less troubling if we as a society could recognize the absurdity of these standards. The worry, however, is that men and women unconsciously equate a woman's worth with her ability to conform. And there is the added worry that the women who are perpetually dedicated to approximating these standards will find themselves living an unbalanced life in which tanning and exercise push out their education and interpersonal relationships.

Fifth, the rise of raunch culture risks promoting an unhealthy model of sexual relationships. There is something peculiar, for example, about men passively consuming displays of female sexuality. This is not a model of mutual and reciprocal engagement. Rather, women perform. Men watch. It makes little room for any discussion of female desire. While women might derive some satisfaction from knowing that they are the object of sexual interest, there isn't a sense of give and take. Or to the extent that there is an exchange between the participants, it is he saying "take it off" and she deciding whether and how to comply. This does not send the message that women and men are equal partners in sexual encounters, but threatens to reinforce old stereotypes encouraging women to serve their men.

Note the contrast with other forms of exhibitionism. Skinny dipping, for example, is joint activity in which men and women share similar goals (swimming and revelry) and occupy similar positions (everyone is naked). There's no push to be as raunchy as a person possibly can and there are fewer opportunities for women to pander to screaming men. Skinny dipping typically occurs among friends and lovers, but the size of the group is irrelevant. Alternatively, we might imagine thousands of people marching naked through the city. This might be a collective act of protest or a simple expression of camaraderie. Like skinny dipping, there is common participation in a mutual goal. While superficially similar to women going wild, skinny dipping and naked marches do not promote the same kind of unhealthy sexual relationships because they do not reinforce power asymmetries or the objectification of women.

None of these considerations are conclusive, but they do suggest that women should think carefully about whether they ought to want to bare their breasts, drop their pants, or simulate sex with other women for a crowd of cheering onlookers. Men should think carefully about what screaming "take it off" says about their values, interests, and ideals.

It is possible for a woman to go wild with self-respect. I can imagine a self-confident woman who quite consciously decides to take a walk on the wild side. She retains the right to forgo any activity that violates her personal standards or conflicts with her considered values. She may live to regret the choice, but she is aware of the various pitfalls just described.

For example, having spent several years as nude model for art classes on campus, she is prepared to live with visual representations of her nakedness. Though a raunchy video is not the same as an artistic endeavor, she hopes it will stand as a testament to her adventurous spirit. If her body happens to conform to conventional standards of beauty, she might be delighted by the prospect of being considered a "hottie." If not, she may enjoy exposing her older, larger, or more ordinary brand of nakedness. Either way, she doesn't equate her sense of self-worth with her physical attributes, and she will not give up other worthy pursuits in search of unrealistic standards of beauty. Moreover, she is not unduly influenced by jeering men. She performs, but she does so on her own terms. She might even use the immaturity of men to her advantage and think "if showing my tits will get me free stuff, then I'm okay with that." She recognizes that this is a warped form of sexual engagement, and she is well aware of the fact that healthier forms exist. She may dabble in this peculiar brand of sexuality, but she doesn't believe that it is the source of meaningful interpersonal engagement.

Most importantly, this adventurous woman has reflected upon whether going wild is something that she ought to want. She concludes that a wild evening or two will not affect the core of who she is as person. She is willing to go wild responsibly and live with the consequences. She is reflective about her values and consistently adheres to her personal standards. Further, she derives her sense of worth from her ability to direct her life accordingly. I can't know how many of the women going wild on camera or on spring break actually share the adventurous woman's sense of self-worth, but I do hope to have shown what features must be present for a woman to go wild with self-respect.

Thoughtful Sexuality

My goal is not to endorse sexual repression or offer an unduly narrow conception of acceptable sexual expression. To the contrary, any adequate account of college sexuality will need to allow for a wide variety of personal expression, including public nudity. College life is about book learning, but it is also a time for experimentation and self-creation. My aim is to encourage all of us to be thoughtful about how we choose to express ourselves and this includes how we express ourselves sexually. It is not enough to adhere mindlessly to cultural norms or haphazardly accept some standard of behavior. Rather, we come into our own as people when we decide which values we ought to endorse and why. Self-respecting people are responsive to reasons and willing to alter their values, interests, and ideals when the evidence suggests that they should do so. Despite our best efforts, we sometimes sell ourselves short. Mistakes happen. When they do, a self-respecting person will hold himself accountable. However, it is also the case that some consequences can be foreseen and some values shown to be unhealthy. This underlines the importance of self-reflection. A person's sense of self-worth and her ability to live a meaningful life is tied to this capacity. Given the rise of raunch culture, women (and men) must decide whether such displays are in keeping with their values, interests, and ideals. It is far from clear that this is something that women (and men) ought to want. If a woman has any hope of going wild with self-respect, she must consider the question, take ownership of the choice, and be willing to live with the consequences.

NOTES

1 Thanks are owed to Kimberly Blessing, Julian Cole, Bethany Delecki-Earns, and Jason Grinnell for their comments on previous drafts.
2 Ariel Levy, *Female Chauvinist Pigs: Women and the Rise of Raunch Culture* (New York: Free Press, 2005).
3 Ibid., p. 9.
4 Meghan Daum, "Rauch is Rebranded as 'Confidence,'" *Los Angeles Times*, March 15, 2008, available online at www.articles.latimes.com/2008/mar/15/opinion/oe-daum15 (accessed July 29, 2009).
5 Robin Dillon, "Introduction," in Robin Dillon (ed.) *Dignity, Character, Self-Respect* (New York: Routledge, 1995), pp. 2–3.
6 Thomas Hill, "Servility and Self-Respect," in *Autonomy and Self-Respect* (Cambridge: Cambridge University Press, 1991), pp. 4–24.
7 Ibid., p. 5.
8 Harry Frankfurt, *Taking Ourselves Seriously and Getting it Right* (Stanford: Stanford University Press, 2006), p. 2.
9 For further discussion of this point, see Lynne McFall, "Integrity," *Ethics* 98 (1987): 5–20.
10 Thomas Hill, "Self-Respect Reconsidered" in *Autonomy and Self Respect*, pp. 19–24.
11 Immanuel Kant, *Grounding for the Metaphysics of Morals*, trans. James W. Ellington (Indianapolis: Hackett, 1993).
12 Levy, *Female Chauvinist Pigs*, p. 13.

CHAPTER 16

MUTUAL RESPECT
AND SEXUAL MORALITY

How to Have College Sex Well

Sexual Morality is a Required Course

One nice thing about college is that you will probably have the opportunity to have lots of sex. Sex
is great. Enjoy it. But while you're doing it, put in
some time and effort to make your college years a
period of morally positive growth and sexually fulfilling development. I offer the following reflections on mutually respectful sexual interaction in
the hope that my insights will prove useful to col-
lege students of many philosophical and sexual stripes. I hope my essay
will illuminate your own thinking about sexual morality, but that is all
I can accomplish here, so don't treat this essay as a college student's
exhaustive or definitive manual to sex or sexual morality. When I talk
about sex, I mean the vast range of possible interactions and relationships between human beings – however rare, weird, gross, brief, or tenu-
ous – that arouse and satisfy someone's sex drive. It isn't actually relevant
to my discussion whether your individual notion of sex is heterosexual
petting and kissing with your steady girl or guy, bisexual heavy flogging
and anal fisting with a group of friends, or homosexual hula-hooping in
a tub of green Jell-O with a perfect stranger. My message is that many of
the sexual activities, interactions, and relationships a college student
might have the opportunity to enjoy can be morally right but that sex

poses serious moral quandaries for all of us and that we must address these difficulties before we have the right to enjoy ourselves sexually.

Morality and Sexuality

As a philosopher, I regard human self-consciousness and freedom as fundamental to all other sorts of consciousness. In other words, I believe that our awareness of other things and other people depends on an immediate awareness of ourselves as thinking and active. From a moral perspective, I identify humanity with its free capacity to conceive and will its own goals. Unlike non-sentient or non-selfconscious organic and synthetic things (such as carrots, amoebas, bicycles, and computers), human beings freely determine their own goals (choose and plan what they want to be or to accomplish in the future) and freely will those goals (act to realize their concepts of the future). Thus, because human beings freely determine and will their own goals, they have dignity (or priceless worth as ends in themselves) as opposed to organic and synthetic things that have a price value (for which they might be bought and sold as mere means to an end).

A succinct, simplified account of my approach to morality would run as follows: first, human beings are free, so they have dignity; second, human beings have dignity, so they deserve respect; and third, human beings deserve respect, so they should always treat themselves and others with respect. We should eschew actions that undermine human freedom and dignity – and we should engage in actions that promote human freedom and dignity – in ourselves and in others. Instinctive, or common-sense, notions of basic human decency also suggest that all human relations – even the sexual relations between college students – should involve mutually respectful interactions.

We become familiar with our common human dignity by engaging in interactions with others that display mutual respect for our common human freedom. Some actions regarding ourselves and others preclude mutual respect. Manipulating (with lies or other deceptions) or coercing (with physical or psychological force) another person to perform an action she would not otherwise perform could not promote mutual respect. Seizing or damaging another person's things without his permission, or imprisoning or injuring his body, or attempting to control his psyche, would be disrespectful of his humanity. We would show no respect for ourselves if we compromised the freedom of our thoughts and deeds or sacrificed the integrity of our possessions, bodies, and minds. Mutual respect also requires some actions regarding ourselves and others. Helping (with tangible or intangible charity) or encouraging (with advice or persuasion) another to pursue her personally or humanly needful interests and to realize her morally obligatory goals would support mutual respect. Treating another person's possessions, body, or mind with consideration or benevolence is respectful of his humanity. We should show the same respect for ourselves by using our talents and other resources to their full potential and by caring for our possessions, bodies, and minds.

Your sexual interaction with others is one of many social contexts that you'll experience in college wherein you will come to know yourself as a human being, so your sexual interactions are not morally neutral ground. Our perceptions of ourselves and others as human beings are profoundly influenced by the integration of sexuality within our lives. Sex expresses our individual humanity, but not all sexual interactions involve mutual respect for our humanity. Some reflect an attempt to manipulate or coerce another person without promoting her dignity and freedom or to use another as a mere means without deferring to his humanity. We should avoid sexual actions that undermine human freedom and dignity – and we should engage in sexual actions that promote human freedom and dignity – in ourselves and others. Basic human decency also suggests that human sexual relations should involve mutually respectful sexual interaction.

Some sexual actions concerning ourselves and others exclude the possibility of mutual respect. Mutual respect also requires us to do certain things in our sexual interactions. Coercing another person to perform a sexual action he would not otherwise perform (e.g., by deceiving, manipulating, or drugging him) can't promote mutual respect. Sexually using another person without her permission (e.g., using bodily threat or force when she is unwilling to offer her sexual favors and having sex with her when she is too mentally or physically incapacitated to offer sexual favors) is disrespectful to her humanity. Engaging in sexual activities that pose significant risks to anyone's health and life (because we have not taken due precautions against disease or injury, because we are too incapacitated to exercise due prudence, or because the activities are inherently and unduly hazardous) or engaging in sexual activities that pose significant risk of pregnancy (because we have not taken due contraceptive precaution) for which we are unable or unwilling to take responsibility does wrong to ourselves and others. We show neither regard nor respect for ourselves if we fail to safeguard our consensual participation in sexual activities or to protect ourselves from physical and mental injury in our sexual activities. Helping or encouraging others to realize their personally and humanly needful goals or their morally obligatory goals while engaging in sexual activity supports mutual respect. Treating others' bodies or minds with consideration or benevolence while engaging in sexual activity is respectful of their humanity. We should show the same regard and respect for ourselves by caring for our bodies and minds within the sexual context.

Criteria of Mutually Respectful Sexual Interaction

Mutual respect requires that sexual partners give explicit, or at least implicit, expression of their voluntary participation in the sexual act. Additionally, it demands that each sexual partner exhibits concern for the other's interests and needs insofar as their wellbeing includes and extends beyond their sexual wellbeing. Finally, it compels that each sexual partner attend to the other's desires.

Reciprocal consent means that each partner shows that he chooses to engage in particular sexual activities with a particular partner at a particular time. It is necessary for mutual respect because without someone's indication that she is a willing sexual partner, we have every reason to suspect that she is the unwilling sexual victim of some compulsion or coercion. Reciprocal concern means that each partner demonstrates regard for his partner's personal, human, and moral wellbeing. It is essential for mutual respect because we cannot separate our sexuality from our personality, humanity, or general interests and needs. Without some evidence of each partner's consideration for the other's interests and needs, we have grounds for thinking that the sexual interaction could undermine at least one partner's wellbeing. Reciprocal desire means that each partner expresses complementary expectations and goals for her sexual interaction and that each partner attempts to satisfy those expectations and goals within her sexual interaction. It is necessary for mutual respect because sex without desire results in sensual or emotional dissatisfaction at best and physical or psychological trauma at worst.

We must communicate with our partner in order to assure that reciprocal consent, concern, and desire exist. Communication of consent, concern, and desire could be fairly direct, explicit, and specific or it could be fairly indirect, implicit, and vague. For example, you might say to some enticing somebody, "My, you're delicious; I'd love to jump your lovely bones right now" and this appealing, consenting partner might reply, "You're pretty scrumptious yourself: the condoms are in the bathroom." As you and your delightful partner begin to interact, he might suggest "I'm just crazy about giving oral sex," and you might respond desirously, "My favorite: enjoy." In the course of things, you might murmur, "This is so much fun, but I promised to help my friend with his homework tonight and I've got an early class tomorrow" and your concerned fellow enthusiast might exclaim "Aw, that's too bad: Maybe we can continue where we left off after your class tomorrow. Say, do you like green Jell-O?" Of course, many communications of consent, concern, and desire are not as clearly evident. You can probably imagine how this same series of communications could have been achieved more subtly. The issue is not how the communication was achieved, but that each partner possessed a reasonable, conscientious belief that reciprocal consent, concern, and desire existed.

Achieving mutually respectful sexual interaction would be easy if there were some fail-safe, trouble-free method for obtaining a reasonable, conscientious belief that reciprocal consent, concern, and desire existed. Unfortunately, there are no fail-safe, trouble-free methods. We can sometimes be uncertain about our own volition, needs, interests, and desires, so we can never be certain about our sexual partner's. Moreover, admiration, affection, or even love for a sexual partner fails to guarantee reciprocal consent, concern, and desire. We have only indicators, more or less precise, and signs, more or less ambiguous, to guide our deeds, which, ultimately, we must judge before the rational tribunal of our conscience. Despite these difficulties, we are morally obliged to make a strong effort to solicit, recognize, and interpret compelling evidence of our sexual partner's volition, interests, and desires.

Does this obligation imply that sexual partners must sign a legally binding contract that specifies their desires and expectations, describes their intended activities, and states their voluntary participation prior to every sexual interaction? No. Moreover, no legal contract could provide certain assurance of a partner's consent, concern, and desire. Does this obligation entail that a sexual partner must accommodate his partner's every sexual whim or devote every iota of his energy to making his partner personally, humanly, and morally fulfilled? No. Moreover, no effort could guarantee a partner's fulfillment. There are no certain assurances or guarantees, but there are ways to increase the possibility of reciprocal consent, concern, and desire. We can try to learn as much about our partner as possible by communicating with her about sexual desires, general interests, and other subjects. This reduces the chance of miscommunications and misunderstandings with our partner. We can take time to gain some sexual knowledge of our partner by proceeding cautiously and unhurriedly in the initial stages of a sexual relationship. This increases the chance of correctly interpreting and addressing expressions of consent, expectation, and desire. Before, during, and after sexual interactions, we can solicit more explicit, specific expressions of our partner's thoughts and feelings; observe our partner's reactions carefully; and reflect diligently on what we hear and see. This enhances the possibility of reciprocal consent, concern, and desire while improving our sexual technique and our opportunity for a repeat performance (or maybe even the addition of a hula-hoop or two).

An additional way of keeping sexually charged relationships and inter-actions in moral perspective is to compare them to analogous non-sexual relationships and interactions. If you were intoxicated, ill, distraught, exhausted, or if your capacity to choose and to communicate were other-wise compromised, would you think that you consented for someone to borrow your car or debit card simply because you left your keys or purse readily accessible? Probably not. Thus, you should probably question a sexual partner's consent if his capacity to choose and communicate is somehow impaired. For example, when the new-found object of your desires gets food-poisoning, flunks his physics exam, and spends the rest of the afternoon crying and drinking shots, you should probably put him to bed rather than take him to bed.

If you were involved in a relationship or interaction that served the other participant's needs and interests but undermined your wellbeing, would you believe that she was concerned about you? Most likely not. Thus, you should most likely doubt your own concern for a partner if your sexual relationship or interaction seems to undermine their needs and interests. For example, when aspects of your sexual relationship and interactions lead your main squeeze to neglect his studies, lose interest in the things that matter to him, abuse drugs, or tell lies, you should most likely change those aspects of your relationship or change sexual part-ners. If someone begged, threatened, pestered, bribed, or cajoled you into doing something for her that you didn't appear eager to do, would you consider that your expectations and desires had been addressed? Surely not. Thus, you should surely suspect that your partner's expecta-tions and desires were disregarded if you begged, threatened, pestered, bribed, or cajoled him into doing something sexual for you that he didn't appear eager to do. For example, when you express expectations and desires for things – like marriage, or anal sex, or green Jell-O – that your sexual buddy can't or won't give you or when your sexual partner never asks you for sex, tries to avoid sex, or seems ambiguous about their enjoyment of sex, you should surely revise your notion of what each of you is willing and able to do, have a thorough discussion about how each of you can better satisfy the other, or get out of that relationship.

Moral Issues Associated with Specific Sexual Relationships and Activities

Many seemingly innocuous activities could violate the criteria of reciprocal consent, concern, and desire, whereas many seemingly harmful activities could satisfy the standard of mutually respectful sex. In short, few sexual activities need preclude reciprocal consent, concern, and desire, but any might encumber mutual respect and most do pose specific challenges to those criteria. Every particular sexual interaction with a partner must be conscientiously evaluated with due attention to its unique characteristics. In the following paragraphs, I'll give just a few examples of the moral hazards associated with some sexual activities and relationships.

One example of a sexual behavior that is commonplace but morally problematic is objectification. Objectification involves treating a sexually appealing characteristic – such as an act, a prop, or a body part – as more important than the unique individual who has that characteristic. There is nothing bad about preferring buxom girls or tall boys, but if a sexual partner's arousing feature becomes indispensable while the partner becomes dispensable, i.e., if the appealing feature might as well be attached to anyone at all, then he has been objectified. Most of us probably wouldn't consent to being depersonalized in this way. It is difficult both to objectify a person and show concern for her. Unless both partners are similarly obsessed with the sexually arousing feature, their desires aren't reciprocal. Objectification threatens the possibility of mutually respectful sexual interaction. Fetishism is a less commonplace sexual obsession with some act, prop, or body part that is important for sexual arousal and satisfaction. It can involve reciprocal consent, concern, and desire, but it presents a high risk for objectification. Whether a person merely prefers or fetishizes certain features is not morally important. The moral issue is whether a person regards their partner as a thing with a feature or as another human being who can share in his delight with that feature.

Another example of a mundane sexual behavior that includes moral hazards is manipulation. Manipulation involves misusing sexual favors to control another person's emotions and behaviors or misusing emotions and behaviors to extort another person's sexual favors. Our sexual interactions are usually contingent on the satisfaction we achieve in our general interactions with our partners. Sexual interaction is comforting and cathartic. It makes us feel valued and valuable. However, when we use sexual performance to reward and punish our partner's behavior, or to obtain gifts and niceties from our partner, and when we use emotions to extract sexual performance from our partner, we aren't showing respect. Many people use sex as a way of dominating their partner. Others turn dating into a barter of sex for gifts, entertainment, or other little luxuries and services. Some people take advantage of their prospective partner's sense of kindness and compassion (or his need for kindness and compassion) to get sex. These manipulative sexual activities indicate negligible reciprocity of concern or desire.

Some other examples of ordinary sexual behaviors that create moral problems include irreconcilability and inattentiveness. Irreconcilability and inattentiveness jeopardize reciprocal desire and concern. It is okay that everyone enters the bedroom with different expectations, unequal levels of lust, and disparate desires (e.g., one of you wants a little R&R after finals, and the other wants to feel like Homecoming Queen; or one of you is ready to take on the football team, and the other will settle for the school mascot; or one of you wants to try felching, and the other wants to try tantric yoga). It is wondrous that sexual interaction challenges us to cultivate our range of desires, to match our libido against another's, and to exert ourselves in the effort to please our partner. Nonetheless, when sexual partners' desires are profoundly incompatible, their sex drives are radically disproportionate, or their expectations are markedly opposed, they simply cannot have a sexual relationship based on mutual respect, because someone will always feel deprived or abused. It is normal to lose track of things (like your socks, your homework, or your wits) while you are enjoying sex. However, when you lose track of your partner's needs and interests, you are not treating him with concern. You must pay attention to your partner and your sexual interaction to achieve reciprocal consent, concern, and desire. Disregard for sexual incompatibility and inattention to sexual activity amount to a lack of mutual respect.

Casual sex and casual sexual relationships are examples of less traditional behaviors that can be morally acceptable but pose particular moral issues. Casual sex between almost total strangers seems to defy the criteria of reciprocal consent and concern. Likewise, casual sexual relationships between partners who are relative strangers outside the bedroom seem to imperil the criterion of mutual concern. The shorter, the shallower, or the narrower our sexual relationships, the more caution we must exercise in gauging the reciprocity of consent, concern, and desire. In the context of casual sex with strangers, this involves insisting upon very direct, explicit, and specific communication and avoiding scenarios and substances likely to impair good judgment and clear communication. In the context of casual sex with acquaintances, this involves soliciting direct, explicit, and specific affirmation that your partner's needs, expectations, and interests are being served by your relationship. So there's nothing intrinsically morally wrong with casual sexual interactions, but the participants must be morally responsible and honest enough to communicate openly and respond considerately.

Group sex and non-exclusive sexual relationships are other examples of sexual behaviors that can be mutually respectful but that involve specific moral complications. Group sex and non-exclusive sexual relationships also seem to threaten mutually respectful sexual interaction. There are some special moral risks associated with group sex and non-monogamous relationships. Each additional sexual partner complicates the dynamics of the sexual interaction and multiplies the difficulty of achieving mutual respect, so extra care is needed to achieve reciprocity of consent, concern, and desire between multiple partners. This requires extra communication between partners and extra attentiveness toward partners. Sexual relationships are always emotionally charged, which sometimes leads sexual partners to compromise their own or their partner's needs in order to achieve sexual satisfaction, preserve a relationship, or to serve other confused and confusing goals. Non-monogamous relationships can increase emotional tensions as well as possibilities of partners feeling jealous and neglected or otherwise discontented and dissatisfied. Extra care must be shown to assure reciprocity of consent, concern, and desire. This means especially candid communication about partners' needs, expectations, and interests. It also means especially frank discussion of limits (e.g., regarding temporal and emotional commitments or regarding disease and pregnancy prevention) and equity (e.g., regarding the fair extension of the liberties enjoyed by one partner to the others). So there's nothing intrinsically morally wrong with group sex or non-exclusive sexual relationships, but the participants must be emotionally sensitive, fair-minded, and morally diligent enough to address the needs, interests, and wellbeing of all of their sexual partners.

Sadomasochism is yet another example of a more unusual sexual behavior that can involve reciprocal consent, concern, and desire, but that does raise important special moral considerations. Sadomasochism involves taking sexual pleasure in inflicting or receiving pain. Sadomasochistic interactions pose many special hazards and responsibilities to the participants. Sexual partners sometimes change their minds about volition. For example, a partner might be initially eager to experience certain sensations and then might find those sensations unbearable, so it is crucial that both partners be communicative, attentive, and responsive lest they end up engaged in a non-consensual interaction. Sadomasochistic partners often communicate in seemingly ambiguous or contradictory ways. For example, a partner might cry out "Oh, please don't hurt me" when they really mean "Oh, please hurt me more," so it is important that the partners communicate in advance about their desires, that they quickly and accurately interpret ambiguous sexual gestures, and that they know each other well enough to respond properly to subtle signs of pleasure, satiation, fear, or distress.

Another very grave moral risk associated with sadomasochistic sex is physical danger. Even light sadomasochistic sex can result in serious injury or death, especially if the partners are uninformed or inexperienced. Concerned partners will become informed about risks and safety precautions and about their partner's specific health concerns (such as low or high blood pressure, sickle cell anemia, AIDS, or diabetes) in advance and will remain attentive to possible injuries during and after their sexual interaction. Since intense sensations can impair judgment, one partner must assume responsibility in advance for setting limits on physical risk and injury. A concerned partner must withhold additional stimulation even though their partner might very much like more when it poses some physical danger. Risks are multiplied when sadomasochistic sex is combined with inebriants that alter sensation, release inhibition, or impair judgment and communication. So there is nothing intrinsically morally wrong with sadomasochistic sex, but the partners must be morally conscientious enough to be well-informed and cautious about safety, communicative and attentive enough to respond promptly to their partner's needs, and psychologically mature enough to exercise self-control and good judgment.

A final example of a sexual behavior that is not necessarily odd but that ranges from humdrum delights to extreme thrills is the use of danger or substances to improve the sexual experience. Sexual pleasure can be enhanced by taking social or physical risks, or by using inebriating techniques or chemicals. For example, some people find the risks of having sex in public arousing, whereas some enjoy sex play with knives or guns. Others use electricity, piercing, hanging, or various forms of asphyxiation to produce pleasurable sensations. Of course, many people use chemicals, ranging from supposedly aphrodisiac foods, stimulating gels and lotions, alcohol, amyl nitrite, pot, or other drugs to increase arousal, reduce inhibition, or augment sensation. Most of these forms of sexual enhancement present some moral risks, which must be addressed responsibly if partners are to show mutual respect. Many of these activities, techniques, and chemicals create social or physical dangers, which could compromise reciprocal concern, whereas others impair sensation, judgment, or communication, which could compromise reciprocal consent and concern. Mutually respectful partners must be very well informed and must exercise extreme caution with risky techniques and dangerous chemicals. Many intelligent, informed, careful, and concerned people have injured or killed themselves or their partners using some of these techniques and chemicals. Some of these activities are simply too dangerous for morally responsible partners to do. Mutually respectful partners never use inebriants to impair a partner's judgment and obtain non-consensual sex or to deaden a partner's sensation to coerce them into performing sexual acts they find painful or loathsome. So there is nothing intrinsically morally wrong with sexual enhancements, but the participants must be intellectually informed and morally concerned enough to protect themselves and their partners from coercion and from social and physical danger.

Don't Flunk Your Test

One of the most important things you can learn in college is that in order to have mutual respect between sexual partners everyone must assume responsibility for engaged, informed, communicative interaction. That might sound like it involves some embarrassment, a lot of physical and mental effort, or a great reduction of immediate sexual opportunity. It does. But if you aren't man or woman enough to communicate about sex and to exert yourself with consenting and eager partners, then you aren't man or woman enough to get laid. If you aren't prepared to be a morally conscientious sexual partner, start a vigorous exercise regimen, become a masturbatory virtuoso, or donate your time to a good charity, but don't muck up something as important as another person's sexual experience. Yes, being a good person is tough, but if there's someone somewhere in a tub of green Jell-O waiting around for a stranger with a hula-hoop, then there's probably someone somewhere waiting around for you. Be ready for that person.

CHAPTER 17

BAD FAITH OR TRUE DESIRE?

A Sartrean View on College Sex

An Authentic Self

As far as sex is concerned, modern college is – to put it mildly – an interesting environment. The communal nature of living opens up possibilities for a hedonistic lifestyle. For the first time, many students find themselves freed from the norms and opinions of the outside world; it is finally possible to be what you truly are and do what you really want. Don't be prudent, life is short, you are only responsible to yourself, so "Just Do It!" as the famous commercial suggests. This captures the mindset of many students. The stage is perfectly set for the players to play the game of free love, but the whole story is not so simple. Perhaps the freedom enabled by college is often only apparent. A place such as college where one is constantly in contact with other people puts extraordinary pressure on social relationships. Could it be the case that in an overtly social setting you do not express yourself as you truly are, but instead act in a way that others think you are supposed to act? To make things worse, perhaps you truly want to be the kind of person you think others want you to be. But what then is your authentic being, your "true self"? A philosophical analysis may help you find out the answer.

French philosopher Jean-Paul Sartre (1905–80) belongs to the group of philosophers who have been troubled by the problematic human condition. One of the main themes in Sartre's philosophy is the question about the relation between the self and others. When interested in sexual relations, Sartre is a good philosopher to consult. He was a known womanizer and admitted that his relations with women greatly influenced his philosophical views. Sartre's views on human sexuality focus on abstract relations between different philosophical categories that are to be found in his work; he tries to rationalize sexuality. Perhaps this tells something also about the nature of Sartre's actual relationships.

A full understanding of Sartre's philosophy would require an in-depth analysis of various aspects of his philosophical system, a task which cannot be done here. What I will do instead is discuss aspects of college sex by drawing quite freely on intuitions that are inspired by Sartre's philosophy.

College, the Place to Feel Inadequate about Sex

Sartre's philosophical system is expressed in his monumental work *Being and Nothingness*.[1] More familiar to non-philosophers are probably his plays and books of fiction, both of which are essentially intertwined with his philosophy. In *Being and Nothingness*, Sartre emphasized that a human being is a being that can view itself negatively. Why evolution has produced creatures with this capacity is puzzling. Maybe it is just an unfortunate byproduct of self-consciousness. A human being is a dissatisfied being whose needs are often projected towards the distant future. Whereas the desires and needs of other animals focus on the present, a human finds himself desiring something that is waiting in the future or something that is already in the past. The capability to imagine is a double-edged sword because one can always summon new desires that need fulfilling. As we all know, with every unfilled desire the risk of feeling bad about yourself increases; a human filled with desires is apt to be disappointed. To make things worse, we seem to cling on to our desires. Satisfaction resulting from the suppression of a desire is usually disappointing, after all. Moreover, it is often the case that we *do* manage to satisfy our desire but remain unsatisfied still.

Among human desires the desire for sex is one of the strongest. So powerful was his desire for oral sex that a former president of the United States was willing to risk quite a lot just to satisfy it. There are endless examples of situations in which members of both sexes have lost their mind and behaved in an absurd way just to fulfill their cravings! Sexual desire is obviously not immune to dissatisfaction. As any college student knows, a sexual desire can be fulfilled in a satisfying way, but quite often the resulting satisfaction turns out to be dissatisfying. Why is this so? Perhaps we should start by asking what is it that we actually desire when we feel sexual desire. We desire a person, satisfy the desire by having the body of the person, but feel dissatisfied after all. This is a familiar phenomenon, especially in college, where sudden urges and desires are sometimes satisfied without much deliberation. One hears that in college sex should not be taken too seriously; experimenting cannot be bad. Yet in hindsight, we often conclude that the satisfying events were not so satisfying after all and sex actually becomes a serious issue. Why do we often conclude this?

This question can be explored by asking what the general nature of dissatisfaction is. Sartre noted that shame, which is an example of a negative feeling, is an intimate relation of myself to myself: I am ashamed of what I *am*. But when feeling shame, Sartre notes, "I am ashamed of myself as I appear to the Other."[2] I recognize that I am as the Other sees me. The same can be said about dissatisfaction; it always reveals something about *me*. As philosophers would put it, through dissatisfaction one can discover an important aspect of one's being. But one can also be disappointed to oneself, so to speak, before somebody. I can be disappointed to myself because I do not succeed in a certain way that I take to be relevant from the perspective of others. Disappointment is thus often a feeling with three dimensions. I am disappointed to myself before the Other. This is especially true with respect to dissatisfying sexual experiences. The inadequacy before somebody else than oneself is symptomatic of our consumer society, in which a man is measured by his material achievements and success. We are being offered paradigms of sexual success and cannot keep up with them. Because the standards of success are ultimately set by others, an individual is never fully in charge of her destiny as an achiever of things. In the end nothing is ever enough because there is always somebody who is better off than you. The great gift of the Western culture is that you can always feel inadequate with respect to somebody else who has something more than you. There is always somebody who is richer, who has a more beautiful wife, who is healthier, or who works in a nicer job than you. The worst thing is that there is always somebody who is having better sex than you. Actually, there are *lots* of people to whom this observation applies.

Although philosophy aims at universal truths, a discussion about college sex must acknowledge the fact that an average student is perhaps 20 years old and that college is an institution with a specific purpose. The essential purpose of college is to evaluate students by comparing them to each other. College is thus an example of a place where one encounters the feelings of inadequacy and dissatisfaction. If you are an unsuccessful student, it is because there are others who are better than you. If you are an exceptional student this is because there are others who fail. You are never really evaluated as an individual. In addition to the evaluation by teachers and professors there is the constant evaluation of an individual by her peers. This evaluation infiltrates all areas of life. Others evaluate your background, how you look, talk, and act. Sexual behavior is, of course, one of the most interesting topics to be evaluated and again you are evaluated through comparison to others. College is an environment where a person's identity and self-image is in many ways constituted by others. This in turn has the consequence that college students become increasingly focused on the question of how they look in the eyes of these others. What matters the most are aesthetics of the surface.

Given the central role that sex has in our lives it would be surprising if the basic negative human feeling would not apply to it. *The* feeling of the twenty-first century – dissatisfaction – applies more and more to relationships and to sexual relations as well. Can sexual relations in college be genuine or are they corrupted by the fact that an average student is paradoxically and tremendously self-centered but also extremely sensitive to outside influences and to the opinion of others? A college student is both an active subject and a passive object in the plainest sense of these words. He is active by constantly evaluating other students, but has also a passive role as a target of others' evaluations. How is he going to deal with others in the most intimate relations?

The Look

If college is a place where people become increasingly focused on the question of how they look, what consequences does this have for the relations between the self and others? Sartre claimed that one of the fundamentally important relations between the self and others is the look or the gaze. This relation, according to Sartre, is in some sense the basis for interpersonal relations. The self's concrete relations with others are essential aspects of Sartre's philosophy.[3] These relations are vividly and beautifully described in Sartre's non-philosophical works. The famous slogan from the play *No Exit* concludes that "Hell is other people."⁴ Without going deeply into Sartrean philosophy, a few things about the look are worth noticing.⁵

In some sense another person is always a stranger to oneself. Sartre thought that the "otherness" of others is something that is created by the subject's awareness that she is the object of the look of another. A crucial dimension of human existence is individuals' awareness of being the object of a look. On Sartre's account, the look of the other is objectifying, it takes its object to have fixed characteristics and a deterministic nature. This goes against the self's own understanding of itself as a radically free being without a fixed nature. A person feels that he is free, but the look of the other characterizes him in a certain way. There is thus a conflict between the way a person sees himself and the role placed on him by others. In our society, it is often claimed that especially the male gaze objectifies woman when it reduces woman to a mere sexual object. Women claim that men do not appreciate them as they are, they do not see the beautiful and interesting person they are because they do not see beyond the physical appearance.

Sartre's observation about the objectifying nature of the look is much more profound. That one is being seen by another person is an inescapable fact of personal experience. The result of the look is the subject's realization that she is no longer a person but merely an object. By the objectifying look of the other, one is robbed of one's freedom. The result is a feeling of alienation, which is something uncomfortable that anyone wants to escape. A vicious circle is created when somebody tries to escape the alienation by directing the look at the other person, thereby rendering the other as having a fixed and deterministic nature. By objectifying the other person the individual tries to neutralize the other's judgment which made him an object in the first place. The other person – now feeling alienated – will respond in the similar way and so the "battle of selves" continues.

The conflict between a person and others can be summarized in the following way. A person finds the objectification of herself as being uncomfortable and alienating. She tries to avoid the alienation by objectifying the other person in directing the look to that other person. This is done by denying that the other has an ability to conclude from behavior that a person has such and such characteristics or a fixed nature. The person thus tries to take away the other person's capacity to objectify him. As a result, the other person becomes alienated and tries to categorize the person again in order to evade her own alienation. About this phenomenon, Sartre claims the following: "While I attempt to free myself from the hold of the Other, the Other is trying to free himself from mine; while I seek to enslave the Other, the Other seeks to enslave me."[6] Conflict is thus in the center of interpersonal relations, although each person needs the other in order to safeguard their own existence. It is only through the other that I can recognize myself as a self.

All this may sound awfully confusing, and Sartre's work is indeed notoriously difficult and frustrating to read. The Sartrean word-monsters like being-in-itself, being-for-itself, and being-for-others do not really invite us to study what lies behind them. Isn't this just excessively heavy philosophical jargon? What could it tell us about college sex? There are three important questions worth considering. First, what is the nature of the look in college and how does it affect sexual relations? Second, how interpersonal relations essentially involve conflict and how this affects sexual relations. Third, how the self essentially depends on the other and how this affects sexual relations. In the following, I shall briefly consider these questions.

The Nature of College Sex

If college is a place where people are overtly worried about how they look in the eyes of others and if college is a place where one is constantly the object of the look, it could be concluded that college students often find themselves alienated. On the one hand, people in college are almost constantly being looked at by their critical peers. If, as Sartre would claim, the look is objectifying, a student in college is apt to feel alienated. She is being reduced to an object by the look of others. As a result of how one acts, others ascribe to her a fixed nature. On the other hand, even if one is not actually being looked at in a given moment she is always a potential object of the look. Michel Foucault famously suggested that once people start to believe that they can be observed it is no longer necessary to observe them.[7] The behavior has already changed to one that takes into account the possibility of being seen. In an environment where a person is the possible object of the look of others, she is keen to start acting in a way which is a result of the fact that she could be seen.

In his own way, Sartre emphasized this aspect of the look by noting that "the look" does not always need to be visual. For example, an empty house staring at you from the hill may give the presence of the potential look.

For Sartre, a look can be "a rustling of the branches, or the sound of the footstep followed by silence ... or a light movement of a curtain."[8] The possibility of being seen is disturbing because it reminds us of the fundamental aspect of our being in the world; we are always a potential object for someone else. It is the case that "For the Other I am seated as this inkwell is on the table; for the Other, I am leaning over the keyhole as this tree is bent by the wind."[9] For the other person, I am merely an object with certain fixed characteristics. I cannot control the traits that are being attributed to me and cannot affect the way in which I am being judged. What are the consequences of such a situation for sexual relations?

Usually, the object of sexual desire is the physical body of the other person. This is especially so in environments – such as college – where people are being constantly looked at and where people are therefore particularly interested in how they look in the eyes of others. Male students are worried about their abs, female students are worried about their breasts, and insofar as one is satisfied with one's physical appearance one wants to show it as well. This kind of environment creates a space for a desire for the other's body, it opens the possibility for such a desire. But the desire for sex is not merely a desire for a physical body, it is not merely a physical urge waiting for release. If sexual desire were just a desire for physical pleasure, masturbation should be enough to satisfy it, as Sartre notes. In sexual desire we ultimately seem to desire something more; we desire the person whose body is the object of our physical desire. At least sometimes sexual desire attaches to a particular human being. This, so it seems to me, is how many of us would like to be desired. We are not satisfied if the other person lusts merely after our bodies because we desperately want the other person to desire us and recognize our existence as equal persons instead of objects merely fulfilling the other's desire. We need the other's desire to be special; it must be *me* – as a person – that is craved, and not the contingent body which I happen to have. Perhaps this is why failure as a lover is sometimes an extremely personal and devastating experience. Although you should think that you are being compared to somebody else and rated as "crappy" in comparison to others, this is not how you interpret the situation. It is you and only you who just won the Worst Sex Ever Award. (It should be obvious that I am not talking from personal experience.)

A college student does not engage in this kind of speculation after a drunken one night stand. But students often feel dissatisfied even when their physical desires are fulfilled. I raised the question why this is so and perhaps we here have an answer. A sexual desire is actually a desire to be recognized as a self rather than merely as an object or as a tool for the

ⱵⱵ   ANTTI KUUSELA

other person's sexual satisfaction. When one desires a person sexually, one desires that person as somebody who would appreciate one's own special character. Without being too sentimental, it could be claimed that a sexual desire for somebody is actually a hidden desire for love. It is of course not the way a college student would usually see his sexual desire. A male student sees the desire as purely physical and desires the female because she has "beautiful breasts" or a "super cute ass." In doing so, he sees the other as a mere object and is fascinated by the physical appearance of this specific object. In the worst case, the consequence is that he starts to treat other people as objects. Although porn movies may be entertaining and harmless fun, the picture of sexual relations that most of them describe is not flattering. It is not just feminist propaganda that in mainstream porn women are treated as objects. Woman has been reduced to the absolute object of the male gaze.

It could thus be claimed that the reason why sexual experiences in college are often dissatisfying is twofold. First, a person desires the other physically without recognizing that she actually desires a contact with another person. Although the desire for the other person may show itself physically, it is not just the body which is the true object of the desire. The desiring self feels also a kind of ambivalence when it recognizes that sometimes it seems to desire just *any* other person, whereas at times the desire is definitely fixed to a particular being. In these latter cases, the self almost gets a glimpse of the true nature of its desire, but fails to act on it because of its fixation on the physical aspect of the desire. Second, the self who is the object of the desire is apt to be dissatisfied when it recognizes that the other desires it as a mere object without admitting that the target of the desire is a unique person as well.

Stripped of the philosophical jargon and placed in the context of college the story could go like this. A boy desires a girl. The boy is increasingly focused on the physical appearance of the girl and on the question how he – as a male college student – is supposed to act with respect to beautiful girls. The potential look of the others influences the way the boy desires. Potentially, he is always in sight of others who have expectations and who thereby shape his character. The desire has become the desire it is because the boy fills the role of a college student created by the environment and by others. However, I believe, part of the boy would like to recognize the girl, not as mere beautiful body, but as a person. We want to avoid alienation, we want others to treat us as persons instead of objects. Given this desire, which is familiar to a normal human being, it could be claimed that "deep down" the boy recognizes that the girl should be treated this way – as a person. Dissatisfaction is the result of the failure to do this. Whereas sex may be physically amazing, when there isn't anything more than just a physical satisfaction the act is dissatisfying in the end because the ultimate goal of the desire remains unfulfilled.

The girl is apt to feel the same pressure on how to fill her role, but the dissatisfaction she will feel is ultimately of a different kind. She is desired and as a result may feel desire as well, but she wants to be desired because of who she is. The look of the boy, which is the result of him not under-standing correctly the nature of his desire, objectifies the girl in a way that leaves her as a self out of the picture. Whereas the sex may be physically amazing, it is dissatisfying deep down because the girl feels she is being treated as an object and the ultimate goal of her desire remains unfulfilled. The relations between the sexes, or more generally between humans, con-tain conflict that manifests itself through the fact that each self tries to fulfill its desires and in doing so objectifies the other. It could be claimed that this objectification is especially harmful for sexual relations, which ultimately involve the desire that one is recognized as a self instead of a body.

It goes without saying that the relations between the sexes can be just the opposite; the girl desires the boy and acts upon it. But the roles that society places upon us should be taken seriously in this kind of analysis. Basically, I described the boy as a "being which desires the ass of the girl," that is, as a being which is fixated on physical appearance, whereas the girl is a being looking for a "connection at the emotional level." This may sound awfully stereotypical, but to a great extent we all *are* prisoners of the roles that have been placed on us. The nature of the self depends on others. Ultimately, the dissatisfaction is a result of not really understand-ing or knowing what you want; the boy wants to act in a certain way, but he is also forced to act in a way demanded by his role. He may feel that both sides are genuine aspects of him. Whereas the pressure of the role applies to us all everywhere, a place like college is, for the reasons already discussed, bound to confuse a person about his or her "true identity." In college it is difficult to be free and act in ways that you really want.

Bad Faith or True Desire

We are almost at our journey's end. I shall finish by introducing one more concept that is essential in Sartre's philosophy. This is the concept of bad faith.[10] This phenomenon has different aspects, but generally it applies to situations in which a self denies its absolute freedom and chooses to behave as an object. We choose to behave like objects because we do not want to be reminded of our responsibility. We want to pretend that we are not free in order not to feel the anguish, pain, and despair of ultimate freedom. Especially on occasions when we make mistakes, e.g., engage in shameful sexual relations, we would rather be able to project the blame for the situation onto someone or something else, rather than place responsibility wholly on ourselves.

One aspect of bad faith is a person's inability to make decisions when faced with a challenge. By doing this, a person avoids the responsibility resulting from his choice. To avoid the choice: "One *puts oneself* in bad faith as one goes to sleep and one is in bad faith as one dreams. Once this mode of being has been realized, it is as difficult to get out of it as to wake oneself up; bad faith is a type of being in the world."[11] How the moment of choice puts the self into the mode of bad faith is well expressed by the following example from Sartre.

Imagine a girl on a first date. She ignores the rather obvious sexual innuendos of her date, in the sense that she does not want to consider what they mean. This is because, like our college girl introduced earlier, she wants to understand the compliments as being addressed to her personality, she wants the boy to respect her as a free self. She is trying to deny that the boy wants her as a sexual object, and imagines him focusing on her intellect instead. Thus, when he tells her "I find you so attractive" the girl detaches this phrase from its sexual background and hears it as an innocent compliment. However, at the same time, not being naïve, she is somehow perfectly aware of the boy's intentions and of the desire she inspires. Moreover, she would not be happy if the comment were only a compliment fitting to the context of conversation – she wants the boy to desire her. As Sartre notes, in this situation the girl does not quite know what she wants. When the moment arrives to decide how she wants to react to the situation, the girl puts herself in bad faith. The moment of decision occurs when the boy takes the girl's hand. In order to avoid the need to decide and be responsible for the consequences, the girl chooses to remain passive. This choice is paradoxically a choice that makes the girl an object. The girl is pretending to be a passive object instead of a conscious being that is free. She acts like she is not aware of what happens to her hand or she recognizes her hand as almost a strange object not belonging to her.[12]

Another example of bad faith is rooted in the self's viewing itself as the other by assuming or taking a role placed on the self by others.

Sartre's example of this pattern of bad faith is a waiter who identifies himself in the role of the waiter. He is in bad faith because he is denying what he is, a free being, and is instead assuming a role and playing in accordance with it. According to Sartre, the behavior of the waiter "seems to us a game. He applies himself to chaining his movements as if they were mechanisms, the one regulating the other; his gestures and even his voice seem to be mechanisms."[13] The waiter resembles the boy from our previous example who is torn between his "true self" and the role that he – as a male college student – is required to play. Both the waiter and the college student know the obligations of their roles and the rights which the role allows. There are people who are so deeply entrenched in this kind of thinking, or as one could also say *being* in the world, that there is no difference between their role and their self; they *are* their role. They mechanistically play the role that society demands of them, to the extent that they live and die having forever been only their role upon the earth. Sartre's illustrative examples include a grocer who cannot dream because dreaming is not allowed to the grocer, a soldier at attention that does not see because his eyes must be fixed to a certain point according to a rule, or an overseer who thinks that his purpose in this world is to deny, whose social reality is uniquely that of the No.

With these patterns of bad faith available, we can end with these questions: Are college students more like girls on a Sartrean date or overseers who have assumed a certain fixed role, or are they capable of rising above the many roles placed on them by the college environment? Do sexual relations in college exhibit patterns of bad faith or can they be based on true desire that grows from the appreciation of the other as an equal person, as a self and not an object? Instead of using a moral or educational tone of voice, we can ask in a philosophical manner: Are students who are engaging in sexual relations ready to accept the responsibilities that their own free choices bring? Are they ready to live with the consequences? Are college students ready to live in accordance with their "true self"?

These questions must be left for the reader's introspection. But it should be noted that a "true self" is of course a philosopher's fantasy. The way every person evaluates his actions, fears, desires, or generally his character are in the end taken from the public categories. We are products of our culture, but this does not mean that there could not be higher and lower levels of authentic being. Despite Sartre's rather pessimistic view about the nature of interpersonal relationships, his philosophical conclusions are in fact optimistic: each of us has unlimited freedom that enables us to make authentic choices. In the worst case, other people may be hell for you, but you are ultimately free to choose how you act towards others; you don't need to be hell for them. An authentic attitude towards oneself and towards others is possible, but one has to work hard in order to realize where the root of the problem lies. One does not need to be a Sartre scholar in order to appreciate the view that "man is condemned to be free," that we are ultimately responsible for our own choices. As persons, as human beings, we do not have an intrinsic nature and are therefore free to determine ourselves and choose how to act towards others. We are left alone with our decisions and ultimately without excuses. These aspects of our being are worth considering. Perhaps opening a philosophy book and spending a little time on the analysis of the human condition could, after all, be helpful in the morning after a passionate night in the dorm.

NOTES

1 Jean-Paul Sartre, *Being and Nothingness: An Essay on Phenomenological Ontology* (New York: Citadel, 1965).
2 Ibid., p. 302.
3 Without going into Sartre's delicate formulations, a "self" can be understood as referring to a person, to a self-conscious individual. In this essay the expressions "self" and "person" will be used interchangeably.
4 Jean-Paul Sartre, *No Exit and Three Other Plays* (New York: Vintage, 1989).
5 For a thorough investigation about the nature of the look, see the chapter entitled "The Look" in Sartre, *Being and Nothingness*.
6 Sartre, *Being and Nothingness*, p. 475.
7 Michel Foucault, *Discipline and Punish: The Birth of the Prison* (London: Penguin, 1977).
8 Sartre, *Being and Nothingness*, p. 346.
9 Ibid., p. 352.
10 For a thorough discussion of bad faith, see part one of *Being and Nothingness*, titled "The Problem of Nothingness."
11 Sartre, *Being and Nothingness*, p. 113, emphasis in the original
12 For a masterful description of the alienation of the self, see Sartre's famous novel *Nausea* (New York: New Directions, 1964).
13 Sartre, *Being and Nothingness*, p. 101.

NOTES ON CONTRIBUTORS

MATTHEW BROPHY, PhD, is a visiting assistant philosophy professor at Minnesota State University, Mankato, where he teaches ethics. Fortunately, he managed to fund his PhD in philosophy from the University of Minnesota without subjecting himself to exploitation – other than serving as a teaching assistant. Matthew lives with his beautiful wife and above-average child in Minneapolis.

MICHAEL BRUCE, MA, received his BA from California State University, Chico, where he took classes with his co-editor, Professor Stewart. Bruce went on to earn his master's degree from San Diego State University, followed by teaching philosophy and mathematics courses at the University of Washington's Robinson Center for Young Scholars. He is the editor of *Just the Arguments: The 100 Most Important Arguments in Western Philosophy*, forthcoming in 2010 from Wiley-Blackwell. He thoroughly enjoyed college sex and philosophy.

SISI CHEN recently graduated with a BA in psychology from the State University of New York at Buffalo. Her ultimate goal is to pursue her PhD in clinical psychology so that she can practice family and marriage counseling with a specialization in sex therapy. She is an expert lucid dreamer and loves knee socks.

HEATHER CORINNA is the queer, rabblerousing, polymath founder and editor of *Scarlet Letters*, *Scarleteen*, the *All Girl Army*, and *Femmerotic*. Her sexuality work and erotica has appeared online in numerous venues and in print. Her work in sexuality information and activism has brought accolades from *Adult Video News* to the Illinois Library Association, *The City Pages* to *Playboy*, and from the *Utne Reader* to the Kinsey Institute. Her pioneering work in women's sexuality on the web since 1997 spearheaded a developing trend towards a greater diversity in the voice of erotic and sexuality work, and put the term "femmerotica" on the map. She is the author of *S.E.X.: The All-You-Need-To-Know Progressive Sexuality Guide to Get You Through High School and College.*

JOHN DRAEGER, PhD, is an assistant professor of philosophy at Buffalo State College. His research interests include ethics, political philosophy, and philosophy of law. He has recently been trying to develop an account of respect for persons.

YOLANDA ESTES, PhD, is a professor of philosophy at Mississippi State University. Her teaching covers all areas of philosophy, and her research focuses on transcendental idealism (especially the philosophy of J. G. Fichte) and ethics (especially the philosophy of sex and love). She is an author and editor of *Marginal Groups and Mainstream American Culture* and *J. G. Fichte: The Atheism Dispute (1798–1800)*.

GEORGE T. HOLE, PhD, is a distinguished teaching professor of philosophy at Buffalo State College who has taught for many years a course entitled "The Philosophy of Love and Sex," which should have made him wise(r). He discovers daily that he is not wise about love. To avoid taking philosophy too seriously he plays racquetball and writes poetry. Socrates is his hero – whom he attacks because of his claim to love wisdom and his ignorance of sex and college.

ANDREW KANIA, PhD, is an assistant professor of philosophy at Trinity University in San Antonio. His principal research is in the philosophy of music, literature, and film. He is the editor of *Memento*, in Routledge's series "Philosophers on Film," and, with Theodore Gracyk, is currently editing *The Routledge Companion to Philosophy and Music*.

ANTTI KUUSELA, MA, is finishing his PhD thesis in the philosophy of mind at the University of Helsinki, Finland. Lately, as a result of reading too much Wittgenstein, he has been increasingly interested in the questions "What is philosophy?" and "What do philosophers think they are doing?" Kuusela lives happily in Helsinki with his girlfriend and a goldfish.

DANIELLE A. LAYNE, PhD, is a researcher and instructor of philosophy for DeWulf-Mansion Centre for Ancient, Medieval and Renaissance Philosophy at the Catholic University of Leuven, Belgium. Her primary interests are Platonic and Neo-Platonic philosophy. In her spare time, she writes children's books in the hopes of inundating the young with idealistic worldviews.

TIMOTHY R. LEVINE, PhD, is a professor of communication at Michigan State University. Levine has published nearly 100 journal articles and book chapters on topics related to communication. Levine's primary area of research is deception and deception detection.

BRETT LUNCEFORD, PhD, is an assistant professor of communication at the University of South Alabama where he heads the track in Interpersonal Communication and Rhetoric. Although a rhetorician by training, he enjoys a wide range of research interests and has published in *American Communication Journal, ETC: A Review of General Semantics, Northwestern Journal of Technology and Intellectual Property, Review of Communication*, and *Theology and Sexuality*, with forthcoming articles in *Explorations in Media Ecology* and *Media History Monographs*.

ASHLEY MCDOWELL, PhD, earned her BA from Virginia Commonwealth University and her PhD from the University of Arizona, and is now an assistant professor of philosophy at Kalamazoo College in Michigan. Her current favorite philosophical mission is the translation of academic philosophy (especially epistemology) into useful advice for actual people. If she were a tree, she would be a birch tree.

PAUL A. MONGEAU, PhD, is a professor at the Hugh Downs School of Human Communication at Arizona State University in Tempe. His scholarly interests center on sexual practices on modern university campuses and how they influence relationship development. He serves as editor of the *Journal of Social and Personal Relationships*.

KELLY MORRISON, PhD, is an associate professor in the department of communication at Michigan State University, where she teaches classes in interpersonal communication and gender communication. Her research examines issues in close relationships.

GUY PINKU, PhD, received his MA in cognitive psychology from Ben-Gurion University and his PhD in philosophy from the University of Haifa, Israel. Pinku went on to do post-doctorate work at Washington University in St. Louis. His main research interests are in philosophy of mind, philosophy of psychology, self-consciousness, and free will. His essay in the current volume is inspired by questions he had when he was a college student.

BILL PUKA, PhD, is a professor of philosophy and psychology at Rensselaer Polytechnic Institute where he teaches philosophy and psychology. He completed his doctoral work at Harvard. He has worked as a legislative aide in the US Senate (for Gary Hart), director of an urban economic development program, staff member in a Connecticut "just community" prison unit, professional puppeteer and actor in children's theatre, and a songwriter-recording artist for Columbia Records (where he wrote and recorded very sexy songs).

BASSAM ROMAYA, PhD, has taught widely at Penn State University, Widener University, San Diego State University, and Temple University. His past publications and research interests are in the areas of social and political philosophy, GLBT studies, aesthetics, and ethics.

KELLI JEAN K. SMITH, PhD, is assistant professor in the Communication Department at William Paterson University. In addition to friends with benefits relationships, her research interests include complaining, unrequited love, and stalking.

WILLIAM O. STEPHENS, PhD, is a professor of philosophy and of classical and Near Eastern studies at Creighton University in Omaha. His research interests include Stoicism, naturalism, environmental philosophy, ethics and animals, personhood, and philosophies of love. Though he is a lover of wisdom, he is uncertain about the wisdom of sex.

ROBERT M. STEWART, PhD, is a professor of philosophy at California State University, Chico. He received his PhD from the University of Michigan, Ann Arbor, specializing in ethics and social and political philosophy. Stewart currently teaches courses entitled "Ethics and Human Happiness" and "Philosophical Perspectives on Sex and Love." He also edited *Philosophical Perspectives on Sex and Love*, an influential text in the field.